TONY WHEELER'S

DARK

LANDS

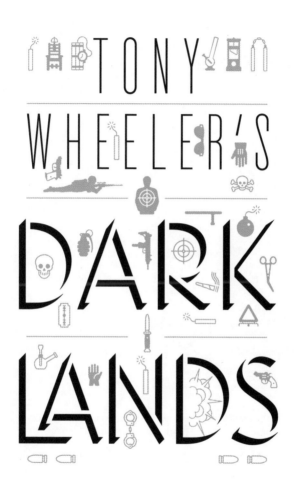

TONY WHEELER'S DARK LANDS

LONELY PLANET PUBLICATIONS

Melbourne · Oakland · London

Tony Wheeler's Dark Lands

Published by Lonely Planet Publications 2013

90 Maribyrnong Street, Footscray, Victoria, 3011, Australia
150 Linden Street, Oakland CA 94607, USA
201 Wood Ln, London, W12 7Tq, United Kingdom

Edited by Emma Schwarcz
Cover Design by Roberto Devicq
Design & Layout by Leon Mackie

Printed by Hang Tai Printing Company, Hong Kong
Printed in China

1st Editon

978 1 74321 846 4

CONTENTS

INTRODUCTION

My first thought, when George W. Bush announced his Axis of Evil, was 'I want to go there.' Well, who wouldn't? He'd inadvertently created an adventurer's travel wish list: Iran, Iraq and North Korea, three countries that were worse than bad; they were positively evil. The fact that Iran and Iraq were sworn enemies who'd fought each other for eight years didn't seem to matter.

So I trekked around Mr Bush's Axis of Evil and then, for good measure, added six other countries that for assorted reasons had been labelled 'bad' to create my 2007 book *Bad Lands*. Afghanistan, home of the Taliban and temporary residence of Osama bin Laden, was – pre-invasion at least – clearly rotten to the core. Burma? Well, imprisoning a heroic Nobel Peace Prize winner would earn any country a bad tag, even before you ran the economy into the ground. Cuba was clearly a wicked place: for fifty years every American president had dedicated himself to getting rid of Fidel Castro and imposing some regime change. Gaddafi, thoroughly evil and with a Michael Jackson–like enthusiasm for theatrical outfits, still ruled Libya at the time so his desert dictatorship deserved a place on the list too. Saudi Arabia was a shoo-in: not only did they oppress women, condemn most of us as infidels and chop hands and heads off, but they also provided almost all of the 9/11 hijackers.

Finally I tossed in Albania, not because the poor Albanians had been very bad to anybody apart from themselves, but because it had been such a weird little locked-away place, with a man – Enver Hoxha – who ticked that important box for any ruthless and corrupt bad-land leader: having a big-time personality cult. None of the friendly Albanians I met during my travels were particularly worried about being lumped in with a bunch of genuinely bad nations; their response seemed to be, 'call us bad, call us anything, just notice we're here.'

My travels through the bad lands turned out to be interesting, educational and, perhaps surprisingly, enjoyable, so a follow-up seemed an obvious plan. I'd even concluded the first book with an extended list of other troubled places I could have tagged on; a number of them feature in this book. 'Bad', however, wasn't the word I wanted. Apart from a little shonky banking, Nauru wasn't really bad; it was more misguided, silly, credulous and exploited. 'Troubled States' is certainly accurate;

they were all in trouble of some sort or another. 'Failed States' is also a precise, or perilously close to precise, definition for some of them. 'Weird Lands' is pretty truthful too: in one way or another visiting each of these countries turned out to be a weird experience. Eventually 'Dark Lands' emerged, and felt right: each had some distinctly dark shadows in its story, which to a greater or lesser extent coloured the atmosphere of the country today.

Mr Bush managed to sneak through once more with a secondary theme. On 1 May 2003 he stood on the deck of the nuclear-powered aircraft carrier USS *Abraham Lincoln* and announced, 'Mission accomplished.' As in any good opera, the words were surtitled above him, across the ship's 'island'. The invasion of Iraq had succeeded and democracy and peace would inevitably follow (although those pesky weapons of mass destruction had yet to be ferreted out).

He might as well have said, 'Pandora's box opened.' We'd done it: we'd marched into Iraq, got all the way to Baghdad, pulled down some statues, got rid of that mosaic of Bush Senior at the entrance to the Al Rashid Hotel and had not only found Pandora's Box, hidden away in one of Saddam's palaces, but we'd levered the damn thing open.

Pandora, in Greek mythology, is the first woman, given a box by Zeus, father of the Gods, with strict instructions not to open it. (In fact it was a jar, but perhaps a box sounded better.) Naturally Pandora opens it and quickly discovers that her little gift contains all the evil in the world – and, once all that trouble has escaped, there is no way of stuffing it back in. Plenty of people had warned Bush, Blair and Howard not to invade Iraq – not to open that Pandora's box – but they were ignored. By May 2003, when he stood on the aircraft carrier, Mr Bush hadn't yet conducted an inventory of what, exactly, had escaped and which impossible problems might need to be overcome before the mission could really be accomplished. Clearly, however, a box had been opened.

Just as Iraq turned out to be a Pandora's box, full of problems we'd rather not have to address, each of my new dark land destinations also triggered memories of myths and fairytales. The ancient Hydra found a new setting in the hills of Pakistan; Rumpelstiltskin and King Midas echoed through the mines of Papua New Guinea. The morals of each tale were clear as I moved from country to country, some better heeded than others. I'd set out to travel through dark lands, but they ended up being fairytale lands too, which I suppose makes sense when you consider how dark fairytales can be.

Well before the Iraq invasion I'd concluded that most of modern life's dangers and pitfalls could be neatly summed up in fairytales. One of my favourite contemporary examples, *The Princess Bride*, borrows a warning from recent history. 'You fool,' the Sicilian outlaw Vizzini announces to his rival. 'You fell victim to one of the classic blunders. The most famous of which is: Never get involved in a land war in Asia.'

We're regularly warned of the dangers of ignoring history's lessons, but why wait until we're old enough to study history? We tell our children fairytales to warn them about how life works, the risks that lie in wait for them. Perhaps we too should be listening a little more closely the next time someone brings out Cinderella or Heracles.

COLOMBIA

In the fairytale of the birthday-suited king, parading in front of his subjects in a non-existent new outfit, nobody is brave enough to state the obvious: he's stark naked. It's left to a small child to announce. Colombia has been a front-line in the war on drugs for many years and an increasing number of people – not just observant children – report that it's an unwinnable war. Nevertheless, there's a big lobby that insists the war must go on, despite all the evidence that it's pointless to continue, ruinously expensive and horrifically damaging. In recent years, the role of the small child, insisting that his eyes see accurately, has been assumed by several Colombian presidents: the king has no clothes and banning drugs doesn't work.

The kidnap victims probably stumbled down this way. Eight of them, in the pre-dawn light of a September morning ten years ago.

We wade across the river. We've made plenty of river crossings by now and this one is only knee-deep. Many of them have been easy rock-hopping exercises, or little more than ankle-deep wades, but the all been through crystal-clear and swift-flowing water. Santiago, the archaeologist who knows this walk better than anybody, insists some of the crossings can be chest-deep after heavy rain. On the other side of the river there's a little parting in the jungle and we can see the stone stairway curving steeply up into the enveloping green. The steps themselves are mossy and numerous – I count more than 1200 before I get to the entrance to Ciudad Perdida, Colombia's 'Lost City'.

To the north, Latin America's great civilisations of the pre-colonial era include the Aztecs of central Mexico and

the Mayans, whose territory spread from the Yucatán region
of Mexico south into Guatemala and other areas of Central
America. To the south, there are great Inca centres, most
notably Machu Picchu in Peru. We're in the territory of the
Tayrona people of Colombia, only 30 straight-line kilometres
from the Caribbean coast, and the four of us, plus our guide,
have spent the last three days climbing up into the Sierra
Nevada de Santa Marte. It was here that the Tayrona built
their great city, Teyuna, starting over a thousand years ago.
The city reached its prime around 1200 AD, before the Spanish
arrived and European diseases decimated the local population.
By the sixteenth century, Teyuna was abandoned and soon
disappeared into the jungle.

Not until the early 1970s was the lost city rediscovered,
first by *guaqueros* – we would call them 'tomb raiders'.
Archaeological protection arrived from 1976, but it's only in
the past ten years that tourists have started to arrive in serious
numbers, typically making a five-day walk to and from the
remote site.

Colombia's chronic problems kept tourists away through
the 1990s, but by 2003 walkers were drawn by the trek up
to Ciudad Perdida. In September of that year, though, an
unfortunate group of international tourists found themselves
caught up in the local guerrilla warfare. The tourists were
asleep in the refuge at the site when guerrillas from the
National Liberation Army (ELN) burst in. They divided the
tourists into two groups, and eight were marched away on a
journey that, for most of them, would last for more than three
months. Colombians joke that two Australians were quickly

discarded as unsuitable for kidnapping; they were too fat and their rubber flip-flops, or thongs to Australians, were not cut out for a fast tramp through the jungle. I can picture them being told to 'lose weight and get better footwear if you want to be kidnapped'.

The eight successful candidates were soon reduced to seven when a young English backpacker managed to escape, but the others – a German woman and six men, four Israeli, one Spanish, one British – set off an educational tour of the region. Kidnapping wealthy Colombians for ransom had been a local business for some years, but this tourist grab had a different purpose. The guerrillas' intention was to show the terrible living conditions endured by rural Colombians, then to negotiate the hostages' release and send them home with an understanding of the reasons for the country's political strife. Unfortunately for the guerrillas and their captives, Álvaro Uribe had been elected president just over a year before, with a mandate to stamp out the smouldering insurrection. Negotiation didn't feature in President Uribe's vocabulary and he unleashed the Colombian army in pursuit of the guerrillas and their hostages. Still, it was a Catholic priest who eventually managed to make contact with the ELN and organise the release.

The Spaniard and the German woman, who had been unwell, had been freed a month earlier, but for the four Israelis and the Englishman, the ordeal lasted 101 days. Poor Reini Weigel, the German hostage, suffered a second ordeal, a financial one, after her release. The German government charged her for half of the helicopter costs for lifting her out of the jungle. The Spanish government didn't bother chasing their man for the other half of the chopper charter, but poor Ms Weigel ended up taking the matter all the way to the German supreme court. Today various European governments, led by the Greeks, could tell her that Germany doesn't forgive debts easily; she lost her court case and eventually had to fork out €18,000, including legal costs.

Soon after I arrive in Bogotá, the Colombian capital, I check into Germán Escobar's Casa Platypus in the Candelaria area of the old city. Germán was a tourism pioneer, establishing his first backpacker hostel when the old city was looked upon as a danger zone where no sensible person would linger.

'Getting my first customer was incredibly difficult,' he says. 'I handed out cards to anybody who looked possible, but eventually a Canadian guy came and stayed and then somehow the word spread all over South America. Three months later I was full, and I've been full ever since.'

Today a host of competitors have sprung up, so many that Candelaria feels rather like Khao San Road in Bangkok, the backpacker centre for all of South-East Asia.

'We're still not overrun with tourists,' Germán continues.

'Probably because some people still view Colombia as dangerous,' I suggest.

'Well, that's good,' he replies. 'I don't want it to become like Thailand.'

And the rationale for the name? 'When I was travelling in Africa in the 1980s the Australian travellers were the best ones I met.' Germán's moved on from backpackers, taking the platypus name with him to the comfortable small hotel where I'm staying.

I do the standard Bogotá sights: wander the student-crowded Candelaria, hang out in the city's main gathering place, the Plaza Bolivar, visit the Museum of Colonial Art which has, of course, lots of colonial art, and the Santa Clara Church Museum, which covers the religious side of the same period and is stuffed full of paintings and statuary. The Ciudad Perdida kidnappers may have rejected fat people but Fernando Botero, dubbed 'the most Colombian of Colombian artists', certainly didn't. The Botero Museum is crowded with the artist's 'volumetric,' paintings and sculptures of unashamedly rotund and often nude male and female figures. Half an hour later I'm puzzled. Botero is so prolific and yet much of his art is exactly the same. A great many of the pictures are labelled simply '*Mujer*', woman, or '*Hombre*', man, (okay, sometimes it's '*Hombre y Caballo*', man and horse). I did like the plump Mona Lisa and there's no question Botero paintings are not always routine, as his extensive series of paintings of the events at the Abu Ghraib prison in Iraq emphasised. The city's biggest tourist attraction, though, is the wonderful Gold Museum, and you can see why the gold-hungry conquistadors discovered Colombia with their eyes wide open and their tongues hanging out.

On my last morning in the city, Germán and I make an early ascent of Cerro de Monserrate, the hill towering over the old centre of the city. Bogotá stands at twice the altitude of Kathmandu, so I'm already slightly breathless before we start out on the 600-metre ascent. There are warnings about the danger of being mugged on the walking trail, but it's okay on weekends and on our early morning climb we're surrounded by people using it as a morning workout or dog-walk trail.

We talk travel and visas, and then get onto the Colombian drug scene. Germán wouldn't allow drugs in his hostel, emphasising the problems it causes for Colombia and the environment. Amazon rainforest falls for coca leaf production just as it does for cattle ranching. Germán has had his own encounters with Colombia's drug reputation. Escobar probably isn't the best surname for a Colombian, but he insists it's a common name. Once, flying into Los Angeles from Tokyo, he was pulled over and given the full two-hour working over, including a strip search. And was then asked to sign a document stating that he was not carrying drugs and had no complaints about the procedure he'd endured. 'And if I refuse?' he asked.

'Well, we could find something, and you wouldn't want that.'

I fly to Medellín and immediately make a side trip to Santa Fe de Antioquia, a delightful old town less than two hours' bus ride away. The town's museum of religious art has a nice old lady to show me around and tell me about everything, in Spanish. I like the life-sized collection of wooden statues of Jesus and the disciples, used for religious parades, and the glass cabinet full of naked cherubs, waiting to be dressed up in angelic attire and, as a finishing touch, have their wings attached.

I leave the museum and, with perfect timing, encounter a children's religious parade, the little disciples with blacked-in sideburns and facial hair each standing on a platform carried by four other kids and looking extremely serious. Which is nothing at all compared to the degree of seriousness the Virgin Mary brings to her platform. A big and very vigorous – and probably not so serious – band accompanies them; if you closed your eyes they could be the Orangemen on parade on the glorious twelfth in Belfast.

I'm charmed by the town even before lunch, which I find in a busy restaurant with art-crowded walls: one patch religious, another architectural, another all portraits. Beside the cathedral in the square, Indian Bajaj auto-rickshaws are lined up, their pilots all dressed in Hawaiian shirts. One of them, his chatty little daughter in back with me, working on improving my Spanish, takes me on a tour to the Puente de Occidente – the 'Bridge of the West' – a fine old nineteenth-century suspension bridge spanning the Rio Cauca, just 5 kilometres out of town.

The bus back from Santa Fe de Antioquia conveys me to the northern bus station in Medellín, from where the metro whisks me to the Plazoleta de las Esculturas, crowded with Botero sculptures; I'm becoming increasingly familiar with their sturdy style. I grab an empanada from a snack bar and sit down among the artwork to think about where to stay. People mill about, each with a sign around their neck announcing '*minutos a cellular*', '*minutos* 250' or some other variation on this message, perhaps just '250'. It means you can rent their mobile phone by the minute, 250 Colombian pesos is not much more than 10 US cents. The really organised ones have safari jackets with a phone in each pocket, each phone attached to their owner by chains, so they stand there with callers arrayed around them, connected by chains like octopus arms. Motorcycle taxis shuttle by, their drivers wearing reflective jackets with their licence plate numbers on back and front. It's an excellent place for people and Botero sculpture watching

Medellín is the country's second-largest city and hometown to two of the country's most famous (or infamous) citizens – cocaine king Pablo Escobar and artist Fernando Botero. The two come together in the Museo de Antioquia in a Botero painting which depicts the shooting of the drug lord, a hail of bullets freeze-framed in the air as he tries to escape across the Medellín rooftops.

In the Parque San Antonio nearby, Botero was commissioned to create a Pájaro de Paz, a bird of peace, but the bird is, perhaps fittingly, shattered. Somebody – to this day nobody knows who – set off a bomb that wrecked the statue and killed twenty-three bystanders, the youngest just seven, the oldest forty-one, one of them never identified. What stupidity. Which is precisely what Botero said about the outrage. The statue was deliberately left in its ruined state.

Say 'Colombia', and for many people 'cocaine' will be the first word that comes to mind. And for years, within Colombia, Medellín was cocaine central. If the world's war on drugs is ever abandoned as the hopeless project it has always been, there will be lots of production relocation. In the developed world scientifically grown marijuana is already cultivated much more productively – and potently – than the old artisan stuff. If it becomes legal, why bother with Afghan heroin, when the Australian state of Tasmania already produces it very efficiently for medical purposes and could easily shift more fields over to poppy growing if they could add recreational use to their market? But come legalisation, South America – and Colombia specifically – is likely to remain cocaine central. For an assortment of reasons, it's where those coca leaves plants grow best.

Plan Colombia, the multi-billion dollar US plan to wipe out cocaine production in Colombia, was a total failure from the American drug consumption point of view. Just as many tonnes of marching powder are marching up American nostrils and there's been no dramatic price increase per gram, which is what you'd expect if the war on drugs had succeeded in cutting production. Even if Plan Colombia had succeeded, drugs are a wonderful example of that immutable law about nature abhorring vacuums. When one drug becomes unavailable, or too expensive, users simply switch to something else, often something much less desirable for a variety of health and safety reasons. In Australia, for example, cocaine is expensive, but its scarcity certainly doesn't mean the country has been relieved of a drug problem.

Plan Colombia, even if it didn't wipe out cocaine production, or even diminish it, did bring lots of benefits to the Colombian government. The plan was always more stick (Black Hawk helicopters) than carrot (finding alternative crops for coca farmers whose crops had been aerial sprayed), but all that military hardware did help a great deal in the Colombian government's assault on the guerrilla forces. Sorting, or more correctly containing, the Colombian cocaine problem may have dramatically improved the situation in Colombia – there's much less narco-crime and much less narco-financing of the revolutionaries – but plenty of other people are still paying the price for the war on drugs. Production may have continued in Colombia and been backed up by new production further south in the continent, but much of the narco-crime profits – and the costs in deaths and general mayhem, a great deal of it suffered by the general population – has shifted north to the countries of Central America and, most dramatically, to Mexico. Getting all that drug production up to its ultimate consumers in the US is an expensive operation with lots of profits to be fought over en route.

In the end it's in America where Colombia's drug problem lies. Wars need two sides if they're going to continue. If one side wins and the other side loses, or one side simply gives in through sheer exhaustion, the war is over. At the moment the US is financing both sides of the war on drugs. American taxpayers front up for the military, the equipment, the stamp-out-the-drug-production campaign. Meanwhile, American consumers front up to maintain the drug production, the drug transportation and distribution and all the drug profits along the way. Americans may not pay for the costs suffered by innocent Mexicans caught up in the US-financed drug turmoil, but they certainly pay plenty in social costs in their own country. Legalising drugs and, as a result, downsizing American jails could work wonders for the American economy.

Not to mention that an expense (funding the war on drugs, funding the prisons, trials, policing) would be turned into income (they'd tax it).

I don't encounter Colombia's drug problem while I'm in the country, and drug-keen visitors are probably wiser to buy cocaine in Manhattan, Manchester or Madrid – all big consumer zones – than in Medellín. If you're going to end up on the wrong side of the law, they'd all be more comfortable places to do it. Nevertheless on my first visit to the country I did have lunch with a drug-book author. Rusty Young's memoir *Marching Powder* recounts the adventures of a British would-be cocaine smuggler in a Bolivian jail. You have to support yourself in jail in La Paz and Thomas McFadden does this by putting on backpacker tours of the prison; Lonely Planet even recommended them as something to do while you were in the Bolivian capital. Rusty introduces me to narco-submarines – he's been investigating them and later sends me the narco-submarine chapter from a novel he's working on. If you can't fly the stuff in and the Mexican border gets too tricky, why not employ some out-of-work Russian submarine designers to produce narco-subs? I thought he was spinning a yarn at first, but a week later I read about it in the British press.

Politicians often have plenty to say about rethinking the war on drugs – at least, until they're elected, when it's quickly shuffled back into the too-hard file. For American policymakers, facing up to the drugs question is probably in the same vote-losing basket as facing up to the National Rifle Association. Colombian politicians, on the other hand, living right on the bleeding edge of the problem, have become an exception. In the early 1980s, when cocaine was only a big problem, not yet an enormous one, President Belisario Betancur told American journalist Maureen Orth, 'We would not have these problems if you were not such excellent clients.'

Two decades later, the problem was exactly the same, only bigger, when President Álvaro Uribe said, 'If not for illicit drugs we would have defeated these groups long ago.' Uribe tackled the problem head on and with considerable success, but his successor, Juan Manuel Santos, still had to go to Europe in late 2011 with the same message, that solving the drug problem is not something Colombia can tackle alone.

From coca leaves to lines of white powder, there are many steps and money to be made at each of them. A few weeks after I depart Colombia I have lunch with its ambassador to Britain, Mauricio Rodríguez.

Rodriguez echoed his President's analysis: 'Cocaine production is like a balloon. We may squeeze it out of Colombia, but it pops up in Peru. And today the big price is paid further down the line. In Mexico 70,000 people have died in the drug wars. If seventy people were to die in London in a conflict over drug distribution there would be immediate action, but Mexico has suffered a thousand times more. Mexico will survive, it is a big country and the problem is mainly in the north along the border. Now the problem is shifting south to the small countries of Central America and there it is doing unbelievable damage.'

Cartagena, on the Caribbean coast, is one of those places where you feel the postcard must have been designed first, and

the city followed. There are lots of balconied buildings with
flowers cascading down towards the streets, which are packed
with restaurants, cafés, bars, galleries and boutiques. It's
simply a very pretty place with tourism as a major industry.
I turn up at what my guidebook called an 'old mansion into
flashy boutique place', where they're somewhat surprised to
have a walk-in, even though the place only has a handful of
guests. The receptionist takes my passport to the manager,
who later announces that my interesting selection of passport
stamps ensured I got a room.

I conclude my first day with a sundowner at a bar on the
fort wall, and then dinner at a restaurant whose menu suggests
that for US$25 I can have starters, main course, dessert and
'a bottle of wine per person'. Really? That has to be a typo,
but when I say *tinto*, red wine in Spanish, a bottle of Chilean
cab sav is plonked down in front of me. It's a good place for
people glimpsing, if not watching, out the open door of the
restaurant. There's a constant to and fro; the nearby Plaza
Santo de Domingo is full of open-air restaurants and there's a
steady stream of restaurant-goers interspersed with guitarists
and other entertainers. People are arriving by taxi or horse
carriage; skateboarders trundle by; there are guys on the prowl
along with single women, couples and families. At one point
a group of porno-devil girls passes by, dressed in short red
dresses and sporting red horns.

Early the next morning I stroll through the plaza. The
fat, reclining Botero nude contemplating the Santo Domingo
Church is having a morning sponge bath, the statue washer
thoughtfully polishing her stomach. Then I'm off on a circuit

of the town's many sites, starting with the Palace of the Inquisition, followed by a variety of churches, museums and galleries. It's getting uncomfortably hot by the time I drag myself back to the hotel for a siesta.

Mid-afternoon, I walk out to the Castillo San Felipe de Barajas, a fortress built by the Spanish in the colonial era to fend off attacks by land and sea. I go mainly to see the statue of Blas de Lezo out front. He must be the model for Monty Python's 'brave knight' – he'd already lost an arm, a leg and an eye before facing up against the huge English fleet of Edward Vernon at Cartagena. This time he lost the other leg, but still repelled the piratical English and their nearly 200 ships. The statue, standing on a peg leg, waving an empty sleeve, appears to be sticking its tongue out at the would-be invaders. Earlier in the day I'd seen a cannonball displayed at the Santo Toribio de Mangrovejo church, fired by one of Vernon's ships. It came flying in through a church window, but did not injure anybody in the assembled congregation.

I walk back from the fort by the India Catalina statue. She's clearly up for *Sports Illustrated*'s swimsuit issue; Colombian women regularly win beauty contests, although they are also reputed to have a huge enthusiasm for plastic surgery. I conclude my sightseeing where I started the day, at the Santo Domingo Church. It's an impressive structure with a nice legend about the devil, in the form of an engineer, trying to tempt the architect to tack on a more ostentatious tower. The pure-as-the-driven architect realises what's up and says no. The engineer-devil, annoyed, gives the church tower a kick as he departs. The fact that the tower is less than vertical and straight, therefore, has nothing to do with any architectural or engineering miscalculations.

After dinner I wander the streets a bit. At one point last night's porno-devil girls – without the horns tonight – stride by in short shiny dresses, like ballet outfits, with gold high heels and followed by a guy in black tights and a black singlet with a red sash. Where are they going? They march through the Santo Domingo Square and disappear into somewhere at the wall.

A bus takes me along the coast to Santa Marta; there's an unexpected stop in Barranquilla where I switch to another bus, but as long as I keep the sea on the correct side we can't go wrong. Lots of stops, including one stand-against-the-bus-and-get-patted-down military checkpoint, stretch the promised four-hour trip by a couple of hours.

A few years ago, Santa Marta had just one restaurant and one bar and you took a taxi to them, but with much of its old city area pedestrianised and the development of a crush of bars and restaurants, particularly around the Parque de los Navios, today it's a new story. There's also a picturesque old cathedral, another interesting gold museum, a little strip of beach at the waterfront and a major port just off to the east.

The pull of scuba diving distracts me. Only a few minutes by minibus from Santa Marta, Taganga is Colombia's backpacker beach resort. It's even attracted a semi-permanent Israeli population, a certain sign of establishment on the backpacking circuit. I drop my bag at Casa de Felipe, a French pioneer in the town, and wander down to the waterfront for lunch. Boats are pulled up along the beach, where the international blend of visitors move from café to bar to restaurant to dive shop. I sign up for a couple of dives the next morning.

Despite the numerous operators, the dives aren't that exciting – there's quite a swell running and some fairly fierce currents at the bottom. The second dive, after a break at a scruffy, stony little beach, is better. There's improved visibility, less current and more marine life. What makes the day's diving interesting is the company. Trevor, an Englishman, is clearly on a busman's holiday since he's a fish farmer in Panama. Like any good British fish farmer (read or watch *Salmon Fishing in the Yemen*), Trevor started his fish-farming career with salmon in Scotland before moving on to Turkey and finding an attractive Turkish wife. I can't work out her name – Ozden or Ausden – but 'nobody can remember it,' she says, 'so call me Rosie'. She's wielding a big underwater camera so she's clearly serious about fish as well.

Turkey – and its sea bream and sea bass – was followed by a hopeless Gaddafi-era project in Libya before Trevor and Rosie turned to raising extraordinarily expensive grouper near Komodo in Indonesia for the Hong Kong live fish trade. Today it's cobia and ling for the US. They say that the Americans are not very involved or expert in the business, they just buy the fish.

'When you want to eat them,' Trevor says, 'it's not being near fishermen and the sea that matters, it's being near a fish market. If it means constantly dealing with fishermen, the restaurant will probably prefer to buy something frozen that they can sling in the freezer and get out when necessary.

Sydney fish market was the best I've ever seen.'

I head out for fish and chips in the evening.

It's from Santa Marta that I make the five-day trek up to
Ciudad Perdida. I'm making the walk with Vincent Michael
and his wife Felicity, who are from the US, and Santiago
Giraldo from Bogotá. Vincent heads up Global Heritage Fund,
an organisation that looks after archaeological sites in the
developing world, and Santiago is GHF's expert in Colombia.
I couldn't ask for better, or better informed, companions. A
colourful *chiva*, looking like the Colombian equivalent of a
Filipino jeepney, rattles us out to the start of the walk and half
an hour later we've already waded across two stream crossings,
started up the first steep ascent and begun to slip and slide in
the mud. The wet season hasn't arrived yet, but it's certainly
been raining and after a spell of misty drizzle it sets in to rain
for real just before we arrive at our night halt.

I'm sodden. It's not that hot, but it's certainly humid.
Santiago suggested that raingear is unnecessary 'because if
it rains it will rain so hard it gets through anything'. In fact,
the rain doesn't need to get through – you could hang me on a
clothesline and I could make my own rain shower; you wouldn't
even need to wring me out. 'Nothing will dry while you're on
the walk,' I've been warned. 'Keep your dry clothes dry for
nights in the camps and put up with wearing wet clothes while
you're walking.' It's good advice. At night the humidity seems
to drop with the temperature, but I sleep very comfortably in
hammocks or bunks, never too hot or too cold.

The night's refuge is an open shelter slung with lines of hammocks. I'm muddy, sweaty and weary. 'This is not fun,' I think as we hang our damp clothes out, where they will be just as damp in the morning. Things start to look better after a cold shower, a cold beer and a hot meal and over the next few days they get far better, but on night one all I want to do is get in my hammock and sleep. I barely notice the cacophony of noises outside, frogs most prominently. Any jaguars on patrol? Tracks have been seen.

In the morning, it's Old McDonald's Farm around the refuge. For the first couple of days, until the trail gets too steep and rocky, we've got mules and a mule driver to carry our gear. He's camped out around the farmhouse verandah, where a caged female turkey is being courted by a male, a tom or a gobbler, doing an elaborate and noisy display outside the hen's cage.

'Come outside, honey,' the tom demands.

'Just open the door and come in, big boy,' the hen responds.

It's a vivid display of turkey frustration – there's no way he's getting in or she's coming out. Eventually the encounter tapers off into much cooing and clucking, but with no chance of consummation.

I pack away my dry clothes and put on my pre-dampened gear, recalling as I do my grandmother's warning of the dangers of wearing wet clothes: 'You'll get a cold in your kidneys.' On the first day the trail was more heavily used than I expected and the surrounding country was mainly agricultural, not jungle or even forest. That soon changes as we climb higher towards the Lost City. Along the way, we have numerous encounters with local indigenous people from the Wiwa and

Kogi tribes. Santiago has made the walk so many times he seems to know all of them. They're always traditionally dressed, a loose shirt and trousers in white going off-white for the men, Mother Hubbards in far more off-white for the women. The men almost always wear rubber Wellington boots; the women have bare feet, shy smiles and, if they're lucky, lots of beaded necklaces. Both sexes sport long, black hair, 1970s rock-band style, and the men are usually chewing coca leaves and carrying lime to go with them in a gourd known as a *poporo*. They also have large plastic-handled machetes. They're all very friendly. A couple of times through the day another tourist group passes, on the descent from Ciudad Perdida.

There are traces of ancient Tayrona agricultural terraces beside the path, and sometimes we find short sections of ancient stone stairways. At times the trail goes into deep jungle-like forest and then it dries out, but usually it's muddy. There are some devastated-looking slash and burn areas either side of us. Ant trails regularly cross our path – they're mostly leafcutter ants, each ant in one direction holding up his green-leaf triangle, like a long line of windsurfers. Sometimes there's a little collection of 'sails' lying down, where the unfortunate ants have been stepped on by passing walkers.

We pass a refuge run by Wiwa people and then a large Kogi village, Mutanzhi, with a big *nuhue* or 'world house', where the men meet, at one end of the village. Soon after, we stop at a solitary house where Rosita, a noted singer, lives with her husband. Santiago has brought him a drum. The hut is almost totally bare; there's not much more than a tattered mattress, a blanket, a hammock and a saucepan.

We walk alongside the very beautiful Buritaca River, which we'll follow all the way to Ciudad Perdida. The river is punctuated by stunning swimming holes, including one, complete with refreshing waterfall, right beside our night stop. The mules stay here, we have to carry our bags the rest of the way. Not that mine is very heavy; you don't need any cold weather gear or a sleeping bag so it's just a few changes of clothes and then a shoes-versus-sandals choice. A big group comes through on the descent, one guy hefting a huge backpack. 'What's in there, his mother?' we ask the guide. It's close to the truth; his mother follows a little later and he's carrying some of her gear.

The next morning, almost immediately, the trail becomes narrow and rocky – not mule friendly – and there's a suspension bridge, recently constructed by GHF, over the surging river. The first tribespeople we meet are two guys walking their pigs on strings. I continue to be amazed that although the temperature is not that high, the humidity certainly is. My glasses constantly steam up, and I'm forever wiping them with my soggy shirt tails. A long climb is followed by an extended up-and-down descent to another crossing of the Buritaca River, and then we walk through the final refuge before the steep stairway to the city.

A few steps into the site there's a big stone slab inscribed with what could be a map. Except it doesn't match the city layout in any form – the city is all circles linked by multiple paths with repeated forks. Soon after our entrance we come to the Monumental Stairway, another 300 or so steps which take us up to the much-photographed platforms of the Central

Axis, dating from 1100 to 1200 AD. The city today is just
platforms and connecting paths; the buildings that once stood
on the platforms must all have been wood and have long since
disappeared. There is no information on what the Ciudad
Perdida buildings might have been like. The Spanish invaders
recorded no descriptions of the architecture and although the
Tayrona people made figures and jewellery showing people,
animals and other devices, they never illustrated buildings
or structures. The Spanish contact was only fleeting and the
city was abandoned soon after, its population devastated by
multiple onslaughts of European diseases.

When the tourist group was kidnapped ten years ago, they
were staying at a refuge right on the site, but it's since been
demolished, so today visitors stay at that final refuge, an
hour's walk and those thousand-plus steps below the site. I'm
very fortunate to be able to stay right at the Lost City, in the
archaeological department guest house. It's a rare privilege. At
dinner the guest-house cat, Pilar, makes itself at home on my
knee. Every place along the walk seems to have a resident cat,
each of them small but sleekly well fed and content. A handful
of soldiers from the encampment just above the site hangs
around the guest house. They've been stationed here since the
tourist kidnapping to ensure there's no repeat performance.
The soldiers are young recruits, eighteen or nineteen years
old and all bored stiff, but they can take calls for an hour each
evening on the archaeologists' satellite phone. The calls are all
either from mum or a girlfriend.

We're at the site for two nights. There's plenty to see – the
site sprawls over more than twice the area of Machu Picchu

and there's a lot more waiting to be investigated. It's completely surrounded by jungle; all you can see are trees in every direction. Everything becomes moss-covered and overgrown if it's not constantly hacked back.

Apart from paths and platforms the site boasts lots of wildlife, particularly the birds for which Colombia is noted. We've been seeing them all along the trail. I only ever catch a brief glimpse of a toucan, but the crested oropendolas are easier to spot. I really like their sock-like suspended nests, long flashy yellow tails and white beaks. There's a tree branch hung with their nests, like a line of washing, just below the big platforms on the Central Axis. Not to mention the hummingbirds – as I'm having a pee one with a long curved beak hums by and works over a line of flowers directly in front of me. There are lots of butterflies too, the brilliant big blue Morpho and the equally large owl butterfly, so named for the owl-eye likeness on its wings.

There's some other wildlife that I thankfully haven't encountered. The walk has a bad reputation for mosquitoes, but they've been nowhere near as bad as I expected. At least for me. Felicity has certainly suffered from them and Vincent has also had problems with ticks; again, they've left me alone. And, wonderfully, there are no leeches in Colombia. Plenty of places with a climate and jungle like this would be prime leech territory.

At lunch a young boy comes by and clears the food left on my plate. Our eating habits are evidently way too fussy; he's one of ten and it must be a case of eat when you can at his place.

The next morning we start back early and stop for lunch and a swim at Tezhumake, our night-two refuge. A dog picks up with us soon after we depart, and I manage, accidentally, to kick it when I try to persuade it to forget us and go back. Santiago threatens it with a stone and it slopes away; we're not the new life it might have envisaged. The final stretch has become very muddy and I have my long-awaited first spill of the walk, but I come away with not much more than a muddy hand. Finally, we continue past Afredo's, scene of that first morning's turkey romance, and arrive at the next refuge, Adan's, for the night. We're greeted with the sound of Vallenato, the enormously popular local version of country and western, with a similar emphasis on 'my woman done me wrong'. There's time for a cold beer and a quick swim in the refuge's river swimming hole before darkness falls.

Having slept really well every night on the walk, tonight I don't. I toss and turn in my hammock – I've learned to get in it diagonally; if you simply lie down straight along the hammock you're locked in place – and then around 2 am it starts to deluge. The rain finally drops back from downpour to straightforward shower, but by this time I'm too awake and worrying about the rivers rising or the track becoming impassably muddy. Of course, when I do get up I realise the rain has stopped hours ago; I've been listening to the river and thinking it was rain.

I start the day in luxurious fashion, putting on dry clothes since conserving them doesn't matter any longer. By the time we complete the first steep climb from the refuge my luxuriously dry shirt is soaking wet. We stop at the store at the top of the first long ascent from the trail head, our final descent, where I have a Coke, my first and hopefully last of the year. We've been swapping the lead with an Australian–German group we met at the Lost City and soon after they stop for a final swimming-hole break. An army contingent watches them in the water.

We're finally at the end. I wash my muddy shoes off in the last river crossing.

Although tourists were the target of the Ciudad Perdida kidnapping, it was more often the local population who suffered from this form of fundraising. By the final decade of the last century Colombia's long history of political turmoil had created a chaotically divided society. The government was opposed by an assortment of revolutionary guerrilla forces, a matching hodgepodge of right-wing paramilitary organisations also opposed the left-wing guerrillas and the drug-producing and -smuggling cartels, often with their own private armies, added further confusion. Throw in American drug war advisors and it's no surprise that the result was bedlam.

Unrest in Colombia goes back to its earliest days as an independent nation. Colombia had a two-party democracy with power tossed back and forth between Liberals and Conservatives, but in fact a large slice of the population was excluded and ignored. The struggle between the groups was often bitter enough to be labelled a civil war; there were eight of them in the nineteenth century alone and the new century rolled in with the Thousand Day War, its death toll 100,000.

Coffee powered the economy through the first half of the twentieth century, but the underlying discontent remained. In 1946, when it looked like the Liberals might be led to power by Jorge Eliécer Gaitán, a genuine man of the people, Gaitán was assassinated. That kicked off La Violencia, a ten-year civil war which killed 200,000 people.

Even that death toll did not bring a lasting peace. By this stage, two-thirds of the population were living in poverty, unable to secure a fair deal from wealthy landowners. Leftist groups started to call for land reform. The biggest and best of them, FARC, the Revolutionary Armed Forces of Colombia, arose in the 1960s with the aim of overthrowing the state and redistributing land. The conflict was not simply FARC versus the government; the rival Marxist-inspired ELN – the same ones who kidnapped the Ciudad Perdida walkers – were also active in the rural areas. Meanwhile, in the urban areas M-19 took up the struggle. To further confuse things, an assortment of right-wing paramilitaries defended landowners against the left-wing guerrillas with the AUC (United Self-Defence Force of Colombia) as an umbrella organisation of these groups.

And then there were the cocaine cartels, which often had their own private armies. Taxing cocaine production, or even getting directly involved with its production and distribution, provided funding for both sides of the left–right split. If cocaine didn't provide enough cash, then kidnapping upped the income flow. Throw in the national army, along with cash, equipment and even personnel from the US war on drugs and it's hardly surprising that much of Colombia became a no-go zone, or that the number of displaced people, refugees within their own country, was greater than anywhere else in the world apart from Sudan.

It was a situation that simply could not go on forever. As with other revolutionary organisations, FARC's money-making operations began to overwhelm it. You can't be preaching land redistribution if you're also seizing land for coca leaf production for your cocaine operations. As FARC's popularity plummeted, Álvaro Uribe was elected in 2002 with anti-guerrilla operations as his central aim; unlike with previous governments, negotiations didn't enter the picture. The results were dramatic and by 2008 the ELN had been sidelined, FARC was on the run and the paramilitaries had been disbanded. Roads were reopened, rural areas brought under government control and people began to move back to the villages they had fled.

Uribe was replaced by Santos, with a promise to follow the same crackdown, and even their fiercest critics would agree that Colombia today is a far safer country than it was ten to twenty years ago, although there are still big problems to be faced. Cocaine production has devolved from the all powerful mega-cartels to smaller *cartelitos*. Then the 'false positives' scandal, when army units upped their body count of guerrillas by grabbing innocent young men off the street, dressing them up as guerrillas and killing them, tarnished the government's reputation.

The worldwide brotherhood of terrorist organisations didn't seem to include FARC in their international cooperative movements too often, until the IRA turned up in 2001, presumably to transfer some of their explosives expertise.

The IRA has often seemed intent on proving that it was a truly Irish terrorist organisation, so although tragedy (killing and maiming innocent people) was part of their game plan, the dial still often turned towards comedy or farce. As if to confirm that when all else failed they were indeed the clichéd Irish incompetent, the IRA seemed to blow themselves up much more often than the average terrorist for whom suicide wasn't part of the game plan. When the IRA bomb squad visited their friends at FARC, the dial was twisted well towards the farcical end of the scale.

For a start, they weren't even Irish, according to their passports. One of them was Sinn Féin's man in Cuba, but all three arrived with false British passports thanks to their Northern Irish origins. Second, they said they'd come to Colombia to go bird watching, which had become such an overused excuse – from cocaine importers to IRA terrorists – that claiming you were in the country to see the crested oropendola or the red tanager made you an immediate object of suspicion.

After they were arrested, all three were convicted of passport offences. The more serious charge of working with FARC failed to earn a conviction and their prison sentences were changed to fines. The government then appealed the verdicts and, second time around, convicted them of working with the rebels. By then, however, the trio had done a runner and returned to Ireland. The local assumption is that they exited the country to FARC-friendly Venezuela and then hopped across to the Caribbean island of Trinidad. Ireland, or rather the Irish in general, ultimately paid for their crimes as the Colombian authorities brought in visa requirements for Irish citizens, unlike most other Europeans. The restriction lasted for six years.

Back in Santa Marta I have one final Colombian journey, which will be with an Irish trio. We're heading out to the Guajira Peninsula, the finger of land curving over the eastern corner of Venezuela and pointing towards the Dutch 'ABC Islands', Aruba, Bonaire and Curaçao. Germán flies up from Bogotá and we head out for lunch at his favourite seafood restaurant. I've already caught the announcement of Chavez's death before I made the Ciudad Perdida walk; now we step inside the restaurant just as another piece of South American history is about to unroll.

Every head in the restaurant is turned to the news on the TV. It's after dark at the Vatican City and there's the white smoke emerging from the Sistine Chapel chimney – the *nueva papa* has been chosen, but who is he? We focus instead on our delicious little lobsters, with rice and plantains, and just as we're departing, the Vatican spokesperson fronts the microphones to announce it's the Argentinian contender, the first New World pope.

'Oh no,' groans Germán. 'The bloody Argentinians are so up themselves, they're always claiming to be the most stylish, to have the best football players. And now they've got the pope.'

The next morning the five of us are picked up outside the hotel at 5 am. Germán and I have been joined by the hotel's owner, Patrick from Ireland, his brother Jim and Jim's wife Berry. From Uribia the road runs parallel to the railway connecting the Cerrejón coalmines to the port of Puerto Bolívar, but first we stop in the shonky little town to load up on supplies. And booze – lots of Venezuelan Polar Beer and three bottles of rum. The Irish trio rapidly start to confirm all the clichés about the Irish and their capacity for alcohol. Germán seems to have no trouble matching them bottle for bottle, but I'm left behind even before we leave Uribia, and fall further behind over lunch. By beer o'clock, I'm a non-contender. The Venezuelan beer comes in tiny 222 ml bottles, but it's dirt cheap at around 50 US cents a bottle and that's a 100% mark-up on the Venezuelan price.

We stop briefly at Manaure to see the salt production process and then it's unsealed road until we head across country to the coast and Cabo de la Vela. It's a dusty one-street town, which has become popular as a remote beach retreat. We inspect the pretty bay at Playa del Pilón and retire to El Faro – the lighthouse – for sunset.

In the morning, our guest house is a messy shambles. There's water, but it doesn't seem to get to the toilets, the sole working sink is only half working, the tap falls off, there's no mirror, so I don't bother shaving, and even the showers are close to useless. The refuges on the Ciudad Perdida trail begin to seem quite luxurious.

We set off and soon arrive at the terminus of the railway line, marked by rows of big wind fans and a gang of photographers shooting a Renault car advertisement. When the railway peters out so does the road, but we press on to Bahía Portete, an abandoned village marked only by the remains of two piers. A paramilitary dispute about ten years ago led to the massacre of the Wayuu villagers here. We continue east through bleak salt-flat country and past a couple of half-hearted children's 'road blocks' (we pay them off with candy) until we suddenly stop at a house and compound which turns out to be the Restaurante Marlene and its *abastos*, a small shop. The shop is surprisingly well stocked in a very picturesque and old-fashioned way. The whole compound is extraordinarily tidy and we're soon tucking into plates of very tasty prawns. With more bottles of beer, of course. The Guajira Peninsula may be one of the more remote corners of Colombia, but it seems to have excellent mobile phone coverage. We phoned ahead to place our lunch order.

After lunch the trails get worse. If they were in Australia, they'd be outback tracks overdue for the grader to come through. Eventually we reach the huge sand dunes of Playa Taroa, a sand tsunami facing off against the sea, according to my guidebook. The dunes are also home to *langosta* – they're not lobsters, but colourful locusts of almost lobster-like proportions. Despite the inhospitable scenery there always seems to be some remote shack or settlement in sight: local cyclists weave by with surprising frequency and while we're sitting on the dune a small boy toting a large plastic container strides down to the beach, fills it with seawater, clambers back over the towering dune and then simply disappears.

'Where did he go to?' we all wonder.

We have lobsters – real ones, not the insect substitute – for dinner that night at Punta Gallinas. Our drinking endeavours include knocking off the third bottle of rum, along with a lot more of those little Venezuelan beers. Next morning, after

a boat excursion to visit a colony of flamingos, we drive to
the pointy end of Punta Gallinas, as far north as you can get
and still be in South America. Another lighthouse marks this
northern extremity.

We push on east. The road is rarely more than potholed,
crumbling, ridged and otherwise generally awful and the
scenery could be Australian outback, if not for the cactus. Or
perhaps somewhere in Africa – I keep expecting to see lions
lounging in the shade under a tree. In reality, the animal
life is a lot of goats, less frequent donkeys and cows, iguanas
that periodically shuttle across the road and those lobster-
size locusts that flutter away at our approach. For the whole
day's drive we see pedestrians, occasional bicyclists pedalling
resolutely from who knows where to who knows where, and a
number of motorcyclists, but the only larger vehicle is a petrol
tanker, five minutes before the end of the drive to Nazareth.

The road has been so bumpily appalling I'm rather surprised
to find we've arrived at a town large enough to boast a school,
a church and even a library. Plus, right on the main square, a
property fronted by a barbed-wire fence and surrounded by
a high wall topped by coiled razor wire. When night falls the
razor wire is floodlit so you can't miss it. I thought it was a jail
at first, but the town tale is that the owner is a narco-profiteer
who clearly has something to worry about. The compound
shelters his underground bunker, we're told, along with the
three Hummers in his garage. The only other thing they know
about him is that he's a vegetarian.

Patrick, Germán and I climb to the Mirador lookout, where
there's a shrine looking over the town, and then out towards

the pointy peaks of the park, where we will go walking tomorrow. The sun is setting when we meet the others at the local drinking-hole-cum-petrol-dealer. The half-dozen locals are all in various states of inebriation, and one example of extreme inebriation rumbles by in a pickup truck. A few minutes later the sound of a mighty tumbling of beer bottles rings out. Just around the corner he's fishtailed into a tree, crumpling the rear tray comprehensively and then colliding head on with the next tree. The occupants of the truck, astonishingly, are unharmed, although the crates of empty beer bottles are scattered across the road.

The next morning half our group has come down with some mystery stomach bug, and the rest are led into the Macuira National Park. Our guide Ricardo knows uses for every plant, tree and cactus along the trail – this one mends a broken bone, that one heals a scar, others to cure baldness, dislodge a retained placenta, deal with dandruff, even deflect the evil eye. On our walk back into town we catch up with a beautiful barefoot girl, her mother and a donkey hefting a big suitcase; they're taking her to boarding school in Nazareth. We have lunch at the home of a local patriarch, a real Renaissance man – he's a published poet and his highly symbolic naive art hangs, crookedly, on the walls around the compound.

Driving back to Santa Marta the next day is the same trip in reverse, but condensed into one day. Once we get back onto the good roads we speed along, but then we slow down, partly from heavier traffic and a slower road, but also due to incessant police, military and assorted other checkpoints. Most of them wave us through, but there are enough that do stop us to make progress tedious. The final stretch takes close to an hour and includes a customs check, which requires all the bags be on the roof to be checked and then, almost immediately, a police check where all the males have to get out and have their ID examined. It's the price you pay, perhaps, for the new secure, safer Colombia.

So the cocaine business is still going, but the associated chaos, deaths, gangs and crime have moved north to Central America and Mexico. The guerrillas, FARC and their offshoots, are under control or on the run. The paramilitaries have been disarmed and the army is behaving itself at least some of the time. The cities are safe and city dwellers are able to venture out into the country, for so many years a closed-off region. Crime is down, tourism is up; the 'don't go there' government tourist advisories have been scaled back or even deleted. Everything is hunky dory, or at the very least pretty safe and sound, right?

Well, not quite. On my last night in Bogotá before heading north to Medellín, I have a leisurely look around the wonderful Museo d'Oro, then grab a couple of empanada de pollos at a small café, withdraw some money from an ATM and stroll Candelaria, mainly around the busy, colourful student area where there's interesting graffiti, street art and shop paintings. I'm only one of several people photographing the graffiti in the late afternoon light as I start to move back towards the hotel, only a couple of blocks away. The pavement narrows and the two young guys ahead suddenly spin around and collide with me.

Hey, I'm being mugged, I suddenly realise when one of them grabs at my bag. That surmise is solidly confirmed when the other one waves a knife at me.

'Take it, take it,' I shout, too shocked to try thinking in Spanish.

They do and then disappear at high speed. I'm left running my hands down my shirt and feeling my chest. Have I been stabbed?

I haven't and all I've lost is my camera (there were better cameras in use around me), my daypack, my guidebook and Spanish phrasebook and my cap. Later I recall I also had an umbrella in the bag. Fortunately, my passport and other important stuff are back at the hotel and the street was too crowded for my muggers to hang around and demand I hand over my iPhone, wallet or watch. Bystanders are looking bemused or shocked, however you react when somebody gets done over right in front of you. A group of students come over to ask if I'm okay. Of course, having things stolen can happen anywhere – it's happened to me more than once and I usually conclude that perhaps I should have been a little more cautious. And when it doesn't happen, I've patted myself on the back. This is my third visit to Bogotá; I'd certainly not had any problems on the first two.

I walk back to Germán's flat, across the road from the hotel. He lowers the key down to the street from his fourth-floor window, and I let myself in and climb the stairs to his apartment.

When he opens the door, I tell him, 'I need a beer.'

DEMOCRATIC REPUBLIC OF THE CONGO

I'm at the New York Met, well past the ride of the Valkyries and into the final turmoil of Götterdämmerung, when I realise that Wagner's Ring Cycle bears a very close resemblance to the story of the Congo. In the opera, the evil dwarf Alberich steals the Rhinemaidens' gold. Then all hell breaks loose and it takes sixteen hours of opera to sort it out. In Africa, the evil Belgian King Leopold stole anything going in the Congo, all hell broke loose and over a century later it still hasn't been resolved.

Don't go unless you absolutely have to. If you're already there, think about leaving. And if you absolutely have to go, then take care, don't go out after dark, take a taxi – don't walk – and keep the windows wound up and the doors locked. Don't take photographs. Watch out for pickpockets. Watch out for the military and, most important of all, watch out for the police. Oh, and don't fly anywhere.

The travel advisories for DRC were not exactly reassuring, but they never are. I was confident that the on-the-ground reality would not be as bad as the advisories warned. It usually isn't, and, besides, what a country! Only the Amazon pumps out more water than the mighty Congo River. The jungles are still home to weird and wonderful creatures, like the cross-between-a-zebra-and-a-giraffe Okapi. Or the even-more-closely-related-to-us-than-chimpanzees bonobos. Plus there's the chance of an encounter with those musclebound mountain gorillas and the opportunity to climb one of the world's most spectacular volcanoes.

Then there's the history, which bounces between weird and shocking. There was the colonial period, described by Joseph Conrad as 'the vilest scramble for loot that ever disfigured the history of human conscience'. Then the breakneck race to independence in 1960, led by a charismatic leader who enjoyed only sixty-seven days as prime minister before being badly beaten and finally shot by a firing squad supervised by the just departed Belgians and urged along by the Americans, who were fearful that the Congo would become a foot-in-the-central-African door for the Soviet Union.

This was followed by a long period of dictatorship by Mobutu, a 'friendly tyrant' (the CIA's definition), who took African kleptocracy to previously unheard of heights and ran the economy steadily backwards. All the while, he was dividing his time between chateaus on the French Riviera and a remote jungle palace equipped with a runway suitable for chartered supersonic Concordes. When his army complained that they weren't being paid, his response was, 'You have guns, you don't need a salary.'

Mobutu eventually reached his use by date in 1997; greedy pro-western tyrants were no longer necessary once the Soviet Union was out of the game. His removal, triggered by the 1994 genocide in neighbouring Rwanda, only led to more trouble, as half a dozen other African nations scrambled in to grab some loot. Some of them – like Zimbabwe – not even bordering DRC.

By the time 'Africa's World War' had ground to a halt, five million people, most of them civilians, had lost their lives and countries like Rwanda and Uganda had suddenly become major gold and diamond exporters, even though they didn't happen to have any gold or diamonds of their own. The Russian cargo planes, seen in so many troubled corners of the world, and the Swiss private jets lined up at Congo airports tell their own story.

But I'm getting ahead of myself. To talk about Congo, we have to define the place, since its name has changed regularly and there are two countries with confusingly similar names, both named after the river. (It's a very impressive river to name two countries after, it should be said.) The smaller Congo is the Republic of the Congo, sometimes known as Congo-Brazzaville after its capital city. Back in the colonial days this was French Congo.

The one I'm visiting is the big one, the Democratic Republic of the Congo, or Congo DRC, or simply DRC for short. We could start with the handy shorthand that any country that puts 'democratic' in its name is clearly not democratic, but the country's name incorporated a falsehood even in the colonial era. It started out as the Congo Free State, clearly a complete lie since the Belgian King Leopold's greed left no room for anything free. His colony's economy was based on slavery and appalling cruelty. Under Leopold, the *chicotte*, a whip made from hippopotamus hide, was routinely used to flog his Force Publique's victims; women were kidnapped to force their husbands to meet rubber collection quotas; and hands were chopped off as souvenirs and to prove that bullets had not been wasted. And it was emphatically *his* colony: only when international condemnation boiled over did he reluctantly transfer the management to the country of Belgium. Leopold's personal Congo Free State became the Belgian Congo in 1908.

The scramble for loot wasn't quite so vile under Belgian management, but the Belgian Congo was still a very profitable operation. Leopold went from looting ivory to looting rubber and under national management the profits came from mining. By 1959 it was probably the most orderly, developed and profitable colony in Africa, pumping out almost ten per cent of the world's copper, fifty per cent of its cobalt and seventy per cent of its industrial diamonds. Of course, the whole place was about to crash and burn, but even after independence the Belgians were reluctant to let go of that profit stream. The breakaway Katanga Province was able to break away from the rest of independent Congo because that's where the mines were – the Belgians hoped they could keep on hauling the minerals out, even if they had to part company with the rest of their lucrative dependency.

So Katanga Province is where I decide to kick off my travels in DRC, but first I need a visa, and I'd be disappointed if there aren't some difficulties in getting one. I read up on it and check the London embassy's website, which features a long list of requirements starting with the usual application form, photographs and airline ticketing confirmation. My first immediate problem: I won't have a return ticket to DRC; I'm planning to exit from Goma across the border to Rwanda and then fly back to London from Kigali. I also need a photocopy of my yellow fever vaccination and something that proves my UK address. They don't ask for it, but I'm told a recent bank statement is nice, because it shows you can afford to go there.

At least it does if there's enough money in your account. I produce a neat little itinerary – stay in this hotel, take that flight – although it's all just intentions; I've got nothing booked. Next is a letter from your employer or educational institution. I write that for myself since technically I'm retired.

Then there's the impossible request for 'proof of accommodation', impossible because I can't get a hotel in Lubumbashi, my first stop, to respond and no hotel booking agency seems to book rooms in any of Lubumbashi's excellent list of hostelries. I make up an official-looking email confirmation from the Park Hotel. Remarkably, I get an authentic confirmation from them a few days later. And finally there's the real crunch: 'a legalised (stamped) invitation letter from partner/host in DR Congo'. Where on earth am I going to get that? I decide to ignore it.

So at 9.30 am on a Monday, I turn up at the DRC embassy entrance, just off Oxford Street and a stone's throw from the BBC's Broadcasting House. There are already a few people milling around the doorway and the process seems to be that you're let in one at a time through a glass door, where a young woman has a makeshift desk set up. She's watched over by a large guy in a very colourful shirt. There's no indication if my sheath of paperwork, minus the invitation, is going to work, but first I've got to pay for the visa – and not by handing over crisp pound notes; it has to be transferred to the DRC Embassy bank account. It works out to be fortunate that I've not done that in advance because the website was out of date – the cost has jumped by £20 and by another £30 if I want a double entry visa, which I figure I might as well have. So

I march down the road to a nearby bank, deposit £90 and return with the deposit slip.

'Come back at 11 am on Wednesday,' I'm told.

Which I can't do because I'm out of town until the weekend.

The following Monday is a public holiday so at 11 am on Tuesday I'm back at the embassy entrance. Pointlessly, as it turns out. When she said 'Wednesday' she did indeed mean 'Wednesday'. Friday will also do, but Monday, Tuesday or Thursday aren't DRC visa collection days. So Wednesday morning I'm back at the door again. There's the usual queue-jumping, but everybody seems to take it in a relaxed fashion and when I get to the bottom of the stairs I'm handed my passport, complete with a very bureaucratic-looking visa. No problems at all.

A side trip to Belgium seemed like a worthwhile addition to my DRC travels. After all, that's where Leopold's share of the vile loot ended up, primarily in the seaside resort of Ostend. Part of Ostend's attraction was that it was far enough away from Brussels to keep the king's extensive collection of mistresses out of the queen's sight. Leopold I, the Congo Leopold II's father, was another Ostend love rat. His popular wife Queen Louise-Marie died in Ostend at the age of thirty-eight and has a memorial chapel in the town's glorious Church of St Peter and St Paul. She's commonly assumed to have died of a broken heart from the king's cheating, lying ways. King Leopold II lavished his Congo wealth on Ostend architecture as well as Ostend sexual escapades. Sadly, both World War I and World War II inflicted huge damage on the town and today there's only the odd architectural gem between featureless modern apartment blocks. His nearly half-kilometre-long, Belle Epoque–style sea promenade, with its endless row of Tuscan columns, managed to survive; an equestrian statue of the royal villain keeps watch from the top. On each side of the regal horseman a throng of his European and African subjects look up at him adoringly. Belgian civilisation seems not to have had much of an impact on the Africans, who are appropriately naked. One gentleman's hand has been chopped off, perhaps a more recent comment on Leopold's colonising techniques.

My Belgium visit also includes the splendid Africa museum on the outskirts of Brussels. Well, the building is splendid; inside it's gloomy, dusty and badly lit, and the displays are well overdue for the renovation due to kick off in 2013. For years the museum's attitude towards their colonial history was neatly summed up by the golden statue of King Leopold II gazing out over the entrance rotunda while a half-naked African cuddles up against his leg. The inscription below the statue describes it as 'Belgium bringing civilisation to the Congo'. It has since taken baby steps towards updating the story in a revised display on 'colonial history'. It will be interesting to see if further revision takes place when the museum is renovated.

Out the window of my Kenya Airways 737 there's a breathtakingly beautiful dawn view of Mount Kilimanjaro and Mount Meru as I fly south from Nairobi to Lubumbashi in DRC. Lubumbashi only came into existence in 1910 and it was purely as a mining town. In the colonial era the town was known as Élisabethville, after the wife of Leopold's successor, King Albert I. The copper belt where Lubumbashi sits extends into Zambia through towns like Ndola, but Lubumbashi's mineral wealth goes much further than copper. The uranium used in the Hiroshima and Nagasaki atom bombs came from this area; during the Mobutu era, however, everything went steadily downhill. Copper production had reached 300,000 tonnes per year at the time of independence and even grew in the following years, but then Gécamines, the nationalised mining business, went into spectacular decline, production fell to less than 20,000 tonnes per year early this century and finally the mine closed completely.

Today 'Mount Lubumbashi', the giant heap of a century's worth of mine tailings, still dominates the city from the south, and a string of new Chinese-owned mining enterprises to the north are reminders that there's still plenty waiting to be uncovered. The mineral wealth of Katanga Province played a key role in the post-independence chaos, which tore the country apart, and it was here that Patrice Lumumba, the first leader post-independence, met his sad end. Figuring they might keep their hands on a large slice of the mineral output if they could carve Katanga Province out of the new nation, the Belgians actively supported local leader Moïse Tshombe in his breakaway efforts. Lumumba's attempt to haul Katanga back into his new nation didn't endear him to the Belgians and when he appealed for Soviet assistance, he quickly fell out of favour with the US as well. President Eisenhower even discussed with the CIA how Lumumba could be eliminated.

Although direct US action proved unnecessary, it's pretty clear the US didn't oppose his murder.

Lumumba was elected in June 1960, Katanga Province broke away in July, and the government was deposed by Mobutu in September and Lumumba placed under house arrest in Kinshasa – surrounded by UN troops to prevent Mobutu's forces from getting in, and by Mobutu's forces to prevent Lumumba from getting out. He managed to escape in November, but was recaptured by forces loyal to Mobutu and handed over to Tshombe in Katanga Province in January. Already badly beaten by Mobutu's men on the flight to Lubumbashi, Lumumba was executed later the same day by a firing squad supervised by Belgian officers.

Tshombe, who may well have been present at Lumumba's death, was shuffled in and out of power in the following years as the Belgians, the UN, assorted mercenaries and various Congolese factions squabbled over Katanga. Today, a statue of the local hero overlooks an ornate fountain which appears as if it has somehow survived all the upheavals since the Belgian departure. It certainly wouldn't look out of place in some Belgian provincial town, but in fact it dates only from 2010, when it was installed to mark fifty years since independence.

I wander the town for a couple of days, peer over the walls at Mount Lubumbashi, check the cathedral, the museum and the zoo, enjoy the comforts of the Park Hotel, shiver on a surprisingly chilly morning and book a flight with Hewa Bora Airlines to Kinshasa, the capital. Hewa bora is Swahili for 'good wind'; it's also, coincidentally, the name of the village where the president Joseph Kabila was born.

In a straight line, the distance between the second-biggest and the biggest cities in DRC is about 1600 kilometres, a two hour flight, and until recently flying was the only way you could travel it. Of course, there were railways and roads back in the Belgian colonial era and in the last couple of years land travel has slowly begun to start up again; there are reports of people making the trip in anything from two weeks by motorcycle to three weeks by public transport, to a month by four-wheel drive. A train service runs irregularly and unreliably between Lubumbashi and Kananga, the halfway mark, from where intrepid travellers can continue by bus and truck.

Apart from its own attractions, Lubumbashi has the secondary advantage that I'm not jumping into the DRC pool in the deep end. Every report on the capital underlines that these days it's Kinshasa the big and bad, no longer Kinshasa the beautiful. It is the biggest French-speaking city in the world, comfortably ahead of number three – Montreal – and number two – Paris. It won't completely live up to its bad reputation for me personally, but after a taxi whisks me into town from the airport, I drop round to my embassy to register, something I've never done anywhere before.

The Democratic Republic of the Congo may suffer from the curse of wealth, a surfeit of natural resources that seems to enrich the chosen few and enslave the vast majority, but it also suffers from a surfeit of quite a few other resources, including soldiers and police. Since they're not paid very well, if at all, the police have to make a buck wherever they can. Shaking down motorists is certainly one reliable way of ensuring a steady income and Boulevard 30 de Juin, the eight-lane highway running right through the centre of town, is marked by regular pedestrian crossings. Each offers the potential for extracting cash from any driver who fails to stop for even a vaguely approaching walker.

I rarely made a taxi or bus trip in Kinshasa that wasn't stopped at some point by the police. One particular incident underlined the problems. While the police officer waited, my driver searched his pockets, behind the sun visors and in the glove box for his driver's licence before finally admitting that he must have left it at home that morning. After more protracted discussions, a satisfactory payment for this oversight was negotiated and we continued on our way. A block down the road he reached into his pocket, pulled out his licence and showed it to me.

'Of course, I had it with me all the time,' he explained. 'But if you show them your licence they may take it away from you and then it can be really expensive to get it back. It's much faster and cheaper to say you've left it at home.'

The easiest way to extract money from a tourist is to catch him taking photographs. In fact, the DRC's 'no photography' regulations don't seem to be enshrined anywhere; they probably fall under Mobutu's famous Article 15 – *débrouillez-vous* – that you have the right, indeed the duty, to 'improvise' or 'get by', making money any way you can. Telling a tourist they shouldn't be taking photographs is certainly one handy way of extracting a few dollars.

Which is why I was pleasantly surprised to be invited by the military guards to photograph the ornate mausoleum in front of the Palais de la Nation, where the successor to Mobutu, Laurent Kabila, now lies. Mobutu's eventual departure in 1997 was prompted by a host of coinciding events. His long rule had turned sour years before; he was no longer a bulwark against Soviet intrusion into Africa and his Western supporters were heartily sick of financing his lifestyle. The economy had gone steadily backward for decades, the infrastructure was crumbling, mines were closing, roads disappearing, education standards had plummeted, life expectancy had lowered and the average Congo citizen was much worse off.

Nevertheless, Mobutu was a deft hand at the old divide-and-rule game, and it was only the genocide in neighbouring Rwanda that finally precipitated the greying despot's departure. Under Paul Kagame, tiny Rwanda had a much more efficient military than the gigantic Congo, despite all the military equipment and training the Belgians, French and Americans had lavished upon their friendly tyrant. And Rwanda had an overwhelming reason to get into the Congo, in pursuit of the 'genocidaires' who had driven the Rwandan killings. Best of all, this pursuit looked like it could be self-financing. Funding the Iraq invasion with Iraqi oil turned out to be a bad plan for the US-led 'Coalition of the Willing', but funding a Congo invasion with Congolese gold, diamonds and, most important of all, tantalum, turned out to be a very wise plan for Rwanda and its friends. Even some of its enemies did quite well out of the Congo free-for-all.

The final piece in the jigsaw puzzle was to source a local freedom fighter, keen to end the Mobutu horror story. But

finding somebody to overthrow the long-term dictator was
not straightforward. Eventually Laurent Kabila was roused
out of retirement in Tanzania and sent off as the figurehead
revolutionary. Kabila had a lengthy history: Che Guevara,
during his failed attempt to stir up rebellion in the Congo in
1965, had met with Kabila and decided that if this was the
best on offer there wasn't much hope for the revolution. For the
Rwandans in late-1996 this was not a problem; Kabila was just
somebody to add a Congolese feel to the invasion.

Mobutu had ensured that his army was best at fighting each
other, so that nobody could threaten his control. Besides, in
the Congo extracting money from civilians was a much more
important skill than repelling an invading army. The First
Congo War lasted barely six months: by mid-1997 Mobutu
was in exile (and soon to be dead) and Kabila was in power.
Unhappily for Kabila, his Rwandan and Ugandan supporters
soon tired of him; politically and economically he was useless
and changing the country's name, yet again, from Mobutu's
Zaire to the current Democratic Republic of the Congo didn't
allay anyone's concerns about democracy.

Soon the Second Congo War kicked off and it was a much
nastier and more prolonged affair than the first. Lasting nearly
five years, from 1998 to 2003, the war dragged in half a dozen
other countries, either to support a side, to protect their own
interests or to grab their share of the Congo's riches. The war
would also be labelled the Great War of Africa or the Coltan
War, after the mineral that can be processed into tantalum,
a vital ingredient of mobile phones. We all tote around a
taste of tantalum in our phones and it has most probably

come from DRC, the world's major producer of coltan. Like a conflict diamond, it may well have travelled down some very compromised paths on its way to your pocket or purse.

Millions of civilians had died by the time the Congo Wars ended, but the extensive death list also included Laurent Kabila, assassinated in 2001 by one of his child-soldier bodyguards. *The Economist*'s story on his death summed up the episode succinctly. 'Who killed Laurent Kabila?' queried the headline, a question quickly answered in the subheading, '50 million people had a motive'. Kabila's possibly adopted son Joseph soon succeeded him and has proved to be only a slightly more able administrator than his father. Slightly more democratic at least – he won a reasonably fair election in 2006, in fact, a very fair election compared to anything else in the country since 1960. The follow-up election in 2011 was probably not so even-handed.

Despite the millions who might've wished him ill, Kabila's mausoleum shows only the respect for a former leader. Gigantic hands hold concrete palm fronds over the late president's tomb and a large heroic statue of the slain revolutionary guards the front. For whatever reason, I can take photos here, but generally visitors should only get their cameras out with great care and certainly not near anything vaguely official – like airports, government buildings, army or police officers or the Congo River. It's wide and brown but if you do want to photograph it, do what I do – hop on a boat, cross the river to Brazzaville and shoot it from another country. The river is 3 kilometres wide at this point, making Kinshasa and Brazzaville the two closest capital cities in the world. The Kinshasa side of the river is distinctly lacking in viewpoints, while Brazzaville enjoys a glut of them. Find a riverside café, lounge back with a Primus beer (the standard DRC beer is also available across the river) and take as many photos as you like.

While enjoying my Brazzaville beer I muse about what fun I'll have on the short trip back to Kinshasa. I've opted for a 'canot rapid', the deluxe, high-speed riverboat , principally because the VIP transport involves fewer bureaucratic hassles. Congo travel is complicated by the complete lack of division between 'landside' and 'airside'. Travel in less colourful regions has a clear division between one side and the other. When you leave landside and go through immigration or security to airside, you can't just wander back to landside. There doesn't seem to be any line drawn between the two in either Congo. When I arrived in Lubumbashi, my first DRC stop, there were all sorts of people milling around outside the terminal; where you, as an arriving passenger with unstamped passport, should go was completely unclear.

Leaving Brazzaville Beach, the romantically named Congo Republic departure point, I go through assorted procedures, escorted all the time by a 'protocol', one of the fixers who are an unavoidable part of the Congo travel experience, and often seem to come included in your ticket cost. My passport is stamped and taken and we then wander back down the street. So I have now left Congo Republic, don't have a passport and yet here I am, back in Congo Republic. My protocol eventually leads me to the boat, my passport is returned and off I go.

Back on the Kinshasa side of the river I stroll the Botanic Gardens, avoid a couple of run ins with the police – once by simply continuing to walk when they hail me – and make an evening excursion to La Creche Hotel's rooftop terrace to catch some excellent rock music. The DRC has a lot of it and, although I've no idea who I am listening to, they are very good.

Brazzaville's attractions included the very fine St Anne's Basilica, with its green-tiled roof, and a peculiar new addition to the landscape, a gigantic statue of Pierre Savorgnan de Brazza, the French explorer who gave the town its name, looking like a malnourished, barefoot travelling hippy from the 1960s. The mausoleum behind the statue houses his remains and those of his immediate family, relocated from Algeria, where they had already been moved from Paris. On this side of the river, however, the statues of the Belgian Congo's colonial father figures don't get the same respect. The crumbling Musée National is also in limbo-land, awaiting funding to properly house its extensive collection. Henry Morton Stanley's Congo River steamboat, said to be rusting away in a museum courtyard, has actually been shunted off to the navy dockyard to be restored.

There is an assortment of Belgian statuary, no doubt retired from more prominent city positions: an equestrian statue of the appalling Leopold and one of Albert, the nephew who succeeded him as king. Figures of noble Belgian workers have been shifted here from the railway station and tucked away behind the museum building is a statue of Stanley, looking as if it has suffered the sort of indignities the US Army's art appreciation squad inflicted on statues of Saddam Hussein. Famous for his 'Dr Livingstone, I presume?' query, Stanley explored the country on behalf of King Leopold between 1874 and 1876.

Stanley, who had established a reputation for shooting first, asking questions later and then blaming it all on unfriendly natives, scattered his name around the country. Kinshasa and Brazzaville stand beside Pool Malebo, which was Stanley Pool in the colonial day, a lake-like widening of the Congo River. From there falls and rapids prevent navigation the rest of the way to the coast. Head east and you can travel for weeks before you reach my next stop, Kisangani – Stanleyville in the colonial era – at a bend in the river. It's the major town upriver and just above it the Boyoma Falls, also known as the Wagenia Falls, marks the upstream end of that long navigable stretch. It used to be known as Stanley Falls.

It's clearly time to head upriver, but once again I'm taking to the skies. The roads fell apart years ago and for a long spell the riverboats weren't running either. This led to shortages of all manner of supplies, but now the barges are once again shuttling back and forth – as long as the river levels are high enough. I put aside Congo River travel for a later date and take another flight, this time on Hewa Bora's venerable 727. As I board I note the small plaque by the door announcing that it rolled off the Boeing assembly line back in 1965. Its original owner was Lufthansa and although it will be coming up for its fiftieth birthday soon, some newfangled winglets tacked on to the wingtips show some reasonably recent love and attention.

Before I board, however, there's another round of DRC fun-and-games. The airport is exactly the sort of shambles you'd expect if you've read about Congo infrastructure, despite which

I make my way to the check-in desk quite easily; they fill out a boarding card; I go to the baggage check-in point, tell them I have no baggage to check and sail through the passport recording process before I hit a small problem at security.

I don't want to have any checked baggage on my Congo trip – from everything I've heard it's just an invitation for more problems, delays, payoffs. People check in with bags wrapped completely in plastic tape, which must show some sort of concern about what happens to your bags. In fact, some travellers even come with carry-ons wrapped in plastic, which must complicate physical inspection at security, but no matter.

The fact that I've planned a near-freezing night on top of a mountain, if all goes well, makes packing light problematic, but I've managed it so far. Kinshasa security makes me wish I had checked luggage instead. The X-ray machine doesn't work, neither does the metal detector, but there are three security guys to search your bags and when I see them taking liquid containers off the guy in front of me, even though they're the less-than-100-ml containers accepted everywhere else in the world, I start to worry. Sure enough, they have absolutely no interest in anything else in my bag – and don't even look at my computer bag with its 250 ml bottle of water – but head straight for the liquids bag, which is right on top. At first they want to confiscate everything, but I talk them out of sunscreen (it's a stick, not liquid), insect repellent (it's a roll on), mouthwash (I take a swig) and deodorant (I spray my armpits), but they want my little hotel-size bottle of shampoo. I show them *lave les cheveux* and tell them I don't want to have dirty hair, but they're adamant. I offer to buy it back for 1000 CDF (a dollar), but no, my dangerous shampoo is gone.

Fifteen minutes later, in the departure lounge, one of the security guys sits down beside me, surreptitiously slips me my shampoo bottle, pockets 1000 CDF and all is well.

The view from the plane is just an awful lot of jungle; deforestation has clearly not infiltrated every part of the Congo. We may not see them, but there are villages, towns, life down below. They've just been cut off, disconnected. Since the Belgian colonial days railways have disappeared; the jungle has grown over the roads and bicycles are often the only way – apart from walking – to get from one place to another. Cargo bicycles, often pushed rather than ridden, are the principal means of transporting goods and freights. Alternatively, you can fly: it's often reported that the more economically viable towns and villages, the ones that can justify a rough and ready airstrip, have become isolated 'islands'. It's as if rising sea levels have swamped the roads, cutting off one place from another.

If the flight isn't full there can't be more than a handful of empty seats. One of the four '*blancs*' on board gets off at Kisangani with me, the other two continue to Goma. The officials inspect my passport and have lots of questions about my 'profession' – it seems to be a major obsession. I always list myself as an engineer: it's a nice, safe occupation and indeed, in a previous lifetime, I did work as a mechanical engineer for a car company. I tell them I'm a designer, on holiday from BMW in Munich.

It's forest country, and busy all the way into town, until suddenly we're there, taking a garbage-strewn dirt track off the river-level airport road into the town. Post-independence Kisangani has done it hard. A painting behind the desk at Les Chalets, the popular foreigners' hotel, shows Belgian paratroopers descending into the town in 1964, when the chaos after independence was at its worst. After the troops broke the siege, journalist Edward Behr made his famous query, 'Anyone here been raped and speak English?'

More bedlam followed through the late 1960s and although money was poured into the town during the Mobutu period his mismanagement soon sent things backwards, as it did in so many other Congo cities. Nevertheless the real anarchy arrived with the First Congo War. The invading Rwandans and Ugandans were as inclined to massacre local people of Hutu descent as they were to kill Hutu 'genocidaires' who had fled from Rwanda. Worse was to follow during the Second Congo War when the Rwandan and Ugandan troops fell out with each other and, of course, the greatest toll was among innocent civilians caught between the two sides. Much of the town was destroyed between 1999 and 2002. Peace and the resumption of riverboat services has allowed Kisangani to turn the corner, although there's still evidence of the damage.

Walking around town I find an ATM and download a supply of US dollars. The Congo cash routine is to get US dollars and then change a smaller amount into Congolese francs. Here, as in Lubumbashi and Kinshasa, there are plenty of pavement money dealers sitting around, fronted by bricks of 500 CDF notes, the biggest denomination. Swapping US$20 nets you thirty-six of those notes, about as many as you can comfortably carry. So the procedure is infrequent ATM stops for US dollars, then more frequent stops to convert the dollars into francs. Small purchases are all made in francs, big ones in dollars.

There's plenty of evidence of the town's new money in the signs for diamond dealers. They're another indicator of the enormous wealth waiting to be dug up in this often shattered country; they're also one of the reasons for the private jets at Congo airports. Despite the signs advertising the dealers' presence it's a secretive business and outsiders are not welcome.

I take some photos of painted supermarket signs and a couple of kids are pleased to be included. I stroll on, down to the riverside, and I'm almost back at the hotel when I stop to photograph the sign for the Champs Elyse bar. Two minutes later I'm 'detained' – it's hard to call this an arrest – by a big guy waving an identity card, which seems to show he's someone important. He's complaining loudly about something which I presume – no, I know – is the photographs. Although Kisangani is a photogenic town I've been cautious, using a small camera, whipping it out and putting it away quickly, keeping my camerawork unobtrusive, whether photographing cross-river canoes, the market activity, the riverside Cathédrale Notre-Dame du Rosaire or the ruins of what had once been the fine old Hotel Les Chutes.

Two 'accomplices' – or are they just passers-by? – jump on board. There's a lot of pushing and threatening and the same things are said over and over again. This is obviously going nowhere in the street and I'm beginning to think that the longer we stand here the more people we're going to attract. Clearly the opportunity to jump in and harass a hapless *muzungu* is too good to resist.

'Let's go to the police station and sort it out there,' I suggest and off we go. The uniformed police in the large area in front – plus one guy cooped up in a small cell – look bemused by our show and we're still getting nowhere except now we have a bigger crowd. I'm marched to an office round the side where the head cop, with a mate, is watching the DRC football team play Cameroon on TV. I enthuse when the DRC goes 1-0 up, although I'm unsure if that helps. An assortment of people come and go, including the original three. The head cop is watching the footy game with one eye and trying to phone somebody at the same time, whether about me or not I'm also unsure.

By this time I'm very thirsty and I suggest to the guy who marched me from the front that perhaps he could go buy me a *boisson*. I give him 1000 CDF and off he goes to get it. Of course, all this is revolving around my not having a photo permit and, although I've suggested that I'm quite happy to get one, there certainly isn't much opportunity to do so when it's a Sunday afternoon and I've just arrived in town. A US$500 charge for a photo permit is proposed at one point, probably by one of the three original jokers.

More people come and go, including an attractive younger woman, and after some conversation I'm told to go with her. She turns out to be the Chef de Division Unique from the Hotel de Ville, the town hall, somewhere up the local power ladder. So we go outside and get into her car, with one guy in the front, and one either side of me in the back. She drives us here and there (nearly colliding with a motorcycle) and finally we drive by the Hotel de Ville, where I'm told I should return tomorrow morning to get a photo permit. She gives my camera back, then I'm dropped at my hotel. All this has taken well over an hour, perhaps two. I must admit that after the first three troublemakers, everybody else has been as polite and friendly as you could ask for. Getting arrested in DRC has been absolutely no hassle at all, just a little sitting around and waiting.

'Nothing special,' says Joe Wasilewski, whom I immediately bump into at the hotel bar. He's had a similar police station interlude on his way out to Wagenia Falls, Kisangani's big tourist attraction. Joe is doing some sort of research project out in the sticks about 120 kilometres from Kisangani. 'It used to take twelve to thirteen hours to drive there, now the road is better and it only takes nine,' he says. 'Of course, a couple of hours are spent waiting for ferries and stuff.'

He works for REDD – Reducing Emissions from Deforestation & Forest Degradation – which has something to do with sustainable forestry. He was also, in an earlier lifetime perhaps, some sort of Steve Irwin–style crocodile and snake wrestler who made assorted TV appearances; he's got a DVD of some of his classic critter conflicts ready to run. He's been here for two years, in six weeks on, six weeks off spells and hasn't learned much French in that time.

Joe and I chat with a guy working on his PhD, at Kisangani University, on Congo rodents and how the chaos in recent years has affected them. It seems there are lots of interesting rodents in the jungle around here, including the zebra rat. We then have a session with two Congolese would-be environment protectors, who turn out to be lawyers as well. Patrick (who, aside from English, also speaks Lingala, Swahili, French and one of the other main local languages, either Kikongo or Chiluba) says he would have come straight to the police station and bailed me out if I'd called him, as a favour to a passing tourist. I take his number in case there is a next time.

Jean Marie Bergesio, the exuberant Belgian patron of Les Chalets also agrees that a visit to a police station is part of the Congo experience, but insists that photo permits are 'absolutely not necessary, it's just another way of trying to make money'.

He's been here for forty-three years, and has clearly seen it all. 'It's been up and down,' he reports. 'Currently it's slightly up,' he makes a gentle incline motion. I mention *A Bend in the River* and he says, 'Naipaul was here for a year.' Kisangani was the troubled setting for V. S. Naipaul's novel, although town, river and even country are never named.

Bright and early the next morning I'm at the Hotel de Ville and soon find the office where I can get a photo permit, except the department head, or *chef*, isn't there yet. There are six people lounging outside the chef's office, but no chef. I'm about to depart when the chef appears and, surprise, surprise, it's Lydie Aganano, Ms Senior Official from yesterday. Another circular conversation stretches my limited French, the gist of which seems to be that in fact they don't issue photo permits in Kisangani – why hadn't I arranged one before I arrived?

We drive round the corner to the Kisangani press office where, very soon afterwards, another chef appears and there's more circuitous talking before he starts writing me a photo permit by hand. There clearly isn't such a thing as a photo permit form. I suggest that perhaps I should summon Patrick, my recently acquired lawyer.

'Oh, it's not that important,' is the reply. Although the speed picks up.

Now to negotiate a price: although US$100 is mentioned and US$500 was floated at the police station yesterday, it's now suggested that US$50 should suffice. I protest that not only is that incredibly expensive but it's also what I'd heard a photo permit should cost for the whole country, not just one town.

'So what do you want to pay?'

'How about US$20,' I suggest.

'Oh, okay.'

The whole process has taken less than two hours.

Once my photo permit is in my pocket, nobody even hints at complaining about my camera again, although I continue to use it as unobtrusively as possible. I ask if taking photos with a phone is okay, and the response is, 'Phones are fine, it's only cameras.'

I head to the market to investigate – and photograph – that tasty bush-meat snack: monkey. The impact on the ecosystem from the Congo's devastating civil war has been horrific. The war killed millions of people, but it also had a devastating effect on the environment. Driven from their villages and farms, many people were forced to become hunter-gatherers, foraging for a living in the jungle. Killing the odd monkey for village consumption is one thing; when hunters come in and wipe out whole troops of monkeys to ship down to Kinshasa on the barges it becomes a big problem. Joe spoke of seeing motorcycles going by with dozens of smoked monkeys on board.

He contrasted Congo to Costa Rica: 'In a day's walk you can see four or five different types of monkeys in Costa Rica. Here they know about humans and get as far away as they can.'

I think about the merry troupe of capuchin monkeys I encountered trying to break into the hotel restaurant in Costa Rica a couple of years ago. The smoked monkey section in the market is a depressing sight.

Wagenia Falls is just a ten-minute ride upriver from Kisangani; a motorcycle taxi ferries me out there to watch the local fishermen scooping fish out of the foaming waters with their conical nets. The calm below the falls marks the start of almost 2000 kilometres of navigable river down to Kinshasa, from where it's a nonstop tumble of rapids and falls for the final 250 kilometres to the Atlantic.

It was the trip upriver from Kinshasa – Leopoldville in the Belgian era – which inspired Conrad's *Heart of Darkness*. Through the years of violent turmoil, transport on the river ceased, a major problem for the people of Kisangani, whose only alternative route was either by air or on those mostly impassable roads. Now the big barges are plying regularly up and down the river and there is certainly no shortage of Primus beer in the town's bars. I wander down to the docks to ask about the trip. '*Le descente c'est deux semaine,*' a trucker tells me about the journey downriver. Upriver takes a month, but you should allow for five or six weeks.

I'm not planning on taking the river back to Kinshasa. Instead I take another flight further east, to Goma, in the troubled Kivu provinces along the border with Rwanda. It was time to check out the two attractions which account for almost all of the small number of tourists who visit the country each year: the magnificent gorillas of the Virunga National Park, and the stunning, lava-spewing Nyiragongo Volcano.

After the killings in Rwanda many of the genocidaires fled east through Goma into the Congo, pursued by the forces of the RPF, the Rwandan Patriotic Front. So it's long been a strategic and troubled area. Today there's a huge UN force in and around Goma and, although the security situation is always up and down, it's probably a little calmer during my visit. My DRC travels so far have been unplanned: I just turned up and waited to see what happened. While the DRC is hardly in a 'tourist boom', if you're going to see another tourist, this is where it will be, so these two local attractions – the gorillas and the amazing volcano – will take some planning and permits.

A little internet research pre-departure had unearthed my Goma guide, and the Western Union office on Earls Court Road in London had whisked US$400 Congo-wards. Now, would Emmanuel Rufubya be waiting for me at Goma's airport? My flight, the same elderly Hewa Bora 727 that had taken me from Kinshasa to Kisangani, banked over the lake, skimmed across the market and landed safely. Three years earlier, another Hewa Bora aircraft had smashed into the market on take-off.

Out in the public area I immediately meet Emmanuel, a pint-sized bundle of energy; if he were Irish he'd field leprechaun jokes. I'm soon in a hotel room by the lakeside, looking across to Rwanda, not much more than 100 metres away.

Goma's gorillas won't be my first Congo animal encounter. The high point of my Kinshasa stay was definitely a visit to Lola ya Bonobo sanctuary, about 30 kilometres out of the city. For a long time bonobos were thought to be just undersized chimpanzees; then, in 1928 someone realised they were an entirely different species found only in the Congo. The sanctuary looks after – and studies – orphaned bonobos. Their matriarchal society and 'make love not war' attitude – chimpanzees are more prone to war – provides plenty of interest for academics.

There are fifty-seven bonobos at the sanctuary and although only orphans are brought in, many of them subsequently breed. I watched the 'bonobo mamas', young women who play with the new orphans in the 'nursery' area, and then walked the 3-kilometre circuit around the outside of the sanctuary. It's fenced to keep the bonobos in and us out. Bonobo numbers in the wild are down from perhaps 100,000 in 1980 to 10,000 today. They can live to fifty or sixty years old, and have their first babies at ten. Their young are breastfed for four years so it's usually five or six years between births. And they're the most 'biped' of the great apes: that is to say they walk a lot.

On our way round the sanctuary I met Dr Zanna Clay, a British researcher who did her PhD on bonobos, spending three months a year here for the past four years. She's now studying empathy at Atlanta University. As we sat and watched the small group she was following, she explained how the matriarchal nature of bonobo society is based on female cooperation.

'Males can be friends, but the bonds between female bonobos are much stronger,' she said. 'So two females can dominate one male, and if another male comes in to support the first male the females will simply bring in another female. Eventually the next male in line thinks, "Forget this, sort it out yourself." So the females always win because they'll always go further in calling in their supporters. As a result, males usually give up immediately, because they know they're never going to win. With bonobos this is particularly seen with food – the females always get first choice.'

Of course, part of the reason males seem to be content with this is sex. With bonobos there's plenty of it. They've been dubbed 'the promiscuous apes' and Zanna, it turns out, has made quite a name for herself on the topic. In 2011 she received lots of media attention after reporting that the more important the sexual partner, the more noise the bonobos make. Google 'Zanna Clay', 'sex' and 'noise' and an assortment of stories pops up.

While the bonobo sanctuary was quite something, visiting animals in their natural habitat is always more exciting. I'd be looking for gorillas outside Goma in the wild. Gorilla tracking is a big deal in neighbouring Rwanda; there's often a long waiting list and you have to lay out US$500 for a permit. Still, it's an amazing experience and plenty of visitors are willing to put up with the wait and expense. Just across the border, in the Virunga National Park in DRC, 50 kilometres north of Goma, you'll find the same mountain gorillas. At US$400, a gorilla-tracking permit is nearly as expensive as in Rwanda – throw in a pricey short-stay visa and you'll actually pay more to see them, but the waiting list is much shorter and the experience is probably a little less commercial, so you'll get your gorilla encounter with a smaller group.

With my guide Moses, I set off for the Virunga National Park on a road which was sealed once upon a long time ago, but has not been maintained for years. So there are traces of tarmac, little potholed stretches, the odd island of bitumen. An hour out of Goma the road is blocked; a truck has broken down more or less in the middle of the road. Another truck, trying to squeeze by, has gone off into a ditch. Then a Land Cruiser has tried to squeeze by on the other, narrower, side and suffered a similar fate. So there's a lot of digging, pushing and unloading going on – the truck had a full cargo of sugar cane on board – and more vehicles are joining the queue in both directions. Another truck has a go at pulling the stuck truck out, without success.

I overhear a lot of comments about the *muzungu* (white guy) while we watch. Meanwhile the time is ticking by, and the gorillas, presumably, retreating further into the jungle. Fortunately, there's a Land Cruiser from the park on the other side of the block and we arrange to go in that, along with three South Africans who are also stuck. The surface gets much worse when we turn off the main road and once again, as so many times over the years, I'm impressed by the strength and durability of Land Cruisers. An outrider on a motorcycle, toting a gun on his back, rides with us as some sort of guide or guard.

At the park's starting point we're briefed: we must wear masks when we're with the gorillas because they're exceptionally susceptible to common human ailments. Now we just need to find them. We're told initially that it will be two hours, but that's soon revised to one, which is just as well because the two South African women are not fit at all. Most of the hour's walk is through potato fields, clearly an important crop here, and we're barely into the forest when we encounter the first gorilla. Or, more accurately, gorilla smell – there's a strong animal aroma in the air. We have two guide-guards accompanying us on the walk, and at the edge of the forest there are two more who seem to have the family pinpointed and know exactly where to take us. One of them is carrying a very sharp machete, which he uses to slash a path through the undergrowth for the next hour or two.

In this part of the park there are four families we could encounter – Rugendo, with seven members; Munyanga, with six; Humba, with fifteen; and Kabirizi, with thirty-six – and yes, we've found the big family. The Virunga National Park is contiguous with the Parc National des Volcans in Rwanda so gorillas can shift back and forth across the border. In fact, Moses tells me, the park personnel on both sides of the border are very possessive of their gorilla families and turn them around if they try to move internationally! But essentially the gorilla experience is very similar in both countries: limited number of participants, strict rules (like face masks), only one group per family per day and only for one hour.

We soon spot one gorilla and see several up in trees, and then, as we're following a track that leads to the main part of the family, there's a polite 'harrumph' from behind: we look around to see one of the gorillas following us. She sits down to look at us, then lies back and scratches her stomach. Then rolls on her side and props her head up on one hand with an elbow on the ground. Then makes a couple of faces. And then indicates 'could we please get out of the way because she'd like to carry on down the path'. So we politely move to one side and, damn me, she does a perfect little forward roll somersault, curls up in a ball and rolls past us down the path! I'd say 'like a black furry gym ball' except she probably weighs over 100 kilograms.

We spend our hour following them around. They're up in the trees, down from the trees, back up in the trees, lounging around, eating vines and leaves. This family has three silverbacks – alpha males, named for the silvery sheen their back fur shows at a certain age and size – and we meet up with the biggest of them. He sits there ignoring us and looking extremely regal. We also encounter a mother with a very small baby gorilla, sitting and feeding, the baby completely intrigued by us. After ten minutes she decides to move on and nonchalantly grabs the baby by one arm and tosses it behind her. It lands adroitly on her back and grabs hold as she strolls away.

It's remarkable how totally unconcerned they are by us and how unthreatening they appear. A couple of times we thought we were following them, only to find one of them following us, and they are *big*. Even the small ones are huge and the silverbacks are humungous – they'd make a sumo wrestler look scrawny – and it's all muscle, there's no fat on a silverback. I was fortunate to have encountered gorillas in the wild once before, in the Central African Republic, and I'd sign up for a repeat visit in a heartbeat.

The next day is DRC independence day; I saw the soldiers marching around in Kisangani, to practise for the celebrations. Moses and Emmanuel collect me in the morning and after a quick shopping session – bread, sardines, chocolate, biscuits, water – we drive to the start of the Nyiragongo Volcano climb, only 17 kilometres from town. Timothy Churella, a young guy from Boston – a non-stop talker – is already there, planning to make the climb for a second time. Two days ago, with half a dozen Americans, he got to the top in miserable weather; they spent the night up there, with rain pouring down, and barely saw a red glow.

There's a long wait for two more climbers: Agate and Lydia, two young French women who were stuck at the Rwandan border. Tim has also come across from Rwanda purely for the climb. There are eleven of us in all: the four tourists, my guide Moses, the women's guide (who carries absolutely nothing, not even a water bottle), three porters (one for me and Moses, two for the women and their guide) and two soldier-guides. Both soldiers carry automatic weapons, held up, as is usual in DRC, by string. This was once a rebel area, although now they're reportedly all gone.

We start at 1980 metres. The summit is at 3470 metres and we make four stops on the way up. It takes us four hours, rather than the projected five. At first, it's a gentle climb on a good path through dense rainforest, then it gets progressively steeper and you're walking over volcanic rubble. There's a view of a smaller adjacent crater and for a while it starts to actually rain rather than merely drizzle. It's not very clear and Tim is worried it's going to be a repeat of his previous ascent.

The last half hour to the top is a tough, steep clamber. Am I beginning to feel my age? I certainly begin to wonder in the last little bit, and the older of the soldier-guides seems to be hanging back to look after me. We finally reach the top, where eight huts huddle just below the crater rim, recent constructions, an indication that more tourists are expected. Although it's cloudy there are glimpses of the lava lake down below so I grab some photos in case this is as good as it gets. The crater rim is probably a couple of kilometres across; the lava lake is a kilometre below us and perhaps a half kilometre across. The view of the lava may be murky and indistinct, but if I had to turn around now I'd still be perfectly happy. In fact it soon gets a whole lot better.

The visibility improves and we're just waiting for night to fall to see how it looks in the dark. Dinner is a slice of bread and a tin of sardines, but by 7 pm it doesn't matter: conditions are clear, dark and terrific. Amazing, incredible, mind-blowing – any adjective will do. There's a continuous background noise like a saucepan boiling over and a constantly changing picture on the lake. At times it's fairly quiet, just a network of red lava and black patterning the lake's surface. Then there are eruptions along an edge or fountains in the centre. For a while it builds up to a crescendo of action, the noise level climbs and it's so bright the whole crater is lit up. Equally incredible is that there's mobile phone reception on the crater rim. So I phone my wife Maureen, who is in Portland in the US, staying with friends after seeing another opera Ring Cycle.

We watch the show for nearly two hours and then it's almost as if there's an 'Okay, time for bed' signal. The lake calms down, the violent eruptions stop, cloud drifts in and off to bed we go.

My sleeping bag – supplied by Emmanuel and carried for me by our porter – is not the best; I'm cold despite sleeping fully dressed, with my Gore-Tex coat zipped right up. In the morning, a clear view of the crater is a non-starter – it's clouded over. We leave soon after dawn and three hours later, we're back at the bottom. We see one baboon on the way and quite a bit of birdlife, including the white-collared ravens that hang around the summit and even fly down towards the lava lake.

Back in town Emmanuel takes me for a traditional Congolese meal at a market café. I'm starving, but not so starving that I can completely knock off a softball-sized ball of *ugali* (cornmeal) accompanied by goat, beans and cassava leaves.

We then set off on a tour of Goma, which is not that exciting – first because there isn't much to see in Goma and second because there is no stretch of road in Goma that does not quickly deteriorate into endless potholes, rocks, ridges, speed humps (well, just humps; there's no speeding in Goma) or road height changes.

We go to the site of the 2002 eruption, and while the town was flattened by lava, there's nothing to see here today. Emmanuel gestures to various places as we pass – this (pointing to a dusty, poor neighbourhood) is where the lava flowed through the town; this (pointing to a blank wall in the distance) is the cathedral, which was knocked down by the eruption. We crawl through heavy traffic out of town to Green

Lake, formed by another crater, and then back into town to the new neighbourhood, where the lava flowed into the lake and lots of expensive houses sprang up along the new shoreline. There's a lot of razor wire and security, but the roads are still as poor as anywhere else in Goma.

What's of greater interest to me are the *tchukudu*, amazing wooden bicycles used in and around Goma in great numbers. There's no chain or pedals; they're propelled purely by pushing and can coast downhill with surprising speed. They're strictly for carrying goods, not for personal transport. I'm fascinated by their sheer crudity and yet they're all exactly the same, varying only in size. They must weigh a ton.

I write 'I've been up Nyiragongo' emails to my volcano-enthusiast friends while I sip a beer by the pool.

The next morning Emmanuel picks me up again; he's got two tourists to collect in Kigali, Rwanda's capital, so I can get a ride. We walk the 100 metres to the uncrowded border and I'm stamped out of DRC and into Rwanda in a flash. Emmanuel has a car waiting just across the border and there's an immediate difference: the roads are perfect. One minute later, I've already travelled along more smooth, sealed, unpotholed road than I have in the last four days in and around Goma.

The Congo's wealth has always drawn an ugly collection of vile scramblers for loot, whether it was King Leopold hauling out his ivory and rubber, Belgian mining companies digging up copper and diamonds, or Mobutu and his cronies grabbing anything they could lay their hands on. Mobutu's

1973 'Zaireanisation' takeover of privately owned businesses consisted of emptying bank accounts, selling off the stock and then feeling affronted when nobody refilled the shelves. For a brief spell Mercedes Benz imports to Zaire set African records.

After all this looting, newcomers are still entering the scene, keen for their own slice. Four months before I flew into Goma, another bunch of loot seekers had flown in from Texas, via Nigeria, in a Dallas-based Gulfstream private jet. On board was an American, Edward 'Carlos' St Mary, French businessman Franck Stephane M'Bemba, Nigerian businessman Alexander Adeola Ehinmola and Nigerian Mickey Lawal, half-brother of Nigerian-born Houston oil tycoon Kase Lawal, who in 1997 had been USAfrica Business Person of the Year and in 2010 was appointed to an Obama Trade Advisory Committee. Plus three pilots and flight attendant Kelly Shannon.

Oh yes, and US$6.5 million in cash. The plan was to swap the cash for 457 kilograms of gold, worth about US$20 million at current values so clearly a bargain. The gold vendor was Bosco Ntaganda, not only a gold salesman, but also a militia leader wanted for war crimes by the International Criminal Court. (He handed himself over to the court in March 2013.) The cash was paid out, the gold loaded onto the aircraft and then one person betrayed another, and plane, passengers, crew, money and gold were all grabbed and everyone sat down for a long stay in Goma.

The crew stayed in the lakeside Hotel Ihusi; perhaps someone even had the same room I occupied just a few weeks later. They checked out and flew home to Texas after six weeks, by which time most of the gold and cash had evaporated. The gold had already shrunk by more than 70 kilograms (say, US$3 million worth) just being transferred from the plane to the bank, when St Mary was issued with a receipt. Another US$3 million was handed over – bribe, fine, payment, who knows? – to get the plane back. At last report Kelly Shannon was suing Kase Lawal and CAMAC, his Houston energy company which had presumably organised the whole thing, for post-traumatic stress disorder. I'm hardly surprised: discovering your job might have helped finance mass rapes, child soldier recruitment and other Congo horror stories is enough to give anyone stress disorder.

A week after leaving the Congo, I open my newspaper to a disconcerting story. The ex-Lufthansa Hewa Bora Boeing 727 I'd flown from Kinshasa to Kisangani, and then on to Goma, never got to its fiftieth birthday. Exactly a week after I'd left the Congo it made its final flight, ploughing into the jungle just short of the Kisangani runway, killing most of the passengers and crew in what would be the worst air disaster anywhere in the world in 2011.

HAITI

Is Haiti Cinderella, stuck in the cellar while assorted stepsisters get on very well above stairs? Kept in tattered clothes, sneezing in the dust, while others are allowed their finery and clean air? As the wicked stepmother in this Caribbean version, we have France, but there's an assortment of ancillary villains, with the US most prominent, as usual. Sadly, there has been no Prince Charming, to date, no glass slipper, no happily ever after. For poor Haiti the clock seems to strike over and over again. Most recently it gongs at 4.53 pm, not midnight, and instead of turning coaches into pumpkins, it tumbles the houses down into rubble.

I start on another length of the short swimming pool, realising as I turn at the deep end that this is where the hotel manager, Mr Brown, found Dr Philipot's body. The doctor had slashed his wrists and then cut his throat as well, just to make sure.

Of course, Mr Brown, the manager of the Hotel Trianon, and the dead doctor, Papa Doc's Secretary for Social Welfare, were both fictional characters in Graham Greene's *The Comedians*. The pool is real enough; it's even full of water, unlike when Mr Brown found the corpse huddled under the diving board at the deep end. The hotel, and its gingerbread architecture, is equally genuine, although its name in real life is the Oloffson. Apart from changing that, Greene hardly altered a thing.

It seems so unfair that Haiti should be the basket case of the Caribbean, indeed of the whole Western hemisphere. Most descriptions of the half-an-island nation start with the note that this is the poorest country in the Americas, right down there with the most ramshackle African nations when it comes to hard times. Yet Haiti's difficult birth was a glorious adventure. After a period as France's richest colony – and home to one of its most punishing slave systems – the nation borrowed some revolutionary fervour from the mother country. As the French Revolution began its consolidation over in Europe, a slave uprising, led with consummate skill by the unforgettably named Toussaint L'Ouverture, bubbled over in the Caribbean. This was followed by French perfidy: the colonial power invited the black leader to a peace conference in Haiti and, instead of finding compromise, L'Ouverture was kidnapped and spirited away to chilly exile in France, where he died in prison.

That didn't end the uprising, though. L'Ouverture's generals, Jean-Jacques Dessalines and Henri Christophe, continued the struggle, and in 1804, after tropical diseases had devastated the French forces, they achieved the impossible. Haiti became only the second modern nation, after the United States, to break free of colonial control; it was the first black republic to boot. Not surprisingly, the Haitians were less than enthusiastic about their former slave masters – their first flag was simply the French red, white and blue with the white missing: 'We ripped the white out of Haiti,' Dessalines supposedly said. And out of the flag.

Things started to go wrong almost immediately. The Haitian economy was a shambles after thirteen years of bitter warfare. The French were in no mood to recognise their former possession. Having lost Canada to the British forty years earlier, and now their wealthiest colony, they gave up on the New World and flogged Louisiana to the newly independent USA. Not until 1825 did France recognise Haiti, and only when the penurious Haitians agree to pay the former slave owners 60 million francs compensation.

Britain, despite its own antipathy to slavery, didn't recognise Haiti until 1833 and, most shamefully, the USA withheld recognition for fifty-eight years. Terrified that accepting the existence of a nation founded on a slave uprising might give the wrong idea to its own slaves, the USA waited until 1862 – and Abraham Lincoln – to recognise Haiti. As a result, international trade doorways were closed off for the impoverished Haitians. It was the sugar plantations that were so important to France, and Haiti's crippling debt to its merciless former slave masters wasn't paid off until after World War II.

The outside world may have made it tough for the Haitians, but the Haitians didn't manage things too well themselves. Dessalines realised that he needed white expertise to get the economy moving again and, not unlike Mugabe in Zimbabwe, invited white settlers to return, before changing his mind. He massacred almost every white in the country. The mulattos he distrusted, for their quasi-freedom from French rule pre-independence, and among the black population he lost popularity when he tried to force labourers back into near slavery to get the plantations working again. The idea that independent Haiti would become a republic went out the window – Dessalines announced that he was now Emperor Jacques I. It's no surprise that in 1806 he was assassinated.

Dessalines' death didn't sort things out; instead, a civil war divided the country between the black north, led by

Henri Christophe, and the mulatto south, led by Alexandre
Pétion. Perhaps taking a lead from Dessalines' Emperor title,
Christophe announced that he was now King Henri I. Things
didn't improve in a hurry, but fast-forward to the second half
of the twentieth century and the Duvaliers, Papa Doc and
Baby Doc, would represent some sort of stability, at least for a
while. When Papa Doc died in 1971, it cleared the way for his
equally venal and brutal son, Jean-Claude, or Baby Doc, to take
over. In 1986, after pressure from the Reagan government to
renounce his leadership, Baby Doc was hustled off to Paris for a
comfortable retirement. And then things got really bad.

For the next twenty years, Haiti saw a revolving door of
military rulers interspersed with a chorus line of hapless and/
or greedy elected leaders. Jean-Bertrand Aristide, the wonder
boy of 1991, was in and out within a year, brought back with
American backing and military muscle in 1994, re-elected
in 2000 and kicked out again in 2004, perhaps with US
assistance. 'They brought him back in 1994,' a street gossip
says. 'They took him away in 2004.' He ended up in exile in
South Africa. Throw in an economic blockade (as punishment
for dumping Aristide in 1991), a boat people exodus (many
ending up with a spell in Guantánamo Bay in the pre-terrorism
era), gang warfare in the capital's festering slums and a
steadily declining – make that plummeting – economy, and
it's no wonder that tourism to Haiti didn't just dry up – it
disappeared entirely.

As if its tragic history, economic calamities and succession
of bad rulers weren't enough, some malevolent deity couldn't
resist giving the country a good kick when it was already on

the ground. Since my first visit, the massive 2010 earthquake had caused huge damage in Port-au-Prince and flattened buildings in many other centres around the country. Remarkably, the dilapidated old Hotel Oloffson had come through shaken and stirred, but otherwise unscathed.

Perhaps the statue of Baron Samedi, which guards the front of the hotel building, kept the tremblor at bay in 2010. The Baron is the voodoo (correctly 'vodou') master of the dead, and manager of cemeteries. He's a lwa, one of the spirit entities that communicate between Gran Met, the 'Great Master', and everyday Haitians, and he's emphatically not to be messed with. The locals keep him happy with strong rum, pungent cigars, dark coffee and black, sacrificed roosters, and he, in turn, cures people of illness and, failing that, ensures a smooth ride to the afterlife. He can also be a charming, romantic figure; a painting I'd bought on my first visit, by the naive artist Fortuné Gérard, shows the Baron dancing nimbly in the graveyard, accompanied by a trio of musicians and five comely ladies, his symbols scattered around him.

I was a rare guest in Hotel Oloffson on my first visit in 2008 and possibly an even rarer one when I made a return trip after the earthquake. Last time I flew in from Miami, collected my bag and took a taxi into Port-au-Prince, through Champs de Mars in the centre of town, and a gentle uphill kilometre to the hotel. This time I come in on a bus from Santo Domingo in the Dominican Republic, the nation that occupies the other side of the island collectively known as Hispaniola. I wanted to experience the difference between the two Caribbean nations. Why should Spanish-speaking DR have a per capita income six times as high as Creole-speaking Haiti? And a life expectancy ten to fifteen years longer? It's a difference so stark that it's visible from space – grinding poverty in Haiti has led to one of the world's worst cases of deforestation. The Dominican Republic forests peter out at the border.

On that first – pre-earthquake – visit it almost seemed like Haiti might have been rebounding. Some recent food riots hadn't helped and, of course, it was still subject to those 'don't go there unless you're nuts' government advisories, but they're led by US state department concerns about kidnapped Americans, almost all of whom are in fact Haitian-Americans, not '*blancs*'. Tourists generally haven't been targeted. The turnaround was triggered by UN intervention in 2004. In response to gang violence, and to general Haitian acclaim, the Brazilian personnel who led the UN forces known as MINUSTAH tended to shoot first and only afterwards check which gang the bodies belonged to. As a result, law and order soon returned and intrepid travellers started to trickle – it was definitely no more than a trickle – back into the country. And then the earthquake shut the tap off again.

The Oloffson may have come through the quake no better or worse than before, but downhill around the Champs de Mars the post-earthquake story is far less happy. The National Palace had looked like a big white wedding cake, ready to wilt under the tropical sun, on my first visit. Now it was a wedding cake that some careless caterer had dropped on the floor, and from a fairly substantial height. Across the road, the heroic statue of

Toussaint L'Ouverture and the iconic conch-blowing *Marron Inconnu*, the 'Unknown Slave', survived, although for two years after the quake they disappeared from sight, surrounded by a tent city of displaced survivors. Just weeks before my second visit, this encampment had been cleared away but thousands of tents still remain around the Champs de Mars. Aristide's unfinished Haitian bicentenary tower also came through undamaged, looking like an ugly oil derrick construction was halted when he was dispatched for the second time in 2004. 'It's a pity that didn't fall down as well,' was an opinion I would hear more than once.

The Champs de Mars features statues of all the heroes of independence. As well as Toussaint L'Ouverture there are appearances by Jean-Jacques Dessalines, Alexandre Pétion, and Henri Christophe, although two years after the quake most of them are still surrounded by tents. Quake or not, Port-au-Prince's learner drivers haven't abandoned the Champs de Mars. A line of rather battered driving school cars still make a daily appearance in the park. It's a strange location for it – rather like Londoners heading to Trafalgar Square for their driving lessons, or Parisians to the Arc de Triomphe. Fortunately the traffic isn't so heavy in Haiti.

The Palace wasn't the only national symbol to collapse; just uphill from the Champs de Mars the Catholic Notre Dame Cathedral is also in ruins. Whether to rebuild the current construction – a European-looking church built between 1884 and 1914 – or level it and start from scratch is still under discussion. The city's real architectural tragedy, however, is midway between the ruined National Palace and the ruined cathedral. Externally, the Sainte Trinité Episcopalian Cathedral was a blocky, dull-looking building. But it housed a superb survey of Haitian art – the thirteen naive artists who had painted the church walls in 1950–51 would be recognised as the country's artistic virtuosos. The quake has brought it all down. Sadly, those masterpieces can't be recreated: even Préfète Duffaut, the last survivor, died at the age of eighty-nine in late 2012.

Before the quake, the walls showed a nativity by Rigaud Benoit, a Crucifixion scene by Philomé Obin, a view of heaven from Gabriel Lévêque, and the Ascension and Jesus' baptism by Castera Bazile, although the most vivid Biblical scene was Wilson Bigaud's Wedding of Cana, with Jesus turning water to wine in a distinctly Haitian locale – there was even a rara band playing. Préfète Duffaut, probably the best known living Haitian painter, had transposed the procession of the cross to his native Jacmel, portraying the location in his distinctive surrealist, fantastic style, the city spiralling up into the sky.

Galleries full of recent paintings and block-long walls of street art underline that Haitian art is still the most vibrant and alive in the Caribbean. If you want to take some Haitian art home, there's plenty for sale around Place St Pierre, the main square in the upscale suburb of Pétionville. This street art is turned out at almost production-line speed, and certainly in production-line uniformity, but Pétionville also has a useful assortment of art galleries, their walls glowing with the work of the best known Haitian artists. I buy pieces by Fortuné Gérard (exuberant line-ups of Haitians and his speciality, mermaids), Eddy Valmont (whose rural scenes looked remarkably like the

Balinese style known as 'young artist') and Frantz Zépherin (a little voodoo St George surrounded by a clockwork array of pointillist fish, snakes, birds and lizards).

But you don't have to go to an art gallery or church to get your daily shot of Haitian art; just stand in the street and watch the local bus service, the *tap tap*, go by. Or better yet, go to a busy *tap tap* station area, like the one near the Sylvia Cator Stadium in Port-au-Prince. *Tap tap* artists paint every available surface on the vehicles, continuing up and across the windows, and then, having exhausted all options, they slap other panels on the exterior until passengers and, more worryingly, drivers have to peer out through letterbox-sized apertures in the artwork.

So what to paint on a good *tap tap*? Well, religion never hurts. 'Thank you, Jesus' in big type across the front will undoubtedly help you reach your destination faster and safer. You might put it in French as well: *'Merci Jesus'*. I also spot 'God Above All', 'The Good Shepherd', 'Christ is the Answer', 'God who Decides', 'Hope in God', and, back in French again, *'Pensez á Demain'*, think of tomorrow. With a name for your wheels decided, illustrating the canvas with a good Biblical scene should complete the picture. Lot and the pillar of salt, the parting of the Red Sea, and Noah and his Ark all make appearances, with enough room for a good bleeding Jesus across the back.

Contemporary culture should also feature, though, so Christ on the cross may be gazing down at a football or basketball star, or some hip-hop hero. Nelson Mandela, Bob Marley and Arnold Schwarzenegger might also make cameo appearances. And we shouldn't ignore sex – a page-three girl might flash by you in traffic, either as a surprisingly realistic centrefold, reclining along the side, or in an Adam and Eve scene, happily combining sex with Biblical allusions.

The other economic activity that is certainly booming, alongside art, is the mobile phone business. On my first visit I'd switched on my Australian phone, wondering if I'd connect to a local provider, and if my Australian phone service had negotiated a roaming connection with this impoverished corner of the world. Within seconds a text message popped up on my screen: 'G'day mate! Digicel welcomes you to the Caribbean's widest GSM network. Enjoy your stay!'

I was impressed. I'd see plenty more evidence of Denis O'Brien, the enterprising Irish owner of Digicel. Haiti has become one of the most connected mobile phone markets in the Caribbean: fifty per cent of the population have mobiles, more than twenty times the number of landlines. Although there are other operators – Voila and Haitel – it's Digicel that has made the big impact: their ads, billboards and card vendors are everywhere. There are also lots of phone 'desks' in the street, little more than small tables topped with what looks like a regular landline phone. Except there's no landline connection; it's hooked up to a mobile phone.

O'Brien seems to be determined to prove that capitalism can have a positive side. Digicel is the biggest foreign investor in Haiti and Haiti is the biggest market in Digicel's international business – they're in the Pacific as well as the Caribbean. As O'Brien has said, 'If you make money in a poor country, you can't just take it and disappear, it would be bad business.'

While government departments and NGOs seem to take forever to get things done in Haiti, Digicel has rebuilt and reopened more than fifty schools since the earthquake. Aware that a school without teachers is a non-starter, they've also invested in teacher training facilities. They've also been involved in general restoration work – Port-au-Prince's classic old cast-iron Marché de Fer has been beautifully restored by the Digicel entrepreneur.

I've made my own, far smaller, contribution to the post-earthquake reconstruction. Jacqualine Labrom, an English-born travel agent and tour operator based in Port-au-Prince, emailed me right after the quake to tell me that St Joseph's had collapsed. The seven-storey building, between the downtown area and Pétionville, operated both as a home for street kids and as a backpacker hostel so it was familiar territory for many young overseas visitors. I chipped in for the rebuilding and on my return I'm delighted to see that this is another structure that has been quickly revived, and in a better-looking and more earthquake-proof incarnation.

As I'm shown around, my guide points out the stump of an old tree beside the colourful new building. When the quake hit, the home's director was on the fifth floor and tumbled down with the collapsing building. Having somehow survived the fall, he would then have been crushed by the disintegrating structure if that side of the building hadn't been held up by this handy tree. Just the stump of it remains.

It's clear that the economic situation now is far from pretty. The most poverty-stricken country in the Western hemisphere is not a good title to aim for, but just how bad is it? Compared to African standards, Haiti would fall somewhere in the middle, well above the bottom-of-the-basket cases. Once upon a time, before everything went belly up and the tourists left, Haiti had quite a few useful industries. It was a manufacturing centre for computer components and clothing, and, despite no great enthusiasm for baseball (unlike in neighbouring DR, where they are positively rabid about it and supply a disproportionate number of the big league players in the US), they still managed to make almost all the world's baseballs. These days they ship out a few mangos but very little else.

The road to Jacmel, in the south, is the best in the country, and it should be since – so the story goes – American foreign aid paid for it five times. Papa Doc, or one of his successors, took the cash, failed to build the road, and then applied to have the highway financed all over again. Although it's only 40 kilometres in a straight line from Port-au-Prince, it's much further by the winding road. The first stretch follows the coast before it climbs up into the mountains – and, as the Haitian proverb goes, *dèyè mòn, gen mòn*: after the mountains, more mountains. Despite its switchback nature, it's a fine drive to the town regularly cited as the most popular in Haiti.

Jacmel has quite an artistic reputation: the artist Préfète Duffaut was from here. It's also the setting of the book I'm reading, Edwidge Danticat's *After the Dance*. Danticat is Haiti's best known contemporary writer, with a number of novels to her name as well as this account of a Carnival-time visit to the town. She starts her tale concerned about the dangers that the carnival can bring, dangers that also appear in Haitian art. I look into a gallery with paintings of street scenes featuring bustling city activity; in one of the scenes a road accident is thrown in to enliven things. A young couple have fallen off their motorcycle and lie, looking angelic, in the street, while worried onlookers gaze at them. In the Florita Hotel there's a similar tableau – a car driver has run into two cyclists, who are lying in the street bleeding ominously while bystanders attend to them; others look perplexed or appalled and a policeman interviews the errant motorist. Fortunately, the follow-up picture hangs right beside it: the hospital scene where the accident victims are recovering nicely, visitors dropping by while in other beds mothers lie with their newborn babes.

Jacmel has lots of fine old houses with a distinct New Orleans flavour, though many of them are crumbling. England may have its haunted houses, but Haiti has a zombie hotel waiting for someone with money and taste to appreciate its battered style and great position overlooking the harbour. The Hotel Manoir Alexandra, now closed, is the home of Hadriana Siloe, Jacmel's most famous fictional resident and heroine of René Depestre's *Hadriana in All My Dreams*. In the novel, the beautiful Hadriana has the misfortune of dropping dead just as she reaches the altar on her wedding day. But wait! This is Haiti, voodoo central, so is she really dead? Sure enough, she's been poisoned by a practitioner of the dark arts and soon rises as a zombie and heads for the mountains where she appears as a voodoo spirit. She's mistaken for Simbi Lasous, spirit of springs and fresh water, before she finally retires to Jamaica. Note well: It's still against the law in Haiti to turn somebody into a zombie.

Since the zombie hotel isn't open for business I stay a few kilometres out of town at Cyvadier Plage, where I have a great view over the little bay from my balcony. To get back and forth to Jacmel I jump on a *tap tap*.

How many passengers can you get in a *tap tap*? goes the Haitian riddle.

Answer: One more.

Tap taps are not designed for comfort: little Japanese pickup trucks with two bench seats, one down each side. Five people on each bench is pretty straightforward; two up in first class, in front with the driver, makes thirteen in all. Of course, you can extend those bench seats to overhang the back bumper and squeeze in six a side, to make it fifteen. Then perhaps three hanging off the back to make it eighteen. And you can always squeeze two more in the middle, so twenty is no problem at all. And then one more.

I stand out on the road, flag down the next *tap tap* coming by, jump on the back and ten minutes later I'm in town. It's a short stroll to Jacmel's wonderful market: its cast iron building is a smaller version of Port-au-Prince's Marché de Fer or 'iron market'. In the bright pink Thank you Jesus shop in one corner, a tiny plaque notes that Simón Bolivar, South America's great 'liberator', stayed here in 1816. He reputedly asked his host how he could repay his hospitality and Pétion suggested freeing the slaves in South America, which Bolivar immediately took on board, once he'd kicked the Spanish out.

The market is crowded, colourful and frenetic. Picture your typical Western supermarket in an especially busy spell – early evening on a payday with a long weekend coming up, perhaps. Now double that crowd, or triple it. And these aren't even the shoppers, they're the vendors, each managing their little corner of the stock. One woman for the onions and garlic, one for the toothpaste and soap, one for the salt and rice, one just overseeing tomatoes and so on down every aisle. You just have to squeeze between them to find what you want.

A local guide takes me on the short trip out of town to the Bassins Bleu waterfalls. There's a river to cross, quite a fording operation for his little four-wheel drive, and then it's up to the end of the road from where it's less than a kilometre walk to the three pools. There's a bit of rope-assisted clambering to get up to the top pool, but it's worth it for a swim under a nice little waterfall.

Finally I take a stroll down Jacmel's not too exciting town beach, where a local lad intercepts me. 'Listen,' he says earnestly, detaching the cigarette from his lips to make the statement clearer. 'I want to have some of your money.' It's said in a remarkably relaxed tone; there's no hint that I'm about to be separated from my cash, just that it would be very nice if some of it could be transferred to his ownership. When I don't take up the suggestion, he strolls away.

After Jacmel, it's north, to the Côtes des Arcadins. Back in Haiti's tourist heyday, the Côtes des Arcadins was the Port-au-Prince beach strip, and for wealthy Haitians it's still a weekend getaway from the capital. Today, the surviving resorts along the coast are definitely on the rundown side of worn out. Having passed Cabaret, the town that featured as 'Duvalierville' in Greene's *The Comedians*, I continue right to the end of the strip to look at Club Indigo, which used to be Haiti's Club Med, but today is a very sadly ragged scene. Perhaps it's a good place to get an idea of what a Club Med was like back in the 1950s or 1960s. Or a Cuban resort for Russians or Poles back in the iron curtain era. Grim. Cheap.

So I back track to the Kaliko Beach Club, which is almost equally frayed at the edges. I was hoping to do a scuba dive from here tomorrow, but that looks unlikely too. My instant unhappiness with the place is reinforced when they try to fit me with one of those plastic wristbands all-inclusive resorts are so keen on. They'll hardly lose track of me; the only other guests are a party of American missionaries.

Google 'Haiti' and 'missionaries' or 'Christian mission' and you'll find plenty of American interest in bringing the word to poor misguided Haiti. Getting rid of all that voodoo nonsense is obviously viewed as a worthwhile task. The time I flew in from Miami I suspected a substantial slice of the *blanc* passengers were evangelicals, who are reportedly in Haiti in big numbers, and strongly opposed to voodoo. One guy on the plane had a T-shirt proclaiming, 'It's a jungle out there, so you need Jesus with you.'

I find my own spot, with my own beer, and look west towards the setting sun. Cuba's a little more north-west than due west, but it's not far away. Less than 100 kilometres of open Caribbean Sea separates the north-western extremity of Haiti from the south-east tip of Cuba. On a clear day you must be able to just about see Cuba from Haiti; it's often said that Haiti makes a good test marker for Cuba. If Castro's mismanagement and pursuit of the Marxist holy grail has crippled Cuba's economy and, presumably, living standards, how does Haiti, with its capitalism and democracy – at least from time to time – compare?

Not very well, and this from the CIA Factbook, which you'd expect to be fairly even-handed on this score. Gross Domestic Product per capita? Haiti US$1900, Cuba US$4500. So with all its communist inefficiencies (and any visitor to Cuba will agree there are plenty of them), the Cubans are still twice as productive as the Haitians. Infant mortality? Haiti sixty-two deaths per 1000 live births, Cuba six. In other words, Haiti is as bad as it gets and Cuba as good. Life expectancy: Haiti fifty-eight, Cuba seventy-seven. And literacy, where everything else stems from, I suppose: Haiti fifty-three per cent, Cuba 100 per cent.

The sun dips below the horizon. At night, at least, both Haiti and Cuba settle into the same darkness.

Back in Port-au-Prince the airport's tiny domestic terminal is crowded and there's a batch of small aircraft waiting out on the tarmac. Haiti is a small country – why are so many people flying places? Because the roads are so bloody awful. I'm flying to Cap Haïtien, which is only about 130 kilometres away and will take less than half an hour by plane. By road it would be seven, if all went well. This is yet another example of how poverty pollutes. Lousy roads take more time to drive and consume more fuel, often in worn-out old vehicles which are environmentally unsound to start with. When things get really bad, those who can afford it simply abandon the roads and take to the air. And nothing is fixed.

When I arrive at Cap Haïtien, my local guide, Madame Gersonne, drives me into town, testing her car horn's continuing function every 100 metres or so before she finally drops me at the Hotel Roi Christophe. What a delight – it's more like something in Guatemala or Mexico, where Spanish colonial flavour often features in hotel design, than somewhere in the Caribbean. Staying in a hotel named after King Christophe seems appropriate, since my number one reason for coming to Cap Haïtien is to make the pilgrimage south to the nearby town of Milot, where he built his fortress and palace.

I walk to the Place d'Armes, the town's main square, which also has a Central American flavour, but without the colour and bounce and joie de vivre of a Mexican zócalo, which adds to my Haitian depression. It's already been increased by a stroll along the messy waterfront road, past a grey, miserable sea breaking on the trash along the shore. I continue along the coast as far as one of the French fort remains: this one is simply a batch of extraordinarily heavy cannons – mortars, I guess – festooned with garbage and washing.

My spirits rise slightly when I get back to the hotel, but why does Haiti depress me so much today? I suppose it's partly the 'pollution of poverty' brought home to me at the airport, the environmental catch-22 when road travel is insufferable. Then there's the water being delivered by tanker because the water reticulation system is so ruined. And all the little plastic water sachets (because the water ... again), which adds to an already overwhelming garbage situation. Generators are used everywhere because the power supply is so unreliable – more infrastructure decay. Throw in deforestation and charcoal burning and it's hard to stay positive.

The women in town seem to be trying to fix what they can control: the next morning I see them sweeping the stretch of street in front of their houses. Madame Gersonne picks me up and off we lurch to Milot; it's only 20 kilometres out, fifteen of which are on either potholed or dusty, unsealed road. The small town is the site of Sans Souci, the ruins of Christophe's 'Haitian Versailles'. The palace fell into disrepair after his death and then was badly damaged by a huge earthquake in 1842, but even the ruins are a magnificent sight. Milot means 'carefree' and that's what Christophe intended his palace to be, elegant proof that the former slaves could be as relaxed and regal as their former masters. Fountains, statues, feasts and dances all added to that impression, but Christophe was to prove as ruthless a taskmaster as the departed Europeans. In 1820 he was crippled by a stroke and shot himself using a silver bullet. Ten days later his successor was bayoneted to death.

A road winds steeply uphill from the airy, lightweight ruins of Sans Souci to the immense and brooding Citadelle, 5 kilometres distance and 750 metres vertically above the palace. Christophe intended his fortress to be an insurmountable obstacle to any French attempt to recapture Haiti and reintroduce slavery. He armed his fortress with cannons, mortars and howitzers; looking down from the towering fortress walls, you can see a large proportion of the Citadelle's 50,000 cannonballs, bombs and other assorted projectiles stacked in neat piles. It's scarcely surprising that the French never tried anything.

You can drive up to a kilometre from the top and I've supposedly paid for a horse for that last stretch, but even if I were a horserider, taking one of these little bags-of-bones would seem positively sadistic. The Citadelle really is an amazing fortress and the prevalence of long, sheer drops with utterly unfenced edges is a clear indicator that foreign tourists are very few and very far between. There are crowds of local visitors, along with a handful of foreigners and UN soldiers on R&R. They'll need to do something about the falling-off possibilities before overseas visitors arrive.

Labadee Beach, just 10 kilometres of winding road along the coast from Cap Haïtien, is the only place cruise ships stop in Haiti. A couple of times a week a Royal Caribbean cruise ship out of Miami anchors offshore and thousands of passengers spend the day riding the zipline above the enclosure, lounging on the beach or venturing into the Caribbean waters to snorkel, kayak or jet-ski. None of them get to see nearby Cap Haïtien or the Citadelle, the most impressive man-made site anywhere in the Caribbean. It's said that once upon a time the passengers didn't even know they were landing in Haiti; they were told the stop was at 'Paradise Island'.

'Oh, are we going to be safe? Should we just stay on the ship?' seems to be the concern of some passengers.

'Don't worry, it's totally fenced off from Haiti,' is the quite accurate response.

It's unfortunate that an artificial creation like Labadee should be by far the biggest tourist centre in Haiti, but that's the reality and, given that reality, I'm happy that at least the one cruise company goes there. However, the cruise ship visits to Labadee sparked a small storm of misguided criticism after the 2010 earthquake.

'How can they take pampered tourists to Haiti to lie on the beach when people are lying dead in the ruins of Port-au-Prince?' roared the critics. 'Security forces are desperately needed in the capital, not guarding cruise ship passengers at Labadee.'

So is the answer to take your passengers somewhere else? Boost the business at a richer Caribbean island? I've seen first hand the effects disasters have on tourist destinations, whether those disasters are man-made (like the 2005 terrorist attacks on Bali) or natural (the 2004 tsunami in Thailand). I know that people involved in a tourist business in such a destination want to get out a simple message: 'Come back.' The very last thing they want is for some concerned tourism idealist to be telling people to stay away.

Norm's Place, where I'm staying the night, is around the headland from the cruise ship enclosure. It's neat, tidy, well kept, but facing away from the sea: it's not a place I want to hang around. The village of Labadee is only a hundred metres further, but the beach has totally disappeared beneath the usual layer of garbage. Walking back, I pick up a nasty big piece of glass, thinking some kid is going to step on this, only to realise it's just one of many nasty big pieces of glass.

I chat for awhile with Norm Zachrin, who came here in the 1970s, lived in Cap Haïtien, then moved out here and built his home and guest house on the remains of an old French fort, so there are thick walls and lots of stone. He married a Haitian woman named Angelique and now seems to make a living out of their guest house, and selling crafts to the cruise ship visitors. What he did before Haiti – the rag trade in Texas – seems clear enough, but what he's done since is still a little mystifying. Like others I've met, he's strongly against Aristide, in fact Norm even looks back fondly to the days of the Duvalier dictatorship, 'when things got done. There were no gangs, no kidnapping, no garbage, and there were good roads in the Duvalier days.'

The next morning I charter one of the regular taxi boats for a cruise along the coast and back again. There's an abandoned resort around the next headland which might become another cruise ship beach, then a couple of Western-owned houses squeezed up against the sheer hillside rising out of the ocean, and little patches of beach. A Gibraltar-registered yacht is anchored off one of the houses. Back at the Royal Caribbean beach, there must be 100 jet skis lined up waiting for the ship to come in. There's a host of other activities, including 'rock climbing' and inflatable 'icebergs'. The three ships anchored ready to take passengers for a quick cruise along the coast are amusingly named the *Nina*, *Pinto* and *Santa Maria*.

Haiti struck me as a land of close connections. I'd swum in the Oloffson's pool and felt that link, via Graham Greene, to Papa Doc, who lurked in the background of the book's narrative. Now, at Labadee, Norm, who had mused that at least under the Duvalier dictatorship things worked, suddenly announces that his wife Angelique's first husband was a colonel in Baby Doc's army, until one day he was one of seventeen officers lined up in front of a firing squad. For no apparent reason.

We all know the six degrees of separation theory – that you can move from anybody on earth to anybody else in just six easy steps. So here it is, via Papa Doc: six steps from Norm to Princess Di.

In 1964 the son of an Egyptian schoolteacher, thirty-five-year-old Mohamed Fayed, arrived in Port-au-Prince. His arrival was noted by Aubain Jolicoeur, the journalist immortalised as Petit Pierre in *The Comedians*. He reported that the 'eminent Kuwaiti Sheikh Mohamed Fayed' had arrived in town.

The eminent sheikh was quickly introduced to Papa Doc and soon had his fingers on everything to do with oil in Haiti (well, he *was* from Kuwait) and was skimming off a nice little percentage from Port-au-Prince's harbour operations. It was rumoured that the sheikh would soon be married to Marie-Denise, Papa Doc's eldest child, but by this time the CIA had become interested in the influential visitor and their enquiries revealed that not only was he not a sheikh, he was not even a Kuwaiti. No problem, by this time he'd been fast-tracked to Haitian citizenship and was toting a Haitian diplomatic passport.

Unfortunately for Fayed the shipping companies were not at all happy about the money that would be heading his way and collaborated on undermining his position. As the heat started to build, Fayed skipped the country in 1964, $150,000 disappeared out of the harbour authority's bank account at the same time.

Thirty years later and Mohamed Fayed was the owner of London's iconic department store Harrods when his son Dodi died in a car crash in Paris. So Norm via Papa Doc to Princess

Di is a few easy steps. Norm is married to Angelique, her first husband was executed by Papa Doc, who did business with Mohamed Fayed, whose son Dodi was in the fatal Mercedes with Princess Di when it ploughed into the side of the Pont de L'Alma tunnel in Paris.

The room I stayed at in the Villa Creole on my first visit to Port-au-Prince didn't collapse in the 2010 earthquake, although other parts of the hotel did. The Hotel Montana, down the hill, was not so lucky. It suffered a disastrous collapse that killed many of its guests.

On that first visit I left the rarified atmosphere of Pétionville for the 10-kilometre downhill run into the city proper. Getting there in the late evening was no problem, but getting back in the early hours wouldn't prove so easy. I was surprised at how empty the streets were already. Port-au-Prince is clearly an early-to-bed sort of place.

Not at the Oloffson however. The main gates into the hotel grounds were shut and the smaller pedestrian entrance gateway was manned by bouncers checking tickets, encircled by a noisy mob. What it takes to get in was extraordinarily confusing, but I eventually managed to convince them that I was staying there. It's more a white lie than a black one: I was staying there and I will be again in a week's time.

There's no shortage of musical passion around the Caribbean, but the rara bands and other musical styles of Haiti have an enthusiasm and intensity that's quite unmatched – the Oloffson is the place to sample it. Most Thursday nights the hotel's resident band, RAM, takes the stage close to the witching hour. They take their name from Richard A. Morse, the hotel's manager and the band's lead singer. Although he is away on my return visit, it's his wife Lunise who's the real front to the band in any case. Behind her gyrating vocals are two equally athletic ladies, amply endowed and ready to shake everything they have. And then there's the twelve-piece band, including my favourites, the three players who periodically put down whatever they're playing and pick up the rara horns. There are no twists, turns or fancy controls to a rara horn, just a straightforward funnel varying from short through medium to extra-long and sometimes played two or three at a time. Quite apart from sounding impressive, they also look terrific.

'Voodoo jazz' propels me into the early hours on both visits. The first time I had to find a late-night motorcycle taxi from the city's ominously empty streets to whisk me back to Pétionville; the second time I simply retreat to the Mick Jagger room overlooking the pool. The next morning I fly out with my ears ringing and a smile on my face. My Haiti depression has been lifted, the rara horns and sheer energy of life consuming thoughts of the nation's ailments. It's a band-aid, of course – how could it be anything else? – but what a band-aid.

For all its difficulties, Haiti has something that draws people back. If not the tourists, at least the ex-rulers. After the quake, a couple of them slipped back in. First Baby Doc turned up from his long Paris exile, just in time for the 2011 presidential election (nobody suggested he might like to run). He quickly found himself under house arrest, although, a year later, it seems to be a rather relaxed form of custody: 'Hang around the Pétionville mansion, don't take too many trips around the country and perhaps at some time we can talk about returning some of the money you stole' seem to be the rules. Then, even closer to the election date, Aristide rolled in as well. Nobody suggested he might make it, fourth time lucky, but there were plenty of other contenders. Michel Martelly, or 'Sweet Micky', better known as a musician than a politician, eventually won the election run-off and is grappling with the country's many problems. It doesn't take anywhere near six degrees to connect the president to the Oloffson or to Graham Greene. Richard A. Morse, the Oloffson's manager, resident band's lead singer and initiated voodoo priest, is Sweet Micky's cousin.

ISRAEL & PALESTINE

The old Uncle Remus tale of Brer Rabbit and the Tar Baby sums up the Israel and Palestine entanglement. Two sides trying to extricate themselves from each other only to find they become further enmeshed as the struggle goes on. You can argue about which side is rabbit and which side baby, but there's no question that the entanglement is a sticky one, and the more the two sides fight the harder it becomes to separate them. Every settlement, every stretch of wall, ties the two countries more closely together.

'At last,' I think, as a boulder hurtles towards me.

Go to Sicily and you'd expect to have a bag snatched by a passing scooter rider. In Ireland you're likely to consume one too many Guinnesses and regret it in the morning. Try to use your French in Paris and you'd be disappointed if it wasn't corrected at least once. I'd already been arrested in the Congo, so getting stoned in Palestine was just another rite of passage.

Israel and Palestine, individually and collectively, were top contenders for a position on my dark lands list. Although it took a week for the first stone to come my way – smaller and less deliberate ones would follow on two occasions – an assortment of other clichés about travel in the region had already lined themselves up.

I flew from Australia via Abu Dhabi to Amman in Jordan, and an hour after my passport was stamped into the country I am stamped out again at the Allenby Crossing into ... well, where am I being stamped into? Is this Palestine? The West

Bank? The Occupied Territories? Or perhaps Judea and Samaria, if I'm willing to accept the most extreme right-wing Israelis, who believe the borders of Israel should extend all the way to the Euphrates River, currently in Iraq.

To my mind, I'm entering Palestine, but the immigration process is under Israeli jurisdiction, and almost immediately, it seems, they confirm all their worst image problems. First the bags are hauled out of the bus luggage compartment and tossed on the ground while we're kept on board. Young people lounge around in jeans toting big guns. Our first step towards entering wherever we are entering is to go through security, a process that always involves a hint of indignity. Here it's laid on with a shovel.

The shoddy queues and boxes the officials sit in shout the message clearly: 'You're a third-world people and we're giving you a third-world experience.' My progress halts at the desk where I'm quizzed on why I'm here, where I'm going, who I'm seeing. I've got an Israeli friend's name, phone number and address in Tel Aviv at the top of my list, but that doesn't do anything and I'm passed on to a second window and a second interview with a very young soldier. He soon tires of looking at a long list from my laptop of 'We'll go here, we'll stay there, we'll add this, we'll walk to here, we'll drive there'. Getting into wherever I'm getting into takes well over an hour. And indignity? I'll soon experience worse.

I spend the first couple of days in Bethlehem, close to that famous wall: the much talked about, much photographed division between Israel and Palestine. Prompted by the terrorist attacks during the Second Intifada, construction of the wall commenced in 2002, and there's no question that there has been a dramatic drop in the number of attacks since that time. So is it the Separation Wall, the Security Wall, the Segregation Wall or even the Apartheid Wall? It depends on who you talk to, but whichever name you decide on, it's difficult to find a weirder example of the wall's idiosyncrasies than at Rachel's Tomb.

Bethlehem and biblical childbirth were connected well before the virgin outing. Rachel, wife of the Old Testament prophet Jacob, died giving birth en route to Hebron from the biblical Shechem, which might be Nablus today. (You can read about it in Genesis.) Jacob installed a pillar at her resting place, on the outskirts of Bethlehem, and, since she was revered by Jews, Christians and Muslims, the tomb became a pilgrimage site for all three religions. It survived right through the Byzantine and Islamic periods, and the Crusader interludes; the current building comes courtesy of the Ottomans. In 1841 Sir Moses Montefiore – English, Jewish and wealthy – financed the restoration of the Ottoman dome and the addition of a vestibule and a mihrab. This was intended to mollify the local Muslims, who were getting fed up with increasing numbers of Jewish pilgrims interrupting ceremonies.

A century and a half later, in 1995, an Israeli military camp was plonked down next to the tomb. Three years after that, it's said that the army destroyed the Montefiore dome and vestibule. Bad, but much worse was to come. In 2006 a finger of the wall was extended into Bethlehem to enclose the tomb and cut it off from the town. From above it looks like a tentacle of the spaghetti monster, or one of those weird US electoral boundaries drawn to ensure a candidate of a certain racial profile is elected.

For Palestinians it meant the tomb was now off limits. For the businesses that had sprung up around the tomb it meant bankruptcy.

I read a lot more on Rachel's Tomb and, of course, there is more than one side to the story. There were regular Palestinian attacks on the tomb prior to the Israeli military arrival. It's also unclear whether the dome and vestibule were destroyed or were simply enclosed within a larger building so the original structure is not visible. Read Jewish websites and you'd think it was never Muslim. Read Muslim ones and the Jews never played a role! It's not unlike the entire country, in that sense.

I start my visit to Rachel's Tomb from near the Bethlehem Intercontinental Hotel. The wall is very picturesquely painted on this stretch and I walk along its labyrinthine path until I get to the checkpoint gate into Israel. I get across quickly because there's no queue, only a handful of people walking through like me. On the Israeli side, I backtrack 100 metres towards Bethlehem, where another gateway blocks the road leading around the wall to the tomb. I'm not allowed to walk the final few hundred metres, so I hitch a ride instead.

After the tomb's annexation, ordinary foreign tourists were not allowed to visit, but things seem to have changed. Still, I'm the only non-Jewish tourist here today; I wander the tomb without a *kippah* (or *yarmulke*, in Yiddish) and after a while, a polite gentleman comes over and offers me one, with the suggestion that it will 'help you to fit in'. Guidebooks suggest that wearing the Jewish skullcap indicates you agree with the tomb being a strictly Jewish site. I say I prefer to remain an outsider. The tomb stands about 3 metres high, shrouded and then covered again in clear plastic. It's surrounded by black-clad gentlemen, most of them bearded and many wearing wide-brimmed hats, most of them facing the tomb and reading. From the tomb I manage to hitch back and it's a quick march back into Palestine. No security or checks in that direction.

When I get back to the hotel I try to trace my convoluted route along the wall, through the wall and then back along the other side of the wall, on Google Earth. The view is remarkably fuzzy and I puzzle over whether I've got a poor connection or if it's something more sinister. It turns out I've run into the Kyl-Bingaman amendment, which stops Google Earth from buying US satellite imagery of Israel at a higher resolution than they could obtain outside of the US. This is Israel at work; it's said they've twisted the arms of other satellite owners like South Korea or Russia to ensure they also don't sell anything higher resolution. This may all change soon: Turkey's Göktürk satellite was launched by the Chinese at the end of 2012 and will also offer higher resolution imagery. The current state of Israeli–Turkish relations means that arm-twisting might not work so effectively with the Turks. It's a Catch 22 situation – once Google can get higher resolution imagery outside the US they won't need to: when that happens they'll be allowed to buy it within the US. In the meantime, don't try to study things too closely in Israel; you'll get a better view of the back streets of Pyongyang than of Bethlehem.

Bethlehem, one of the few places in Palestine that sees a regular flow of international visitors – even if most of them are day-tripped out from Jerusalem and often don't realise they've crossed over – is followed by a visit to Hebron, where you despair of things ever going well in the West Bank. Before I leave Bethlehem, I hit all the Christian sites, starting with the Church of the Nativity in Manger Square, the starting point for all Bethlehem tourism. Is this the exact place where Jesus was born, where a church now stands? There's a fourteen-pointed star on the floor to show precisely where the birth took place, and the site of the manger (a trough or box used to hold feed for an animal) is just a few steps away. It's as good a guess as any, and the micro-drama that plays out here is a fair simulacrum of today's disputes over Israel, Palestine, the West Bank and Gaza. The Christian sects who argue endlessly over ownership of the church are mirrored in the rest of the country by the various Israeli factions, the Palestinian Hamas and Fatah groups and anyone else who'd like to throw their hat in the local property ring. The Armenians, Greek Orthodox and Roman Catholics all preside over their own bit of the church and get extremely annoyed if one of the others encroaches on their territory.

The next day, I walk from the square to the Milk Grotto, another Christian legend site, hollowed out of white rock. Legend has it that, while Mary nursed Jesus, a drop of her breastmilk fell to the ground, turning it white. Then I take a taxi via Shepherds' Field, where they watched their flocks by night, to Hebron. I grab a shawarma for lunch and walk to the old town, where the souq is sadly quiet. This is an overwhelmingly Palestinian city now, but a Jewish settlement right in the town centre has cast a dark cloud, making Hebron the most difficult urban centre on the West Bank. Settlements can be like poisonous weed: once they take root, everything around them dies. In Hebron, about 500 Palestinian shops have been closed by the military 'for security purposes' and another thousand have gone out of business. I wander around the area and down one street in the souq which is overlooked by settlers. The Palestinians have had to stretch wire mesh across the street because of settlers throwing stones, bricks and other debris onto people walking below.

The 500 to 800 Jewish settlers in the heart of the old city require up to 4000 Israeli soldiers to look after them, and all sorts of international observers to make sure both settlers and soldiers behave themselves. I enter the Tomb of the Patriarchs and check the cenotaphs of Isaac, Rebecca and the biggie, Abraham, which is shared between the Jewish and Muslim parts of the building. In 1994, Baruch Goldstein, an Israeli doctor from the nearby Kiryat Arba settlement, opened fire on Muslims praying in the Ibrahimi Mosque section of the building, killing twenty-nine and wounding another 125 before he was killed.

I leave the mosque, walk around the building's wall, down the street, up the next street, across the courtyard and into the Jewish part of the building, where I look at Abraham's tomb from the other corner. You can peer around the corner of the tomb and see people in the other part of the building. A glass, presumably bulletproof, screen means they can't take pot shots at each other.

My religious outing for the day complete, I meet up with Walid Al-Halaweh of the Hebron Rehabilitation Committee. We admire the view of the old city from the rooftop of their fine old building and then walk over to Shuhada Street. This is the controversial separation street that runs right through the centre of the old town and for some distance is off limits to Palestinians and their vehicles. Walid explains that simply driving from one side of the street, once a major thoroughfare, to the other can mean a 12-kilometre circuit for a Palestinian. Hebron is divided into Palestinian-controlled H1, with about 120,000 people, and Israeli military–controlled H2, with about 30,000 Palestinians and 700 Israelis. Palestinians can only approach the settler properties in H2 with special permits. The Israeli army and some contractors are here today – doing something, moving something – and I quickly find I've been appointed the official photographer for Walid's committee. He remonstrates with a young Israeli soldier, but it's all quite polite. I'm left in their office for a spell, uploading the photographs, before we head over to the local Chamber of Commerce, where an agreement is being signed with a visiting Turkish trade delegation.

With a population around 250,000, Nablus is the biggest city on the West Bank after Hebron, and my next stop. The modern town centre is a mainly recent construction after the Israelis did a total destruction job on the area in 2002. The entrance to the souq still stands, though, and this is where most of the interest lies. Posters of 'resistance martyrs' are pasted on the walls, most of them brandishing big guns like kids playing military games. My guide shows me through the Ottoman souq, past the picturesque clocktower in Victory Square, the Ottoman-era town centre. Built in 1901, it has a twin in Jaffa. Clear away the parked cars and junk and you could imagine café tables around the square – charming and pleasant with a distinctly Mediterranean flavour.

Advancing a block further up the hill, I would have been on the main Roman thoroughfare in an even earlier Nablus. The Nablus Museum was once in the building beneath a large girls school dating from the 1980s or 1990s. It too was destroyed by the Israelis and is yet to be reconstituted. Under the museum, which is not locked, is a stretch of that ancient Roman street, way below the current street level. The school building has been dropped straight on top, the modern concrete columns rammed directly into the ancient paving stones. At least they didn't pour concrete foundations.

Still further up the hill is the Roman amphitheatre, today totally surrounded and partially subsumed by modern buildings. The entry gate is locked and nearby shopkeepers have no idea who has the key. We head back downhill, from Roman Nablus into Ottoman Nablus, pausing in Qaryun Square, where, according to the plaques, Israeli bulldozers knocked down houses without warning, killing the families, including children, inside. We stop in what was once a soap factory, and today is a wonderfully cluttered mix of antiques, herbs and coffee. We sip tea in the office, surrounded by cheeping, chirping caged birds.

Back on the modern central square, we visit an olive oil soap factory, one of only four left of the dozens once in Nablus. To make olive oil soap here, you fill a large circular vat with olive oil, caustic soda and salt, heat it up and stir it occasionally. When it's ready, you tap it off into drums and carry them, physically, upstairs. There you pour the liquid out onto the floor to about 4 centimetres deep, you let it solidify, and cut it up into neat little 6-centimetre squares, break them out, stack them in very artistic looking conical towers and leave them for a few weeks to harden. Then you wrap each block individually and stack them in 10-kilogram cartons. The amazing thing about this whole process is that, apart from the mechanical stirring of the original vat, it's all done manually. Even wrapping the individual blocks of soap is done, with dazzling speed and dexterity, by a guy sitting on the floor, completing each wrapper with a thumb-lick of paste from a jar.

After all this work, vicarious or not, some sweets are in order, specifically the best *kunafeh* in town – the best Nablus *kunafeh* anywhere, in fact. I try a dish of this popular sweet and then watch the men prepare it. They oil a metre-wide pan, then spread flour and water which have been ground down from noodle-like shredded wheat across the pan, and top it with a cheese made from blended sheep's and cow's milks. They heat the pan for a few minutes, place a tray on top and flip the whole thing over. After leaving it to cool, they then wash sugar-sweetened water across the top and leave it to cool again for a longer spell. The café dispenses dishes of *kunafeh* with such speed that another of those metre-wide pans has to be set out every quarter of an hour or so.

I've arranged to be driven from Nablus to a Bedouin encampment overlooking the Dead Sea before going back to Bethlehem. After a series of unfortunate and frustrating delays, we end up at the camp as the sun sinks rapidly towards the horizon. What we should be doing is driving to a lookout point perched directly above the Dead Sea, where we would have watched the sunset with the sea at our feet. Now there's so little time we can only race up to a lookout where the sea is visible, but in the distance. We arrive just as the last slivers of sun drop below the horizon. I am more than slightly disappointed, although I keep my mouth shut. The sight of a distant caravan of camels moving picturesquely along a ridge helps to cool any annoyance.

On our way back to the Bedouin camp we pass a deserted police outpost building from the Jordan era. Walkers on the Abraham Path, a long-distance walking track under development, sleep here for a night on their way to Hebron, two more days' walk from here. We pause just long enough for a quick meal with the Bedouin, sitting around a large dish of rice and chicken, with adjacent bowls of soup and a stack of unleavened bread for dipping.

The small road we took towards the Dead Sea was a good asphalt stretch; it leads past two Israeli settlements. Further along, after the asphalt has ended, we encounter a car coming in the opposite direction.

'Oh, they're settlers,' my guide, George, announces in a surprised tone. 'And they're waving at us,' he continues as he waves back.

'Wouldn't they normally wave?' I ask, used to outback roads in Australia, where you'd think it very strange if the driver of an oncoming vehicle didn't wave hello.

'Oh, an economic settler might wave,' George replies. 'An ideological one certainly wouldn't.'

Israel's West Bank settlers can be divided neatly into two categories. The economic ones are there simply because it makes financial sense: the land is cheaper, the housing is government-supported and if they're working back in Israel, there are modern roads, generally closed to the Palestinians, that slice across the territories to whisk them to and from their jobs. The ideological ones are there for much more controversial reasons; they're there to put an Israeli footprint on what is now Palestinian territory. The settlements that are unofficial or illegal – even by Israeli government standards – will all be ideological rather than economic ones. Of course, to many people all the settlements are illegal.

The settlements are a visible example of a penchant for building facts. Who owns this land? Well, clearly we do, look – there's our house on it. Or better yet, our entire village or town. It's not a new idea – Israeli settlers are far from the first to follow invasion with fact creation. Isn't England dotted with castles and churches built by those Normans who turned up from France in 1066? And much of the US is built on land grabbed from the Native Americans. Australians were particularly adept at land grabbing – the English settlers simply classified the whole country as *terra nullius* – uninhabited land – and then handed themselves ownership titles. In fact, Australia's landed gentry are often referred to as the squattocracy, as they simply turned up and squatted on the land.

As well as Palestinian towns, I want to see some Palestine countryside – after all, Raja Shehadeh's *Palestinian Walks* is probably the best book to have come out of the region in recent years, certainly the best book about walking in Israel or Palestine. I've always felt that walking is the best way to come to grips with a place; you see the world at an appropriate pace: slowly. I've got three very different walks lined up, two of them in Israel, one in Palestine, and each just a short taste of what can be much longer excursions.

I meet my Palestinian walking guide, Nedal Sawalmeh, at the Al Fara'a refugee camp near Nablus where he lives, and we continue up the road to Zababdeh, where we will follow the Nativity Trail back to the camp. The trail was intended to follow a 150-kilometre route from Nazareth to Bethlehem, tracing the path Joseph and Mary might have followed on that epic trek two millennia ago. Since a Palestinian-organised walk can't very well start in Israel, the trail kicks off just inside the West Bank border. I'll be walking day two of the trail.

On the short drive to our starting point and for the first hours of the walk, Israeli Air Force F16s zoom back and forth overhead, often very low and very noisily. Like the settlements, they're a regular reminder of who is in charge around here. This loud display brings to mind the line – credited to an Israeli conservative – that despite a history of Arabs being the great warriors while Jews were the great debaters, this time around 'the Arabs have lost every battle, and the Jews have lost every argument'. In the sky above us the air force is playing the Goliath role, and are winning the battle, while down at ground level the Palestinians are the underdogs, the stone-tossing Davids winning the argument.

In Zababdeh we start with a visit to the town's monastery. In the town centre there's a mosque with a particularly tall minaret, but the population is seventy-five per cent Christian. The day's walk is almost all through rural, agricultural land,

very rarely through anything remotely undeveloped. This
has been described as the bread basket of the West Bank and
there's a great deal of farming going on – potatoes, cucumbers,
cabbages, onions, wheat, lots of olive groves and, late in the
walk, greenhouses growing herbs for the European market. We
stop at a village house in Sir for tea, coffee, fruit and effusive
welcomes from an old man, his son and grandson, and end
up at Nedal's home in the Al Fara'a refugee camp. I would
have thought it was just another tightly packed Palestinian
settlement, but Nedal insists it's divided decisively from the
adjoining Palestinian town, which discourages it from spreading
any further or from merging with it.

'It's been more than sixty years since Israel took our land,'
Nedal says, 'and in all that time there have only been two
marriages between camp residents and someone from an
adjoining village.'

It wasn't a long walk and, having arrived at the crowded
settlement, we sit around, talk, look at walk-related stuff on his
computer, eat a big, late lunch and never get out to look at the
camp. When it gets dark I regret not having pushed to do so.

Unlike the walks I would do in Israel, this trail has absolutely
no way-marking. Adding some would make the trail more
feasible for independent walkers, and would also indicate that
this was very much a real local tourist initiative. It might also
discourage the Israelis from building across the trail. Nedal
reckons way-marking might also encourage the locals to be
tidier. The trailside rubbish is not appalling – I've seen far worse
in other countries in the region – but Nedal tries to partially
blame it on the Israelis.

'The Israelis have crushed young peoples' faith in the future,' he insists, 'so they don't care that they make a mess of their land.' It seems far-fetched.

Of course, our conversation gets around to that big Israel–Palestine stumbling block, the 'right of return'. Nedal explains that his kids, and the camp refugees in general, never say they are from Al Fara'a; they may *live* in Al Fara'a, but they're *from* Jaffa. Nedal was born in Al Fara'a, so his children are second generation, but he's been back to Jaffa, where his family home was. It's now a factory.

'Making weapons,' he insists.

When I offer an Israeli, and for that matter a general Western, perspective – that the Palestinian refugees remain stuck in camps and make no effort to move out into the general community, while an equal number of Jewish refugees from Cairo, Tripoli, Baghdad and Tehran have moved into the general communities; there are no longer refugee camps in Israel – he's almost angry.

'That's a problem between them and Iraq and those other countries. Our problem is here.'

Nedal is forty-three and doesn't appear to be doing much else apart from his occasional guiding work. He has twice taken groups of Palestinian kids from the camps to Spain, and when he was younger he worked on labouring jobs in Israel; for six years he worked at the UN-funded centre in the camp for disabled refugees. What the unemployed refugees do for cash is not explained; the issue is simply skated around. What he has had time for is propagating. He has eight children, two boys and six girls. Trying for a boy wasn't the motivation: his oldest child is a boy, but he can't seem to stop, I'm told that taking the pill isn't good for his wife, but methods involving him 'weren't good' for him either. The latest arrival is just six months old. His wife is absent while I'm in the apartment.

I move on to Ramallah, the 'de facto administrative capital' of the Palestinian National Authority. The Palestinians, if they ever get their own country, would like Jerusalem to be the capital, but is that ever going to happen?

It's just outside the city that I am finally stoned. I stop for an excellent coffee at the amusingly named Stars & Bucks before I drop into the former Arafat PLO compound, its major renovation and rebuild nearing completion. Arafat's tomb, guarded by two soldiers, is open to the public so I stand beside it for a photograph. From there, the rest of the day goes somewhat awry. The plan is to go to the Qalandia checkpoint, the major gateway between East Jerusalem and Ramallah. It's 5 kilometres from the PLO compound and I walk a kilometre and a half before I grab a bus, heading in the right direction, but not on the main road. With a couple of kilometres to go, the minibus U-turns and heads back, so I jump out.

At this point I reach a stretch of the wall, but the road heads away from the checkpoint – the wall continues on the correct bearing. So I leave the road, chased by three angry dogs, and follow the wall across country. Or rather I follow the outer wire fence; the wall is well back behind two fences. I'm picking my way through scrub, scrambling over rocks, finding faint meandering tracks every so often. I come upon more dogs, in fact a great pack of them, and pick up a few rocks in case they're as unfriendly as the previous batch, but they just slope off.

By this time the wall has disappeared; it's just the wire fences. There's a Jewish settlement off in the distance, and the way to the checkpoint – from here at least – dives down into a valley (here it would be called a wadi) and up the other side into a populated area, the Qalandia refugee township. The two communities, in close proximity, remind me how to recognise a settlement. The houses are clustered together, often on hilltops or along ridges, and are encircled by wire fences (these are gated communities); they do not have water tanks on the roofs (settlers get guaranteed mains water and use on average 300 litres per person per day; Palestinians get no guarantees – hence their storage tanks – and get by on 50 litres); and the roofs are red (Palestinian roofs may be red, but not always). Finally, of course, there's no minaret in sight in a settlement. The stream flowing along the bottom of the wadi is a trickle, only a half metre or so wide. As I climb up the other side, some kids – big kids – wave at me and then start hurling rocks.

It's been a while since I've had rocks thrown at me, but when I approach the kids, hands up in surrender and waving my Australian passport, they're quickly apologetic. One of them, who speaks a little English, accompanies me through the township, becoming steadily more apologetic as we go. His English isn't good enough to explain what this was all about – was I mistaken for a stray Israeli from the settlement across the valley? It's a change from the evidence of Israeli settlers hurling bricks at Palestinians in Hebron, but it certainly wouldn't have been amusing if one of the rocks had found its target.

I photograph the wall at the checkpoint, which is covered in artwork, and then grab a minibus back to Ramallah.

Rock-throwing Palestinians are quickly balanced out by the other variety: I field a hearty 'welcome to Palestine' from the passengers in a passing car, who presumably think I've just arrived, and when I stop into a bakery for a cinnamon roll I'm waved out without paying. The baker simply says, 'Welcome.' It's the number one English word I encounter during my Palestine visit.

The next day I cross into Israel. Or the rest of this place; the other side of the wall, in any case.

From the bus station in Ramallah I ride to the border where you get out, go through security and get on another bus into Jerusalem. I was depressed by the Allenby crossing from Jordan, but this kicks up to a higher level. If the Israelis had set out to design an entry point which shouts 'you're shit and we're treating you like shit' they couldn't have come up with anything better. If I were an Australian cow I would find the metal-barred corridor up to the gate eerily familiar, remarkably like being processed through an Australian cattle yard. All I'm really doing is going through security; the Palestinians are having their paperwork checked as well; and there are only ten or twenty people in front of me, but it takes half an hour bus-to-bus. Even when I'm through and ready to go I'm stuck behind a metal rotating door, waiting for it to finally unlock.

I'm staying on the East Jerusalem side of the town's dividing line. I walk along the border road between East and West Jerusalem to visit the Museum on the Seam, an edgy, political art gallery, echoing its edgy, political location. Then I head back to enter the old city through the Damascus Gate, which leads into the Christian and Muslim quarters; I'd already stopped for a pita and falafel but now that I'm faced with the old city's treats, I grab some tea and a baklava, and call it a serial meal. I have a spell in the Church of the Holy Sepulchre and work my way back along the Via Dolorosa. The Fourth Station of the Cross T-shirt shop is gone, or at least its sign is; thankfully there's still a T-shirt shop.

I've timed my arrival for the start of the Friday afternoon Stations of the Cross walk with the Franciscans. There are lots of brown-clad monks, one lugging a speaker that announces what's happening, in Italian, with lots of '*Ave Marias*' included, but sadly nobody is carting a cross, as I was promised. I leave them and head to the Western Wall, having been turned back en route to the Dome of the Rock because it's prayer time, or something. I'm walking in circles by this time, unsuccessfully searching for a rooftop viewpoint, but successfully pausing for another tea and baklava.

Emerging from the old city, I'm handed a cartoon brochure by an American woman: 'Love the Jewish People', it announces. I look it up on the web later and discover it's a fundamentalist Christian tract: 'the end is coming and it's because we don't follow the Bible and back the Jews'. I've barely shaken her off when I'm nearly pickpocketed. It's a 'buy postcards' approach – squeezed between bus and wall and then next thing I realise he has his hand in my pocket and is about to remove my wallet.

'Oh, what's happening,' the bastard announces, when I grab his hand – as if it's just sneaked into my pocket with a mind of its own.

I retire to the hotel's bar for a pint of Taybeh. The barman explains: 'We don't sell Israeli beers.'

I look for the fundamentalist's leaflet, but it's gone. Perhaps the pickpocket took it.

The next morning I join three Swedes on a 'Politics of Jerusalem' tour and for the entire three hours Abu Hassan is near apoplectic about the Israelis. And us, for letting the Israelis get away with it.

The tour begins with a drive through the huge Neve Ya'akov settlement. Unlike the West Bank settlements, you can just drive into this one; there's no checkpoint. West Bank settlements are isolated fortresses: only the settlers or those with permission can get in through the security gates. Across the valley from Neve Ya'akov, the Palestinian Hizma area is the polar opposite. Comprising a refugee camp and two villages, Hizma is a walled prison, keeping the Palestinians in. Abu reckons eighty per cent of the inhabitants have East Jerusalem residency, so they can enter East Jerusalem by the checkpoint. The other twenty per cent can only use the checkpoint at the other end of Hizma, exiting into the West Bank.

We drive out to the West Bank through the Qalandia checkpoint – straight through this time, instead of my half-hour process the day before.

'You were lucky, it might have taken you two or three hours,' suggests Abu.

When we head back towards East Jerusalem, we approach an Israelis-only entry point. We can do this because we're in an Israeli-registered car and Abu has East Jerusalem residency.

'But they can still stop us and hassle us,' he continues. 'It depends if they think I look like Ahmed or Shlomo. Usually I'm Shlomo, but today's a quiet day so they might decide I'm Ahmed and ask questions.'

He's Shlomo today, so we drive straight through.

Our next stop is the Sheikh Jarrah neighbourhood, site of an ongoing land dispute, the flipside of the Palestinian 'right of return' demands. The right to return to homes and lands lost in 1948 is a key Palestinian demand, one it's clear they're not going to get, as long as Israel exists. Here it's Israelis demanding the return of homes and land lost in 1948 when this area became part of East Jerusalem and under Jordanian control. The Six Day War in 1967 brought it back under Israeli control and there's a complicated and unpleasant ongoing struggle over the properties. Our last stop is the nearby International Red Cross Headquarters, where a group of Palestinians threatened with deportation had sheltered for over a year. The final two were arrested and deported in early 2012.

I finish the day with a walk around the city walls, and decide on a taxi ride from Dung Gate back to Jaffa Gate. Taking a taxi in Israel always seems to involve some sort of argument and today is no exception.

'Fifty shekel,' says the first driver when I ask him to use the meter. 'It's Shabbat, the meter rate is higher, you'll save money paying fifty shekel.'

'Fine, I'll pay more and use the meter,' I answer.

The agreed-in-advance rate quickly drops to forty shekels, then thirty.

'Look, it's saving you money, why don't you believe me?'

Several drivers all insist, cross their honest little hearts, that it's going to cost more on the meter.

Of course, I don't believe them and finally, when I start walking, a driver reneges on his mates and takes me. The meter fare is just clicking up to twenty when we enter Jaffa Gate.

In the evening I walk from East (Arab) to West (Israeli) Jerusalem to eat in the city centre. After argumentative taxi drivers, stone-tossing teenagers, pushy border officials and inept pickpockets, I'm not surprised to be propositioned by an Israeli prostitute en route. I dine in Adom, 'Red' in Hebrew, a very stylish place where I start the evening with a blueberry and basil mojito and accompany my seafood risotto with an Israeli pinot noir. It's a decidedly non-kosher seafood risotto, since it features mussels, calamari and prawns, all on the forbidden list.

After my meal, the first taxi I ask to take me to the American Colony Hotel, just beyond my hotel, asks for fifty shekels. The next one uses his meter and it's twenty-one shekels; I give him thirty. Jerusalem's old-school hotel is a place with a quirky history and an interesting role in the country today. Like the Museum on the Seam, it sits on the seamline between East and West Jerusalem and claims to be a pocket of neutrality in an often polarised city. As a result, it attracts a steady stream of diplomats, politicians and journalists – well-heeled ones, we're in five-star land – who also want to maintain their neutrality. Name a notable visitor to Jerusalem – including Lawrence of Arabia – and they've probably stayed at the American Colony, but the occupants were colourful even before it became a hotel. The original owner lived here with his small harem of four wives, and after his death a Swedish-American colony of utopian Christians moved in, hence the name. It was established as a hotel in 1902 by Peter Ustinov's grandfather and in 1987 the actor filmed an Agatha Christie movie here. John le Carré wrote one of his books here during his stay, and it's also a favourite of retired US presidents and British prime ministers.

In the basement bar I get talking with a Washington DC–based embassy builder, over here doing some sort of work. After my cocktail, a couple of glasses of wine and now a couple of beers, it's a mildly tipsy reel back to my hotel.

In the morning I enter the old city through Herod's Gate into the Muslim quarter, wander aimlessly and eventually find myself back at Herod's Gate. I make one final sortie towards the Dome of the Rock. It's been closed every time I approached it. Last night I was told it would be 'open at 7.30 am', but this morning it's 'closed all day'. Defeated, I walk back along the Via Dolorosa to St Anne's Church, the 'finest Crusader church in Jerusalem'.

A black American preacher is bringing the roof down with a fire-and-brimstone sermon, which incorporates a great deal of shouting. When I return to the church after wandering around the Pool of Bethesda excavations, his congregation – all white – now have their arms around each other's shoulders and are shouting and hollering together.

'Well, it's a bit different,' a French priest says, when I emerge looking somewhat bemused.

As I walk along the Old City wall, back towards the hotel, I encounter four small boys. Once they pass, they pick up stones and start hurling them at me. They're really only pebbles, but I'll count it as my second stoning this trip.

It's time to leave Jerusalem and head north. The first taxi I approach to go to the bus station won't use his meter. The second will, and the driver, Adan, suggests I take him all the way to Nazareth: 'You'll get there in an hour and a half, instead of four.'

My bus trip was going to involve one bus to Afula and then another from there to Nazareth, staying within Israel proper, but before I know it we've slotted Jericho into the mix and we're through the checkpoint and in the West Bank. Every time I think I've left the West Bank, I find myself back there.

We cruise down Highway 1 towards Jordan, pausing at the sea level marker as we drop down below it towards the Dead Sea. Jericho looks like quite an interesting little town; I regret not overnighting there. Hisham's Palace, the most important Islamic archaeological site in Palestine, is the town's big attraction. In fact, it's somewhat of a mystery; no one's even certain if it's really named after the Caliph Hisham. What is certain is that it has some magnificent mosaics, and I'm a sucker for mosaics. I've visited similar desert palaces in Syria and Jordan and Hisham's follows a standard pattern, incorporating a fortress-like palace, a bathhouse and an agricultural development. In this dry environment the irrigation systems were clearly important, but water was also a necessity for the bathhouse and it's here that you find the mosaics, particularly the wonderful Tree of Life. The truly amazing thing about this site, though, is that I am the only visitor; I have the whole place to myself. It's a sad indicator of how far Palestine is off the tourist trail.

We drive back to Tell es-Sultan, the site of what might be the oldest town in the world – perhaps 10,000 years old and with a claim to the first stairway ever. Oldest city or not, Jericho is certainly the lowest city at 260 metres below sea level. A cable car climbs up over the tell to the Monastery of St George of Koziba, perched high up on a cliff-face above the town.

We depart Jericho and head north on a road that runs parallel to the Jordan River. Jordan itself is clearly visible off to the east the whole way. At Qaser al-Yahud, where John the Baptist is supposed to have baptised Jesus, we peer across at a collection of interesting-looking buildings over the river in Jordan. The river is a tiny affair, perhaps 10 metres wide, although swift-flowing; we can talk to the Jordanians on the other side.

As we approach the checkpoint to leave the West Bank and enter Israel, Adan instructs me to say I'm going to Tiberias, if I'm asked.

'Nazareth is an Arab town. We could get delayed if you say you're going there.'

I am asked, I do say Tiberias – 'for a day or two' – but we're still pulled off to have the car searched and my bags put through an X-ray machine. Total delay? Perhaps fifteen or twenty minutes, but Adan, as calm and gentle as you could hope for, is incensed. He's pleased I'm seeing what happens, though. I relate yesterday's 'Ahmed or Shlomo' tale. It's the usual Arab or Israeli question: Adan is Palestinian, but also a Jerusalem resident. The car is the only completely Israeli thing about us.

In Nazareth Adan drops me at the huge Basilica of the Annunciation and I wander into the old city to find my hotel. It's very quiet; the town is almost completely shut down on Sunday, and after a couple of pieces of communal cake from the friendly inn's communal kitchen I take a circuitous route back towards the Basilica. Just before I arrive, two kids yell something at me and yet another stone is hurled my way. Not very hard, and they run off immediately and keep running when I step in their direction. It's my third stoning of the trip and my second of the day.

The Basilica is the town's big attraction, built on the site of Mary's home, where the angel Gabriel appeared, announcing that she might be a good virgin, but she was still going to have a baby. The church is a curious structure, built on top of the ruins of a Byzantine church, which in turn was built on top of a Crusader Church, and on back through history. There's an international collection of artworks, mainly mosaics, of Mary and child all around the Basilica, inside and out.

By now it's getting cold and dark, so I head back to the inn, where I meet Suraida Nasser and her husband, and Maoz Inon. Suraida is the Arab Palestinian granddaughter of Fauzi Azar, after whom the inn is named. Maoz is the Israeli who turned the fine old house into what it is today. We meet up with two more Israelis, Dror Tishler and Nitzan Kimchi, for dinner. Nitzan has been to Korea and confirms that his name does indeed cause considerable amusement there (kimchi is the fermented cabbage dish for which Koreans have such a strange passion). Dror and Nitzan are two typically entrepreneurial Israelis, creators of Kata, a backpack business which specialises in bags for professional camera and video equipment. The creative office is in Jerusalem, where they're also partners with Maoz in a popular backpacker hostel.

We proceed to have a very talkative dinner. Suraida and her husband muse about visiting Jordan, an Arab country where Palestinians predominate and yet are still treated as second-class citizens. Like other Arab countries in the region, Jordan has a delicate balance between its different sects and tribes, and the Hashemite clan who rules the country regards Palestinians with some suspicion. Forget politics, though – the real argument in this region, no matter what your religion, is where to get the best hummus. Some disagreement follows on just where it is found, but the following day it's halva rather than hummus which provokes discussion.

The next morning Maoz, Dror, Nitzan and I drive to Kibbutz Lavi, from where we'll spend a day walking part of the Jesus Trail. Maoz has mapped out a 65-kilometre trail, starting in Nazareth and ending at the Sea of Galilee, a route Jesus might have followed two thousand years ago. We start our walk from a memorial to the parents and siblings of the kibbutz founders who lost their lives in the Holocaust. Many of the founders were among the 10,000 children evacuated from Germany to the UK in the Kindertransport following Kristallnacht in 1938. A large proportion of their parents and relatives, left behind in Germany, did not survive the war. Kibbutz Lavi was unique in that the children stayed with their parents; usually they lived in communal children's quarters. The kibbutz was established on the site of a village whose Arab population was chased out in 1948.

We soon pass an onion field and I joke that this must have been the spot where Jesus performed the miracle of the onions. It was only later that he got around to fish and loaves. The walk

heads up to the Horns of Hattin, an extinct volcano cone, which
was the site of the battle that brought the Second Crusade to
its disastrous conclusion – at least from the point of view of the
Crusaders. We stop for an extended snack break, the guys are
equipped with a Campingaz-style cooker, so we make tea – and
then coffee – and feast on bread, biscuits, cheese, olives, dips,
tangerines and halva, with some joking about the omission of
pistachio halva from the wide variety of flavours on offer.

After filling up, we move on to the Nebi Shu'eib, the site of
Jethro's tomb and a centre for the Druze. Jethro, father-in-law of
Moses, was – so the Druze believe – the source of Moses' useful
opinions. From there we descend further down the hill to the
site of Hattin village. The Arab villagers here, 1300 of them,
fled or were pushed out in 1948 and were never allowed to come
back. The only surviving traces of the lost village are parts of
the mosque, and we clamber through the makeshift steel bars
– installed to keep minaret climbers out – and on up to the top
of the small minaret. It's a sad little site. We clear the place up;
local weekend picnickers have left quite a mess and Maoz is very
protective of his walk. We then sit down to our own little picnic, a
repeat of the one we enjoyed not that long ago, not that far away.

Maoz's phone rings hot and heavy with calls about the Gospel
Trail. The Israeli Ministry of Tourism came up with a copycat
competitor to Maoz's Jesus Trail – called the Gospel Trail – but
soon discovered that he took the useful precaution of nabbing
the web address for Gospel Trail and is not willing to give it up.

'It's not as good a trail as ours,' Maoz insists. 'It doesn't go
to the Horns of Hattin, one of the most historical sites along
the route, nor does it take you over the Hill of Arbel with its

wonderful views. And it definitely wouldn't take you to a site like this, the remains of a village where the Arab population was driven out in 1948. In fact, it tries to avoid Arab population centres altogether. Walkers tell us that it's the hospitality they receive in both Jewish and Arab communities that is one of the highlights of the walk,' he continues. 'No way am I going to give them that web address.'

With all the talking and eating, this is a somewhat relaxed stroll, and we're not exactly making great time. The decision is made to abandon the rest of the scheduled day's walk and do the first bit of the next, the Hill of Arbel. We've arranged to conclude the day at a guest house where Jesus Trail walkers often overnight, and the owner, Israel Shavit, is summoned by phone, picks us up and drives us to Arbel. We climb to the top of the hill for the great views over the Sea of Galilee and the distant, hazy Golan Heights. I plan to spend a few days walking the Israel National Trail, but I get a preview here, where the two trails briefly converge near the site of those famous incidents of water walking, storm calming and feeding large crowds from meagre resources.

From our hilltop lookout we descend to the ancient synagogue at Moshav Arbel, where Maoz sums up the day – Holocaust memorial, Crusader defeat, Druze memorial, abandoned mosque and now synagogue ruins, all in one walk. A few more steps and we're at our driver's guest house. For lunch! Given that we've already had two trailside 'lunches' and it's only late afternoon, what we really have is an extraordinarily early dinner: Hungarian goulash and a nice bottle of cab sav.

Dror and Nitzan return to Jerusalem, and Maoz takes me back to Nazareth, relating the intriguing story of the Fauzi Azar Inn en route. Like so many young Israelis, Maoz followed his military service with a backpacking world tour. He'd come back enthused about the benefits of backpacker tourism – it brought an international mix of young people into contact with local communities and injected money into those communities at the local level. Nazareth's beautiful but rundown town centre looked like the perfect place to set up shop – part backpacker hostel, part boutique guest house – but that meant finding a suitable building, which would certainly be Arab-owned, and convincing the owners to go into partnership with the enemy: a young Israeli.

He discovered the semi-abandoned Fauzi Azar building and convinced Suraida that restoring her grandfather's house to its former glory not only was possible, but also made good business sense. Convincing Suraida's mother was a more daunting task, but Maoz was a man on a mission.

There's been a lot of talk all day about the state of the nation, or nations – a lot of 'what's happening, where is this all going', with absolutely no conclusions. Demographics are repeatedly cited as the key element in the whole puzzle. If a two-state solution doesn't happen, then it becomes one state, and Palestinians will soon outnumber Jews in that greater Israel state. Then what happens? An Israel that isn't Jewish? Or an Israel with a disenfranchised majority, a non-democratic Israel? This is one reason for the apartheid comparisons: Israel could become like the old South Africa, democratic only by restricting the vote to a minority. Of course, demographics aren't so simple.

For a start, the Palestinian fertility rate is falling, even on the West Bank. In Israel itself it's not that different from the Jewish figure, and Christian Arabs in Israel probably have even fewer children than Jewish Israelis. The demographics were massively disrupted in the 1990s by the arrival of a million Russian Jews, but they tend to have even fewer children than other Jews, so it was a one-off change, not an ongoing factor.

So what about a Greater Palestine? Part of the West Bank could be merged into Jordan, which is already at least sixty per cent Palestinian. This would effectively be a step back towards the pre-1967 situation, when all of the West Bank was in Jordan, and that's the last thing the Jordanian kingdom wants. They're a Hashemite minority ruling a Palestinian majority, and certainly don't want the majority to be even more overwhelming.

Maoz educates me a little more about the Orthodox side of the Israel picture, starting with a handy identikit. The Orthodox Israelis, the men at least, can be recognised by their *kippah*; the ultra-Orthodox go for that fashionable, all-black look which would blend seamlessly into the street scene in Warsaw 120 years ago, sometimes accompanied by a strange hat and usually by a strange hairdo. It's best not to call them ultra-Orthodox – that's a minefield which can be tiptoed around with the term *Haredi*. Contrary to what I expected, they're not necessarily on the far right of Israel's political spectrum. Some of the far right do come from this segment, but many *Haredi* have no right-wing tendencies at all. They're even supposed to be anti-Zionist because they believe there shouldn't be an Israel until the messiah arrives. As a result, many of the *Haredim* don't support the state, and they certainly won't join the army if they can avoid it. At the time of Israel's creation, its first prime minister, David Ben Gurion, foolishly placated the Orthodox end of the spectrum by allowing them to escape army service as long as they were studying. The result is that a great number of them spend their whole lives studying, even when they have no interest and no aptitude for it. The *Haredim* tend to have lots of kids, so from a small base their numbers have increased dramatically. It's just another piece of the demographic puzzle, one which is causing considerable argument in Israel today. Many secular Israelis are becoming extremely unhappy about the *Haredim*: they don't work, they won't serve in the army, they push for all sorts of religious restrictions on life for non-Orthodox Israelis, and the hard-working, military-serving, secular Israelis have to pay for them.

A few days later Ohad Sharav, an Israeli friend, offers another reason for the *Haredi* opposition to military service. 'It's more than just opposition to the Zionist mission,' he suggests. 'They're also afraid that their young men could go into the army ultra-Orthodox and come out secular, seduced by the attractions of the outside world. And by serving with women.'

While I'm in Israel, an incident underscores the increasing level of conflict between secular and Orthodox. A *Haredi* man boarded a bus running from Ashdod, the seaside town just south of Tel Aviv, to Jerusalem but then refused to sit down. Nor would he get off the bus; he just stood in the door so the driver could not continue. His problem? There was a woman who hadn't gone to sit in the back, which is where he felt she should be. Tanya Rosenblit stood her ground: there's no Israeli law that says women have to sit at the back. The police turned up and asked her if she would move, she refused and eventually they hauled the guy off and the bus continued without him. The Israeli media drew comparisons to Rosa Parks, the black woman who refused to give up her seat to a white passenger on a Montgomery, Alabama, bus back in 1955. More likely it's just another example of the *Haredi* mentality, that as long as they can push women to the back of the bus much more important matters can be ignored.

The next morning Suraida reiterates Maoz's tale of how Fauzi Azar's house came back to life and it brings tears to my eyes. Everybody told him it was a bad business decision, quite apart from the Arab-Israeli problems involved, yet the enthusiasm for what Suraida and Maoz had created, both from the local community and from their collection of international guests, was tangible. Later she gives me a coffee-table book on Palestinian painted ceilings – I hadn't noticed the beautiful one over the reception area and the adjacent rooms, created by a Lebanese painter around 1860. Before I depart for Tel Aviv, I walk around the old town with Maoz. He seems to know everybody and everybody seems to knows him: more than once someone takes my arm and informs me 'he's a good man'. It's a worthwhile reminder that, despite the negatives I've experienced, Arabs and Israelis can work together.

A sherut, an Israeli share taxi, hustles me to Tel Aviv where I'm staying in the classy Hotel Montefiore, named after that Victorian-era British philanthropist involved with Rachel's Tomb. My room features a wall of books. I've got time for a stroll to the beach, which takes me past a notable collection of Bauhaus buildings, but I don't know enough about Bauhaus to appreciate them. Back at the hotel I meet Ohad, my walking companion for the next few days, his wife and assorted friends and family for dinner. I've known Ohad for years, although this is the first time I'll be walking with him. We finish early: it's a crack-of-dawn departure tomorrow.

In Palestine I spent a day on the Nativity Trail followed by a day on Maoz's Jesus Trail. Now I'm heading to the opposite end of the country, the Negev Desert, for four days on the big Israel walk, the Israel National Trail. Since it's not much over 400 kilometres, as the crow flies, from one end of Israel to the other, it's quite a feat to squeeze in a 1000-kilometre walking trail. It begins on the slopes of Mount Hermon, the highest point in Israel, whose peak, and ski runs are in the Golan Heights, captured from Syria in the Six Day War of 1967. For the first week, the trail follows fairly close to the border with Lebanon then it runs south to Tiberias on the Sea of Galilee, where I'd briefly joined it on my Jesus Trail stroll.

From there the INT turns west towards Haifa, then south, sticking to the shores of the Mediterranean for several days before turning abruptly east, just before Tel Aviv. Israel is very narrow at this point, so it doesn't take long before the trail approaches that contentious wall, touches on Jerusalem, turns away to the south-west and then skirts around the West Bank before diving into the Negev Desert. This is where Ohad and I will pick up the trail.

It's in the Negev that hiking the INT can get complicated. The population thins out, so there aren't so many places to eat, stock up on supplies or find a bed for the night. Even if you're camping, the sites become more desolate and ill-equipped and for long stretches you hit a big problem: there's no water. Trail walkers are advised to carry at least 5 litres of drinking water per day – you can forget about niceties like washing and showers. The secret of crossing the Negev is water caching – laying in supplies of water to find as the walk progresses. Serious trail walkers do caching trips, driving to points along the trail where they can bury supplies of water for later. Trail notes recommend that you also carry the phone numbers of strategically situated taxi drivers, who will ferry water out should you arrive at your water stash and find some nasty water thief has pinched it. Fortunately, the trail is also populated by 'trail angels', who offer free accommodation – and water in emergencies – to INT walkers. I won't have to cope with these trail tribulations: Ohad has worked everything out and each day we take a taxi to the start or end of the day's walk, shuttling his car along the trail as we go.

Day one starts with a 5 am departure from Tel Aviv, and we're soon at Arad, high above the Dead Sea. A taxi takes us to the start of the walk, avoiding a tiresome march out of the town, and before long we're making a 7-kilometre descent through the *Nahal* Kanfan – *nahal* is the Hebrew word for wadi – a dry and rocky valley that widens out at some places only to narrow down to just a metre or so across at others. Apart from one stagnant puddle in a narrow section, there's no water at all, but it's clear that water does gush down here, and at speed. Our only encounters are a single hiker just a kilometre into the walk, a camel herder on a donkey halfway down the valley and, high above the trail, a shepherd with a bunch of sheep and goats. Oh, and two Hummers with soldiers at the very end.

The single problem with the day's walk is that we do it much too fast. We were told it takes seven or eight hours, but even with a couple of leisurely stops it takes just five. Luckily, Negev taxi drivers seem to be very informed about the trail, even recommending particular points with good mobile phone reception for when we need to call for a pickup. Today's driver whisks us back to Ohad's car in Arad and we drive down to the Dead Sea, passing a string of unusual accident memorials on the winding descent. Roadside memorials have become a worldwide phenomenon in recent years, though they're often short-term affairs in the West. Here, they've become 'wreck art': weird plinth-mounted sculptures of motorcycle bits and car parts.

We're doing the trail in style; our overnight stay in a Dead Sea spa resort even includes a massage – it never gets to my legs, which probably need it the most. Afterwards we float in the hotel's Dead Sea pool; the sea itself, only 100 metres away, is rather chilly at this time of year. The salt burns any cuts, scrapes or scratches, including ones you didn't even realise you had.

It takes a ridiculous amount of time to get going the next morning, but once we're underway it's just a terrific walk all day. Almost immediately we catch up with a group of walkers, but they soon divert off on another track. We climb up a long wadi and then up to the rim of Ha'Makhtesh Ha'Katan, or small crater. The view is of the 'wow' variety and it's certainly not small – it takes us five hours to walk across. Although it's a crater, it's been formed by erosion, not, as it looks, by a gigantic meteorite.

At our lunch stop, halfway across the crater, we bump into two young women. Darya and Yuval are thirty-two days down the trail from the northern starting point; another couple of weeks and they'll be dabbling their toes in the Red Sea at Eilat. Curiously, they started out on the same day, but not together. One day in, and Darya's walking partner decided that long-distance walking wasn't for her and quit. So Darya teamed up with Yuval and her partner, but then a week or two later and Yuval's original companion also cried 'enough'. Appropriately, they are both recently out of the army: walking the Israel National Trail is almost an Israeli rite of passage, part of an extended gap year. You finish your military service, hike the INT, and head off around the world – a bit of trekking in Nepal, some hanging on the beach in Goa – until finally you get around to university or a job.

Having crossed the crater heading due south, we now turn west, walk to the edge of the crater and start climbing. Ohad has not only sorted out the trail technicalities and problems, but he has also chosen some particularly dramatic sections. Darya later emails me that, for her, this was the most spectacular day on the whole Israel National Trail. Ohad and I may have concluded we were speedy walkers the previous day, but we're soon put in our place as we climb out of the crater. Darya and Yuval catch up just as we start the climb and then proceed to surge up the hill ahead of us, despite carrying packs with tents, sleeping bags and cooking equipment, while we only have daypacks.

As we climb out of the crater, Ohad phones ahead for our taxi pickup and we're soon installed in our utilitarian guest house and dining in what has to be the strangest 'Italian' restaurant

I've ever encountered. I'd always thought the Italian menu translated anywhere, but clearly not in the Negev. Ohad opts for Thai noodles, which turn out to be a much wiser choice than the curious interpretation of fettucine pesto I'm served. They were the only Italian words I recognised.

We have walking companions for day three: just as we're finishing breakfast, Moshe Gilad, a journalist with the newspaper *Haaretz*, arrives from Tel Aviv with Ohad's young son Toam. Moshe begins his questioning as we're driving to our starting point.

'So where's the weirdest country you've ever been to?'

I hate being asked what my favourite country is, but strangest is no problem at all. 'North Korea,' I reply. 'Far and away in first place in that category.' North Korea struck me as much more than just a place of Potemkin villages; it was a Potemkin country – the whole place was a fake.

'Okay, second place?' he continues.

'Saudi Arabia.' With its weird religious police and its odd mix of modern (all that oil money, all that bling consumption) and mediaeval (an archaic justice system of hand- and head-chopping, women being treated like chattels and developing-world workers like slaves), I had no problem nominating the oil-rich kingdom for number two position. Our curious Western relationship with the country reinforces their strange status. We beg them to buy yet another squadron of supersonic interceptors to go with their latest platoon of tanks, plead with them to keep the price of oil low, and praise them as reliable partners in the Middle East while turning a very blind eye to their extreme distaste for democracy, not to mention the fact that they supplied nearly all the 9/11 terrorists and continue to promote dissent in the Islamic world.

'And I'll nominate Israel – or Israel and Palestine – for third place,' I add. Moshe is totally unfazed by the comment and quotes it in his subsequent newspaper article about our day's walk.

The day's wonderfully varied walk takes us in the direction of Ha'Makhtesh Ha'Gadol, the big crater, and starts with rolling hills and ridge lines and the remains of Meizad Zahir, a small Roman fortress from the second or third century AD.

From there we climb to an amazing lookout point, descend into a long wadi, passing a group of Israeli walkers on our way, and then run into a herd of ibex. We cross the wadi and climb the canyon wall, an ascent that Italian walkers in the Dolomites would describe as a *via ferrata*, an 'iron road', after the metal steps embedded into the rock and the stretches of chain strung like climbing ropes.

All day there have been glimpses of the Dimona nuclear station and a tethered 'spy' blimp seems to hover overhead.

'It's keeping an eye on us,' I joke, taking photos of the distant station. This is where everyone assumes Israel manufactures its nuclear weapons. The government is silent on their existence, but most people think they are real.

We conclude the walk at the rim of the big crater and drive to Kibbutz Mashabei Sade for the night. Moshe returns to Tel Aviv while Ohad, Toam and I head to the kibbutz canteen for dinner, where a big group of young Americans are enjoying the Jewish homeland experience.

Day four, our final day on the trail, starts in a crouching, cramped pedestrian tunnel under a railway line used to convey phosphate from the Oron mining site. Emerging from the tunnel, we immediately start up Mount Karbolet, which means 'cockscomb' in Hebrew. The edge of Ha'Makhtesh Ha'Gadol is like a sawtooth and much of the time it really is an edge. To my right, there's a sheer drop down into the crater; to my left a steep slope falls away from my teetering progress on the narrow path along the rim. It's not easy walking; it's a continuous up and down, is often rocky and uneven and you feel like you're walking with your ankles bent over. Still, it only takes us three hours to reach *Nahal* Mador. This is an 'escape', a point at which you can abandon the crater rim if time is running short and you're not going to be able to complete the day's walk before nightfall. We're well ahead of schedule, despite the fact that Ohad had been warned not to attempt this section on a short winter's day.

From there it's up and down – mainly up – until we finally descend the *Nahal* Afran, a truly spectacular valley. There's a series of rockpools, empty now, but, unmistakably, water does run through them in large quantities; the *nahal* walls show tilted strata levels and there are jumbled fallen rocks as well as sections with metal foot- and handholds up and down sheer faces and across severe slopes. Then there are the slopes that are just tricky, steep and loose. Altogether, you can see why it's not a good idea to get stuck here after dark.

We emerge onto the plain outside the crater and then it's just a trudge to the night camp, where we're picked up. It's been a fascinating four days and a very different experience from the gentle, fertile country of the Jesus Trail. There are so many walking opportunities in this region. If miracles happen, Palestine's Abraham's Path might one day extend all the way through Turkey, Iraq, Syria, Jordan and Israel, as well as Palestine, to conclude at Abraham's tomb in Hebron. At the moment a major miracle would be required to link the northern end of the Israel National Trail to the southern end of the 400-kilometre-long Lebanon Mountain Trail. On the map the two trail ends are about 10 kilometres apart, but in reality they could be separated by half a world.

I've had lots of opportunities to have my thoughts and opinions pulled in different directions throughout my stay. Even before I arrived, Ohad said in an email, 'It's a bit odd to say, but I don't think I know a single West Bank settler.' It's a reminder that there's no single Israel. During my West Bank travels I regularly bumped into that contentious wall and felt the impact – all negative – it has on the Palestinian population. Yet Ohad reminds me why it was built when he speaks about how intolerable life was during the Second Intifada, when every bus trip could be your last.

'Anna Orgal was our first translator,' he says. 'She translated your India guide. We were still a tiny business and it was the first Lonely Planet book we did in Hebrew.' If anyone asks me which guidebook I'm most proud of I still immediately point to that book. I travelled around India with Maureen researching it in 1980; she was pregnant with our daughter Tashi who was born later that year. 'Anna was a beautiful and optimistic woman,' Ohad continues, 'who always believed in peace and dialogue with the Palestinians. In June 2003 she was working at the Bible Lands Museum in Jerusalem and was on bus number 14a as it travelled along Jaffa Street in central Jerusalem late one

afternoon. A suicide bomber, dressed as an orthodox Jew, got
on the bus and exploded. One hundred people were injured and
seventeen killed. Anna was one of the deaths, she was fifty-four.'

No matter where you are in the world, demographics
are becoming the great determiner. It's like the boiled frog
syndrome. Wars, terrorist attacks, natural disasters – we
recognise them instantly, but like the frog failing to see that the
water will soon be too hot for survival, we fail to notice gradual
changes undermining our existence. So the Italians fail to notice
that not having kids will eventually mean there won't be enough
young workers to pay the old folks' pensions. The Indians fail to
notice that using modern technology to ensure they have sons
instead of daughters will soon leave them with a hopelessly
skewed gender mix. The impact of demographics is rather more
dramatic in disaster-zone countries, where too many young
people and too few jobs leads to violence and instability.

Israel and Palestine are facing a number of demographic
changes, all of which one side or the other – or even both
– is trying to ignore. I left Israel and Palestine saddened,
disappointed and worried. One state, two states – there was no
solution and nobody I spoke to could see one. On both sides,
Palestinian and Israeli, the focus seemed to be on a pessimistic
worst case: 'Things will have to get much worse' or 'There will
have to be some sort of cataclysm'. Neither one state or two, but
no state seemed to be the general conclusion.

Sadly, no state seems to be the perfect solution to many
Israelis and Israel supporters. 'Faced with violence from the

Palestinians, Israel won't negotiate' is one common view, 'and without violence Israel has no need to negotiate.'

So the present situation could continue indefinitely, and with every day that passes, with every new settler moving into the West Bank, with every extension and reinforcement of that wall, the notion of a two state solution moves further into the realm of impossibility. While at the same time, with every additional Palestinian or *Haredi* baby the possibility of a one state conclusion grows ever more ridiculous.

The government decision to extend settlements and walls combined with the relentless progress of demographic change may make the impasse ever more rigid, but one other factor outweighs them both. As Herbert Stein ruled, 'If something cannot go on forever, it will stop.' Trends that can't continue won't. In South Africa, apartheid could not go on forever. In Eastern Europe and the Soviet Union, Communism could not go on forever. And in the Middle East, I seriously doubt that the Israeli treatment of the Palestinians has an infinite future.

COLOMBIA

(**1.**) > CIUDAD PERDIDA'S MONUMENTAL STAIRWAY
(**2.**) > PLAZA BOLIVAR MARKS THE HISTORIC CENTRE OF BOGOTÁ
(**3.**) > IN CARTAGENA COULD BLAS DE LEZO – MINUS AN ARM, A
LEG AND AN EYE – BE THE MODEL FOR MONTY PYTHON'S BRAVE
KNIGHT?
(**4.**) > CHILDREN'S RELIGIOUS PARADE IN SANTA FE DE ANTIOQUIA

(**5.**) > A BOTERO NUDE GETS A KISS AND A CARESS IN
MEDELLÍN'S PLAZOLETA DE LAS ESCULTURAS
(**6.**) > THE SANTA CLARA CHURCH MUSEUM IN
BOGOTÁ'S CANDELARIA DISTRICT
(**7.**) > TONY ABOVE THE PLATFORMS OF CIUDAD
PERDIDA'S CENTRAL AXIS
(**8.**) > TOURIST SHOPS NEAR PARQUE SANTANDER IN
BOGOTÁ

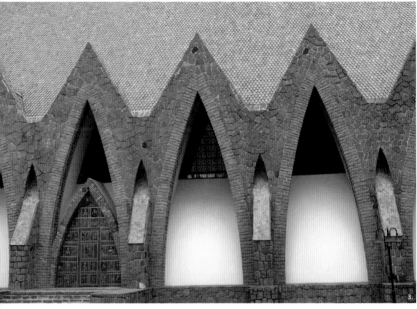

CONGO

(**1.**) > IT'S PIERRE SAVORGNAN DE BRAZZA, NOT A
TRAVELLING '60S HIPPY
(**2.**) > PROBLEMS ON THE ROAD BETWEEN GOMA AND
THE VIRUNGA NATIONAL PARK IN THE EAST OF THE
COUNTRY
(**3.**) > ST ANNE'S BASILICA IN BRAZZAVILLE
(**4.**) > A GIGANTIC HAND HOLDS A PALM FROND OVER
THE TOMB OF LAURENT KABILA IN KINSHASA

(**5.**) > KISANGANI MONEY CHANGERS WITH STACKS
OF 500 CDF NOTES
(**6.**) > CANOE SERVICE ACROSS THE CONGO RIVER
IN KISANGANI
(**7.**) > AFTER DARK THE RED HOT LAVA IN THE NYIRAGONGO
CRATER IS LIKE A CHILD'S IDEA HOW A VOLCANO SHOULD LOOK
(**8.**) > TONY ON THE NYIRAGONGO CRATER RIM

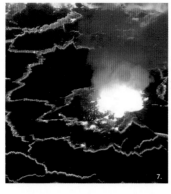

HAITI

(**1.**) > PORTRAITS OF EX-PRESIDENT ARISTIDE CAN STILL BE FOUND ON WALLS AROUND PORT-AU-PRINCE
(**2.**) > RAM CUTS LOOSE FOR ANOTHER THURSDAY NIGHT OF VOODOO JAZZ AT THE OLOFFSON HOTEL
(**3.**) > THE NATIONAL PALACE IN PORT-AU-PRINCE, BEFORE IT COLLAPSED IN THE 2012 EARTHQUAKE
(**4.**) > STATUE OF THE *MARRON INCONNU*, THE 'UNKNOWN SLAVE,' IN FRONT OF THE COLLAPSED NATIONAL PALACE IN PORT-AU-PRINCE

(5.) > A TYPICALLY COLOURFUL TAP TAP IN PORT-AU-PRINCE
(6.) > A STATUE OF THE HEROIC SLAVE REBEL TOUSSAINT L'OUVERTURE
(7.) > NOTRE DAME CATHOLIC CATHEDRAL IN PORT-AU-PRINCE COLLAPSED IN THE 2010 EARTHQUAKE
(8.) > STAIRWAY TO THE RUINS OF SANS SOUCI, HENRI CHRISTOPHE'S 'HAITIAN VERSAILLES'

ISRAEL & PALESTINE

(**1.**) > THE SAWTOOTH EDGE OF MOUNT KARBOLET, 'COCKSCOMB' IN HEBREW.
(**2.**) > WE MET DARYA AND YUVAL WALKING ACROSS HA'MAKHTESH HA'KATAN, THE 'SMALL CRATER' ON THE ISRAEL NATIONAL TRAIL
(**3.**) > THE MONASTERY OF ST GEORGE OF KOZIBA, PERCHED ON A CLIFF FACE ABOVE JERICHO
(**4.**) > DAMASCUS GATE TO THE OLD CITY OF JERUSALEM

(5.) > A SORROWFUL STATUE OF LIBERTY ON THE SEPARATION
WALL IN BETHLEHEM
(6.) > YASSER ARAFAT ON THE WALL AT THE QALANDIA
CROSSING BETWEEN RAMALLAH AND JERUSALEM
(7.) > YASSER ARAFAT'S TOMB IN RAMALLAH
(8.) > TONY WALKING THE NATIVITY TRAIL IN PALESTINE

(**9.**) > A COFFEE IN STARS & BUCKS IN RAMALLAH
(**10.**) > THE OLD CITY OF JERUSALEM
(**11.**) > QUEUEING UP TO GO THROUGH ISRAELI SECURITY AT
THE QALANDIA CROSSING
(**12.**) > LOOKING DOWN INTO THE OLD CITY FROM
JERUSALEM'S DAMASCUS GATE

NAURU

(**1.**) > CHILDREN SELLING MANGOS BESIDE
THE BUADA LAGOON
(**2.**) > A COLLAPSED'S PHOSPHATE LOADING CANTILIVER, A
SYMBOL OF NAURU'S FORMER WEALTH
(**3.**) > THE ROCKY PINNACLES OF 'TOPSIDE'
(**4.**) > THE COAST ROAD HAS TO BE CLOSED WHEN OUR
AIRLINE'S LONE 737 TAXIS OFF THE RUNWAY

PAKISTAN

(**1.**) > TONY AT A ROADSIDE CAFÉ BESIDE THE SKARDU ROAD
(**2.**) > IN 2010 A GIGANTIC LANDSLIDE CUT THE KARAKORAM HIGHWAY NEAR GULMIT, NOW YOU CROSS THE RESULTING LAKE BY BOAT
(**3.**) > YES, SUBMERGING THE ROAD FOR 22KM WAS A LITTLE INCONVENIENT
(**4.**) > THE AIR IS THIN AT THE 4724METRE KHUNJERAB PASS BETWEEN PAKISTAN AND CHINA

(**5.**) > AN ANCIENT BUDDHA FIGURE CUT INTO A ROCK
AT SKARDU
(**6.**) > THE PROUD GUARD AT THE BEAUTIFUL
SHIGAR FORT HOTEL
(**7.**) > A TYPICALLY COLOURFUL TRUCK ON THE WINDING
SKARDU ROAD
(**8.**) > PAKISTANI TRUCKS ARE MOVING ART GALLERIES

PAPUA NEW GUINEA

(**1.**) > WE MAKE SOME IMPROMPTU REPAIRS TO A BRIDGE
BETWEEN BUIN AND ARAWA
(**2.**) > AT THE PANGUNA MINE SITE GIGANTIC TRUCKS
WERE ABANDONED WHEN THE CIVIL WAR BROKE OUT,
TWO DECADES LATER THEY'RE STILL THERE
(**3.**) > ARRIVING AT THE SOUTHERN END OF BOUGAINVILLE
ISLAND FROM SHORTLAND ISLAND IN THE SOLOMONS
(**4.**) > THE WRECKAGE OF ADMIRAL YAMAMOTO'S BETTY
BOMBER, THE 'ARCHITECT OF PEARL HARBOR' WAS SHOT
DOWN IN 1943

(5.) > THE SHELL PETROL STATION SIGN IN ARAWA IS AN
ELOQUENT REMINDER OF BOUGAINVILLE'S LONG ISOLATION
(6.) > NOSE ART OF JOSE HOLGUIN'S B17 'NAUGHTY BUT
NICE,' SHOT DOWN OVER RABAUL IN 1943
(7.) > BANANA BOATS SHUTTLE PASSENGERS ACROSS THE
SWIFT FLOWING BUKA PASSAGE
(8.) > TWO INGREDIENTS FOR CHEWING BETEL – BUAI (THE
GREEN BETEL NUT) AND DAKA (KNOWN AS MUSTARD),
JUST ADD KAMBANG (LIME POWDER) AND CHEW

ZIMBABWE

(1.) > CECIL RHODES GRAVE AT WORLD'S VIEW IN
MATOBO NATIONAL PARK
(2.) > ALERT IMPALAS IN MATUSADONA NATIONAL PARK
(3.) > THE WESTERN ENCLOSURE WALL OF THE KHAMI
RUINS NEAR BULAWAYO
(4.) > ELEPHANT AND TRAIN ON COLLISION COURSE;
THE BULAWAYO-VICTORIA FALLS RAILWAY LINE FORMS
THE EASTERN BOUNDARY OF HWANGE NATIONAL PARK

(**5.**) > CRAIG VAN ZYL AND HIS BIG GUN, USEFUL TO HAVE
WHEN YOU'RE ON FOOT IN HWANGE NATIONAL PARK
(**6.**) > ROCK FORMATIONS IN MATOBO NATIONAL PARK
(**7.**) > THE FINAL ABSURDITY: THE 100 TRILLION
ZIMBABWE DOLLAR NOTE
(**8.**) > ZEBRAS IN THE LEOPARD ROCK HOTEL'S
SMALL PRIVATE GAME PARK

NAURU

Aesop's fable of the ant and the grasshopper is clearly Nauru's fairytale. Instead of behaving like busy little ants and storing the wealth for hungry days to come, the Nauruans behaved like classic grasshoppers, frittering away their considerable wealth on a losing Melbourne football team, a London West End musical flop, bad real estate investments and a crazy national airline. The grasshopper always comes off so badly in this story, though. What about the ants? You could argue there's a counter-fable in this island's history, in which the greedy ants (read: the British Phosphate Company) steal other people's property and hide it away for the winter.

Here's the story of Nauru in two decades: 1970s – richest country in the world; 1990s – bankrupt.

And the wealth was built on? Bird shit.

Really?

Yes, bird shit – guano to be scientific, phosphate if you want its chemical name. Nauru had a lot of it. And it was worth a lot of money.

Right ... and how did they lose it? Oh, stupidity, greed, incompetence, bad advice, getting cheated by international banks, shifty lawyers, ruthless companies. All the usual suspects.

Nauru is a dot in the ocean. Head north-east from Brisbane in Australia for three hours and you'll come to Honiara in the Solomon Islands. Continue in the same direction for another hour and a half and you're there. A stone's throw south of the equator, and nearly 1500 kilometres west of the international dateline.

It really is a dot: just 21 square kilometres. This makes it the third-smallest sovereign nation in the world, right behind the Vatican City and Monaco. Rank them by population and it's the second-smallest; only the Vatican has fewer than Nauru's 10,000 people.

Nauru gained independence in 1968 and, like too many brave new nations, quickly decided it needed an international airline. Having a 'flag carrier' isn't always a good idea; hardly any Pacific nation has managed to make an airline work, and some much larger and more modern countries have failed dismally. Italy's Alitalia is perpetually broke, Belgium's Sabena lost money for forty-two of its forty-three years and even those efficient Swiss weren't efficient enough when it came to running an airline – Swissair went bankrupt in 2001.

Nevertheless in 1974 Air Nauru took off, with a single Fokker F28. That was fun, so another was soon added. They were both traded in for three larger Boeing 737s, before two 727s were added to make a fleet of five aircraft. Quite an airline for a country with a population the size of a very small town. Where to fly to? Well, almost anywhere: Air Nauru was soon flying to thirty destinations with the aim that Nauru would become a hub connecting the most far-flung airports of the Pacific. Anywhere you wanted to go in the Pacific could be accessed via Nauru.

Great idea – except that just because Air Nauru flew there didn't mean passengers wanted to. Airlines need seventy, eighty or ninety per cent load factors to break even, or, if they're lucky and well run, make money. Air Nauru load factors were more like twenty per cent; flights regularly went off to Japan without a fare-paying passenger on board. Any passengers were usually of the non-fare-paying variety: Nauru government officials were keen on commandeering planes for international shopping trips.

An almost complete failure to engage in marketing or advertising didn't help. The fact that visitors to Nauru were not exactly welcomed with open arms only made matters worse. Eventually, somebody in the government woke up to the idea that the airline alone was going to bankrupt Nauru; they dumped the 727s. One 737 was also returned and then a second one, downsizing Air Nauru to a solitary 737. And still they couldn't turn a profit.

By this time money was running short so Nauru followed the pattern fearlessly laid out by others heading towards bankruptcy: don't pay the bills. From 2002 they simply stopped making the payments on their last 737, and at the end of 2005, after repeated offers to renegotiate or come to some sort of agreement, the Export-Import Bank of the United States, which hadn't been paid for three years, repossessed that lonely 737 while it was in Australia, at Melbourne airport.

Chartered aircraft kept the country connected to the outside world for the next few months, but those friendly Taiwanese came to the rescue with another 737. In return, Nauru had to recognise that the Republic of China – Taiwan's China – was the real China, not that Beijing lot. After all, there's no such thing as a free 737.

Nauru's bird-shit wealth took a century to spend, but millennia to build up. It all comes down to the island's remote location. You have to head 300 kilometres east to reach Nauru's nearest neighbour, Ocean Island, also known as Banaba. Part of the Pacific nation of Kiribati, but a long way from all the other islands in that scattered group, Ocean Island is in fact just Nauru II. It's only a third of the size of Nauru and was also, once upon a time, one big heap of bird shit. Just like Nauru, it's been totally mined out.

Ocean Island aside, you have to travel nearly 700 kilometres east to reach the main islands of the Kiribati group, and over 1000 kilometres south-west to the Solomons. It's no wonder a bird was up for some R&R by the time it reached Nauru. The island still attracts regular avian visitors, it's just that mining the guano also took the trees and until some vegetation returns the birds won't be arriving in the vast numbers needed to recreate the island in a few more millennia.

Birdwatchers can still find twenty-seven different bird species on Nauru, most of them seabirds like Audubon's shearwater; Red-tailed and White-tailed Tropicbirds, with their long trailing tail feathers; the brown booby; the great frigatebird, which can stay aloft for more than a week at a time; and five different types of terns. There's even an endemic species, found only on Nauru. At least, at the moment – the Nauru reed-warbler is an endangered species. It lives in shrubland, which has pretty much disappeared along with everything else on the island – the guano, the tree cover and the seabirds that provided the guano and needed the tree cover for shelter during their island stopovers.

To get a feel for what Nauru must have been like in its heyday, pay a visit to Heron Island on Australia's Great Barrier Reef. It's densely covered with trees and, in season, is equally dense with Black Noddy Terns, the same species that call in on Nauru, and wedge-tailed shearwaters. The sheer density of birdlife on Heron Island can be stunning, ditto for the sheer volume of the noise. This isn't likely across most of Nauru now. There's a thin fringe of trees around the coastline, but the dense forest that once carpeted the whole island is gone. The spiky stone columns of Topside don't attract migrating birdlife.

Humans came along much later than the birds, but they've been on the island for at least 3000 years. Like other Pacific islanders, their diet featured lots of coconuts and pandanus fruit, but they also practised fish farming in the Buada Lagoon. A British seafarer stopped by Nauru in 1798 and dubbed it Pleasant Island, but very soon things weren't so pleasant. From 1830 traders and whalers started to turn up, some of them taking residence on the island, bringing alcohol and firearms with them. Eventually petty squabbles degenerated into the Nauruan Tribal War and in the ten years from 1878 the population of the island fell from 1400 to 900 people. In 1888 the Germans, late starters in the colonial game, took over, banging heads together and bringing tribal warfare to a quick end.

Nauru might have cruised along as a quiet German colony if Albert Ellis hadn't taken a closer look at a lump of Nauruan rock in 1899. The rock was being used as a doorstop at the offices of the Pacific trading company where Ellis worked in Sydney. He had it analysed and promptly sailed off to Nauru and Ocean Island to see if there was more where that first rock had come from. Three months later, phosphate mining started on Ocean Island and in 1906 it was underway on Nauru as well.

German colonial ambitions came to a crashing halt with World War I. Australia, New Zealand and the UK jointly took over as the colonial power and the phosphate business was handed over to the British Phosphate Commission, with Ellis, later Sir Albert Ellis, at the controls. The BPC was a very profitable operation, but not for the unfortunate Nauruans. Screwing the Nauruans, and devastating their island at the same time, continued for another fifty years. In 1921 their royalty was reluctantly increased from half a penny a ton to one and a half pence, and then in 1927 to seven and a half pence, but that was still a long way from an honest price. Imposing a fair deal on the BPC would take much longer. In 1965, legal action in the British courts left the Ocean Islanders with an award of the princely sum of £1 and court costs of £300,000. The Australian government was so embarrassed they later paid out £780,000 in reparations.

The Nauruans took over BPC in 1967, a year before they became independent, and in 1970 phosphate mining was taken over by the Nauru Phosphate Company. Professor Helen Hughes, a Czechoslovakian-born Australian with a doctorate from the London School of Economics, was behind the drive for a fair deal. In 1963, with her help, the Nauruans were finally paid the world price for their phosphate. It was a move that soon made them very wealthy indeed. Unfortunately, as Professor Hughes, by then more than 80 years old, observed in

2010, the islanders 'have a long history of being taken to the cleaners by crooks' and there are still plenty of 'sharks that swim in the Pacific'. The Nauruans would meet a lot of those sharks.

Sitting on top of all that bird shit even with royalties paid out by the British Phosphate Company, hadn't encouraged the Nauruans to do the hard work of shovelling it out themselves. The dirty work was handled by less wealthy islanders from Kiribati and Tuvalu, the Gilbert and Ellice Islands during the colonial era. They were still there right to the end. Phosphate extraction finally ground to a halt in 2004 and the following year nearly 1000 Kiribati and Tuvalu islanders were sent home.

So, finally, Nauru was independent and getting a fair price for its phosphate. This was when things really began to go wrong. Putting money aside when you're making it, so you've got cash in hand when you're not making it, is part of life. You save up, put money into a pension fund, superannuation, 401K – you name it – so that when you retire and are no longer earning you still have money to live on. Sensible individuals do it and countries do it too, if they have any sense; Norway has been raking in the petrodollars from North Sea oil and stashing them away for when the oil runs out. Lots of countries have 'sovereign wealth funds', government investment programs to look after things for some future rainy day.

If ever a country needed that long-term outlook it was Nauru – when the phosphate was gone there was no other source of income on the horizon – but 'long-term' and 'planning' were words that didn't seem to feature in the Nauru vocabulary. Air Nauru may have been the country's worst investment, but somehow even rock-solid property investments could turn bad when the Nauruan government was at the controls. During the good years Nauru put together a nice little portfolio of Australian city properties, with towering Nauru House in Melbourne as its centrepiece. When it was completed in 1977 the octagonal fifty-two-storey skyscraper was the highest building in the city. A few years later it suffered from a concrete shedding problem which afflicted quite a few other buildings around the world. I lived just down the road from the Bastille Opera House in Paris in 1996 and tiles were prone to fall off it as well. This little construction issue aside, Nauru House's only other problem was the minor indignity that locals tended to refer to it as 'Bird-shit House'.

Well, there was one other problem. The Nauruan government tended to use it as a party hangout and, even worse, an office where more of the shady, silly or plain stupid deals that would eventually squander billions of dollars were organised. Nauru House might have been a good real estate investment, but there were plenty of bad ones. They'd buy a prime site – Melbourne's Southern Cross Hotel *had* to be a good location; the Beatles stayed there in 1964 – but years later the site would still lie undeveloped and money was running out. Worse, the real property developers could see them coming. So a sharp developer like David Marriner could buy the Queen Victoria hospital site from the Victorian state government for $15 million in 1994 and six months later the Nauruans would happily offer $50 million for it, only to discover they didn't have that sort of money, let alone enough money to redevelop it. Eventually Melbourne City Council took control of the site.

In early 1998 the Melbourne newspaper *The Age* noted that Nauru owned three city 'bombsites'. Their bad property investments weren't restricted to Melbourne; they'd also bought the iconic Grand Pacific Hotel in Suva, the capital of Fiji. In its heyday the GPH was the Pacific equivalent of Singapore's Raffles or Rangoon's Strand Hotel: Somerset Maugham and James Michener stayed there; guests sipped their G & Ts on the rear verandah, overlooking the ships in the harbour. Then, modern tourists began to bypass Suva. Fiji's international airport was at Nadi, on the other side of Viti Levu, and most of the resorts were either near the airport or on outlying islands. The GPH's market had moved on and the last guest departed in 1992. The Nauruans announced they'd restore it to its former glory but, as in Melbourne, time passed, nothing happened and in 2000 the Fiji government announced they were taking it back. A decade later the Fijians have proved equally hopeless at restoring old hotels.

An empty airline and a badly managed property portfolio may have burned the big figures, but the Nauruan investment geniuses were equally good at losing a million here and a million there on smaller and more colourful (if equally silly) investments. In 1994 the Nauru Insurance Corporation signed up to a seven-year, multimillion dollar agreement to back troubled Aussie Rules football club the Fitzroy Lions. Two years later they had to appoint an administrator to try to recoup A$1.25 million they'd lent the hapless club, which was rapidly approaching bankruptcy and soon to be shifted north from Melbourne to Brisbane.

Picking the wrong football club to lend money to wasn't their only entertaining mistake. They also stumped up £1.5 million to back a play in London's West End theatre district. Naturally, *Leonardo the Musical: A Portrait of Love* flopped, and they lost the lot.

Since everything Nauru touched tended to be questionable, they even became embroiled – innocently – in one of Australia's biggest legal scandals, the 1990s Adrian Powles affair. A managing partner of the straitlaced and old-school legal firm of Allen Allen & Hemsley, Powles was running the firm's London office and, to support his gambling problem, talked assorted clients into a get-rich-quick scheme. Getting rich quick was sure to be attractive to Nauru, but other, quite respectable, clients fell for it as well. Powles funnelled $40 million of his clients' money into his 'prime bank note' plan and eventually went to prison for stealing nearly a million dollars. For a spell it looked like his scheme would drive the legal firm into bankruptcy, but fortunately, both for its sleepy lawyers (they hadn't noticed all that money going astray) and for Nauru, most of it was clawed back.

So the phosphate was running out, the investments had gone bad, the airline was losing money and the old Charles Dickens line about expenditure exceeding income leading to misery was in play. When this happens there are three things you can do. Solution 1 is to cut your expenditure, not eat out so often and stop taking the Air Nauru plane on international shopping trips. Solution 2 is to work harder and find some more income streams. The Nauruans weren't keen on belt-tightening so Solution 1 was barely considered. They did try Solution 2, with an interesting new income stream: Russian money laundering. Having 400 different banks all operating from one post office box address soon proved to be a bad idea. The Russian central bank claimed that US$70 billion (that's right, *billion*) of Russian mafia money found its way through Nauru in 1998 alone. Russian gangsters weren't the only ones to find Nauru a convenient banking centre. In 2006 the Inland Revenue sent English conman Ian Leaf down for twelve years for defrauding the British tax office of £54 million via a convoluted scheme involving high interest loans from a bank he'd established in Nauru. Mr Leaf spent his Nauru-funded fortune on a ten-bedroom house on Lake Geneva in Switzerland and the obligatory Porsche, Aston Martin, Rolex watches, private jet charters and three wives before the tax office grabbed him.

Nauru's blatant bad banking eventually led to a severe telling off and the closure of the Nauru Agency Corporation, the government shack from which all those fake banks were established. Running a prison camp for Australia would later bring in some petty cash, but not enough. So they turned to Solution 3, which is to borrow money and hope that the problem will solve itself before you have to repay it.

The bad property investments had been handed back or lost, but there were still some good ones, so Nauru opted to borrow money and pray. General Electric Finance fronted up $230 million, taking the nice Australian properties as security. Unsurprisingly, Nauru couldn't make the payments.

No doubt GE Finance has plenty of experience in repossessing the car when you don't make the payments, and in 2004 they took the buildings. The Royal Randwick Shopping Centre and the Mercure Hotel in Sydney and the Downtowner and Savoy Park Plaza hotels in Melbourne were all taken over by creditors. Even Nauru House, that fifty-two-storey symbol of just how wealthy Nauru had become back in 1977, was lost. Today, it's plain old 82 Collins Street. It's said that when the receivers moved into Nauru House they found twelve crates of classy Grange Hermitage, which had been maturing nicely since the 1970s.

Visiting any dark land is unlikely to be totally straightforward. During the Air Nauru era, when the country should have been desperate to 'put bums on seats', as the airline mantra goes, the island nation never got around to rolling out the welcome carpet. Air Nauru has gone, but even with the replacement airline's single aircraft instead of five it's not exactly standing-room-only on flights to Nauru. Getting a visa is still a task, though.

Air Nauru was reincarnated as Our Airline – but wait, why did they give it that dumb name? One story is that Nauru finally did what lots of small countries should: offer to share an airline with other small countries. After all, Sweden, Norway and Denmark can share SAS, Scandinavian Airlines System, so why couldn't little Nauru get together with some neighbours and share an aircraft? Air Kiribati came on board – you can see the name painted below 'Our Airline' down the side – and then Solomon Airlines made noises about joining up as well. The Solomon Islanders had suffered an assortment of small-country airline problems. Some clever aircraft salesman had even signed them up for an aircraft that, it turned out, couldn't fly to Australia with passengers *and* baggage. One or the other had to stay behind.

'Okay,' said the Solomon Airlines spokesperson, 'we'll join up, so long as it has a neutral name. We're going to share the airline so why don't we call it Our Airline.'

'Awful name,' thought the Nauru airline people, 'but if that's what it takes, then okay.'

So they painted 'Our Airline' down the side and the Solomon Islanders changed their minds.

I contact Our Airline, book a flight and they say they'll email me a visa. It turns out that means they'll email me a visa form, which I duly fill in and email on to the Nauru Consulate-General in Brisbane. The north Australian city is the centre for everything you need to know about Nauru in Australia; wisely the Nauruans realised they could live without an embassy in the Australian capital, Canberra. I leave the boxes for 'residence' and 'business' blank; I'm not planning on moving to Nauru and I am not going to be doing business there. I fill in the box for 'tourist visit', which asks how much money I am planning to bring with me. After all its banking problems nobody trusts the poor Nauruans to handle the stuff and as a result there are no banks, no ATMs, nobody to change your traveller's cheques. It's cash only please and the Australian dollar is the cash of choice. I reckon $1000 should comfortably cover three days, or longer if Our Airline gets stuck in Kiribati or Fiji and doesn't come back as scheduled.

An email quickly bounces back from the charming Charisma at the consulate in Brisbane: 'Will you be travelling as a visitor or for business purposes?' Well, I thought that was clear, but never mind. 'I will be travelling as a visitor,' I reply.

After which it goes quiet for a spell. An enquiry to Our Airline is followed by a counter-enquiry about where I will be staying in Honiara, the capital of the Solomon Islands, which I plan to visit en route to Nauru. Two weeks go by with no visa and I arrive in the Solomons. So, with five days before my scheduled flight, I email the consulate again. The Nauru visa story remains a bit of a mystery. Will something be emailed to me? Or will it be held by Our Airline so they know I am okay when I turn up for my flight? Or will it simply be waiting for me when I arrive in Nauru?

More silence follows. Flights to dark lands also tend to go at dark hours and Our Airline is certainly not going to miss ticking that box. Flight ON 2 departs Honiara at 1.45 am on Monday and arrives in Nauru less than two hours later – not a nice time to arrive anywhere, even with a one hour time change. If my visa isn't sorted out by close of business in Brisbane on Friday I won't be going anywhere on Monday morning.

The Solomons are not exactly wired and on Wednesday I'm out of email range. Thursday I'm in Munda and manage to email the consulate. It's now twenty-four days since Our Airline said they'd email me the visa form, fourteen since they actually did. I'd returned it the same day, but still I have no visa. Friday I'm in Gizo, the Solomons' number two city, which is not saying a great deal, but not only is there email there's also mobile phone coverage. So I email Our Airline and the consulate and point out that this is going down to the line; I've paid $988 for my ticket; where's my visa?

Amazingly, just ten minutes later, walking down Gizo's main street – okay, Gizo's only street – my phone rings. It's Trent at the consulate to tell me I've never sent them my passport data page. This is the first I've heard about sending them my passport data page, but, like any good travelling boy scout, I have done as Lord Baden Powell recommended. I am prepared. A scan of my passport data page is sitting on my laptop back at the hotel. I sprint back down the street, email the damn thing and then phone the consulate to ask if they've got it.

Yes, but what about a hotel booking? Nauru has three places you can stay, all of them pretty well empty, but you need a confirmed reservation before you're allowed in the door. So it's back to the internet where I cannot find any way to book a hotel in Nauru. After some calls, I end up with a confirmation email from the Menen Hotel, offering a choice between a straightforward standard room and a deluxe ocean-view one. Seeing as I may not get back to Nauru in a hurry, I go for the luxe. I email the confirmation to the consulate and finally, just before 5 pm on Friday, my permit comes through, a 'Certification for Travel and Entry into Nauru'. Couldn't have cut it much closer.

Two days later, around midnight on Sunday, I'm standing in a very quiet check-in at a very quiet Henderson Airport. Of course, nobody asks to see my 'Certification for Travel and Entry into Nauru'.

A few hours later I've crossed that stretch of empty ocean and in the pre-dawn darkness of Nauru's airport, I lose my passport even before I get to the baggage area.

'You can pick it up this afternoon from the immigration office,' I'm told. My bag is there and moments later I'm outside in the dark. There's another guy looking as lost as me, but we quickly find the bus from the hotel, which picks up its four passengers and sets off. The other two are on an aid project. My fellow tourist, the lost guy, is 'trying to get to every country in the world'.

'Oh, like Travelers' Century Club,' I respond.

'No, not like them. They count places which aren't even countries,' he insists, adding, 'I've got ten to go.'

I've got no idea which direction we're heading in or how far the hotel is from the airport, but in a few minutes we're there. I check in and a man from the front desk totes my bag to my ocean-view room, right at the end of the block. 'Are you very full?' I ask, as we walk to the room.

'No, not really,' he replies, which turns out to be an understatement.

There's an electricity-shortage warning note in the room and the air-con is set at freezing. I flip it off, slide the door open to check the ocean view – waves breaking on the reef and a starry, starry night – and fall into bed.

When I wake up a couple of hours later I walk along the ocean front back to the lobby. The hotel may not be very full of guests, but it's pretty clear most of the rooms have permanent inhabitants; the washing hanging from every terrace makes it look like a squatter camp. The swimming pool is a potential health risk; it's empty and you could fall into it. The power shortages are due to the island's fuel supply running low, which in turn means they can't run the desalination plant, which in turn means water shortages. There's been no rain for a long time and the tanker ship delivering fuel is overdue. To picture the Menen Hotel think of an anonymous Ibis or Travelodge motel-like place in a salty, rust-supportive environment, a side effect that comes with ocean views. Then encourage squatters to move in, stand back, don't maintain it, wait for things to fall apart for five or ten years and voila, the Menen.

Apart from the electricity warning, the only other printed information in my room is a note advising that meals at the restaurant cannot be charged to your room and to pay in cash. There's no sign of life in the restaurant, but the front desk points me back there, with another warning about the pay-in-cash requirements. En route I look into the hotel gift shop – that's what it says – ideal if you know anyone who needs a gift of canned tuna (a wide variety) or Spam (regular or lite are on offer).

The Chinese restaurant is as rundown as the rest of the place. Flanking the counter are two glass-fronted fridges, where glistening cold soft drinks are usually found. One's empty, the other looks like a warning from your mum (or the health inspectors) about what will happen to your fridge if it isn't cleaned at least occasionally. It contains two half-empty jam jars, some paper-wrapped butter remnants, one bag of dried-up pork chops, one full of browning chopped lettuce, a whole shelf of some other aging salad green and a final shelf of identical mystery bottles. The bottle information is all in

Chinese and the label shows apples, but the contents are a shade of Coca-Cola brown. Breakfast is a poached egg on two slices of toast and a glass of very sweet cordial. I decide to make my own tea back in my room.

One of my Nauru goals is to have a look at whatever is left of the Pacific Solution. In August 2001, just when Nauru and its economy seemed to really be up against the wall, the Norwegian container ship the *Tampa* sailed to the country's rescue. Actually, the *Tampa* sailed to the rescue of 438 Afghan refugees, who ended up in Nauru, and they, and over a thousand more refugees who followed them, kept the Nauruan shipwreck afloat for nearly another decade.

The *Tampa* was heading from Fremantle in Australia to Singapore when it diverted to aid a troubled Indonesian fishing boat overloaded with refugees on their way to Australia. Having rescued the passengers (mostly men – just twenty-six women and forty-three children), where to next? The international regulations on 'what to do with shipwreck survivors' says 'take them to the nearest suitable port', which just happened to be the Australian territory of Christmas Island, about 150 kilometres away, where they may have been heading in the first place. Arne Rinnan, the Norwegian captain, initially set out for the Indonesian port of Merak, about twice as far away, then changed his mind, with some help from his new passengers, and diverted course to Christmas Island.

Refugee arrivals and boats were becoming a political issue at the time in Australia. Prompted by the *Tampa* debacle, prime minister John Howard would later announce that 'we decide who comes into this country'. So the *Tampa* sat off Christmas Island; the authorities in Singapore said, 'Don't bring them here'; the Indonesians said, 'We don't want them back'; and Australia brightly suggested they could always carry on to Norway. Eventually, Australian troops boarded the *Tampa* to stop it landing the refugees at Christmas Island (there was no way the *Tampa* itself could have docked at the small island), the Norwegians complained, the UN made UN-type noises, Captain Rinnan was honoured with Norwegian and UN awards and the Afghan refugees were shipped off to Nauru where two refugee detention centres had been hastily put together as Australia's Pacific Solution.

The clever idea was that refugees setting out for Australia would realise that they weren't going to get to Australia, they would simply be shipped off to somewhere deeply dispiriting to sit for a very long time while paperwork was shuffled around. Somewhere like Nauru. The Pacific Solution had a number of serious flaws. First of all, after the paperwork was shuffled around, sometimes for up to five years, most of the refugees would in any case eventually end up in Australia. Or New Zealand.

Second, it was enormously expensive. If you're going to build a refugee centre and shuttle politicians, lawyers, guards, staff, social workers and God knows who else back and forth, is it cheaper and easier to do it in your backyard (or, in Australia's case, in some isolated Outback location)? Or on a remote Pacific island with infrequent and expensive connections? Costwise, Nauru was a no-brainer bad decision. On the flipside, Nauru

was equally inaccessible to journalists, refugee advocates
and others who might have thought this was a bad idea and
complained about it. Nauru was Australia's own Guantánamo
Bay, a place where you could hide the government's dirty deeds
away, well out of sight. Probably even more important to John
Howard, it showed how tough he was on the refugee question
and helped him win the next election.

So the couple of million dollars a year Australia was tipping
Nauru's way was ramped up to $20–$30 million annually.
About 1500 refugees would enjoy Nauruan hospitality. At a
cost of, say, $100 million overall, that's around $70,000 for
every man, woman and child who experienced the comforts
of the Topside or State House refugee centres. Not everybody
in Australia loved the Pacific Solution and finally, in 2007,
the controversy helped to unseat John Howard and the new
government promptly brought the Pacific Solution to an end.
Of course, like any good movie monster, it refused to die and
in late 2012 we didn't even have to wait for the Australian
opposition to win the next election for them to revive the idea
of the camps. They promised to reopen them if they got elected,
and start pumping money back into the Nauruan economy.
Good money after bad is something Nauru knows all about
and, sure enough, the Pacific Solution Take II is back in action,
courtesy of a government that got into power at least partly on
the promise of getting rid of it in the first place.

After that very unexciting breakfast at the Menen I set out
to walk into town. This is a mistake, I soon discover, because

Nauru has no 'town', just various places scattered all around
the island coast road. I'm past 3 kilometres and beginning
to wonder how far the drive was from the airport last night
when a large Nauruan lady stops and picks me up in her ute
for the last 500 metres to the government offices. In one handy
package you get everything, including the President's Office,
the Parliament Building and what I want, the Border Control
& Immigration Office, where I hand over A$100 and get my
passport back.

'You get a better stamp when you leave,' I'm told (I don't)
and if I want I can stay for up to thirty days. 'We average
thirteen visitors a month,' the guy behind the counter says.
'They come from all over,' he continues, explaining that the
arrivals flow ticks up when it's cold in Europe.

'How many came in on this morning's flight?' I ask.

'Just two of you,' he answers. That would be me and the
visiting-all-countries American, Albert Podell.

The government offices are right opposite the airport
terminal so I cross the runway and have a look at the now
deserted building. At an internet café, I check my emails.
My banker back in Australia alerts me to the arrival of a
gratifyingly large deposit to my account. 'Take care of it,' I tell
him. 'I'm in a country where bankers and bad advice managed
to run through a much larger figure.'

A few steps further and I'm past the island's second hotel to
two phosphate loading cantilevers, rusting and collapsing, with
signs warning you that further disintegration could occur at
any moment. It's lunchtime so I stop at a Chinese place next to
the hotel; about eight per cent of the population here is Chinese

and, as is usual in the Pacific, they run most of the shops and restaurants.

I start back to the hotel, now nearly 5 kilometres away, but I'm soon picked up by a guy on one of the postie bikes that seem to be the two wheels of choice on Nauru. A postie bike is Australian slang for the small Honda utility motorcycle used by postal workers, usually post office red in colour and with just one seat, but with a big, sturdy carrier rack on which I perch. In Nauru the rack needs to be sturdy because, like McDonald's fries, the islanders only come as large, extra large and gigantic. A generation of sitting around, not doing too much and eating lots of fast food has resulted in the most obese people in the world: more than forty per cent of the population has diabetes.

Just before we arrive at the hotel I notice Albert, walking along the coast road in an outfit the travel fashion police should give him a good bollocking for. All he needs is a sign hovering above him shouting 'serious travel nerd'. The singlet from Uxmal is the crowning touch.

I've arranged an afternoon island tour, which turns out to be the two sweeties from the front desk – Frances and Persephone – jumping in the hotel minibus and whisking me away. After driving by the airport again we leave 'Oceanside' and turn up into the centre of the island to 'Topside', where we stop by the 'tank farm' (short on petrol right now) and roam around various sites. There is still some phosphate being mined, but at a much lower output than in Nauru's heyday. In the old days it was conveyed in little railway trucks, which are now scattered along the roadside; you can still see the tracks in the road in places.

We also stop in at the Topside refugee centre, occupied at
the time by the NRC – the Nauru Rehabilitation Corporation.
They're quite happy for us to come in and look around.
The refugee housing was simple, container-like rooms, all
repainted, but also all derelict. With shared toilet facilities
it looks a little like a utilitarian backpacker hostel. The
Australian government's Pacific Solution may have described
them as 'refugee detention centres', but in fact the refugees
were free to wander Nauru during the day, as long as they
came back to the centres for the night. They certainly weren't
going to escape the island. They didn't just sit around either;
it's said they managed to grow fruits and vegetables – no
diabetes for them. The NRC seemed to be using the site as a
plant nursery although they would have needed a much, much
bigger nursery if they were seriously going to revegetate Nauru.

Whatever the plus points, a few years in a Nauru refugee
detention centre was nobody's idea of fun. It clearly didn't
appeal to Alexander Downer, Australia's foreign minister when
the Pacific Solution Mark I was dreamed up. At a tourism
conference we both spoke at in Sydney in 2008, Mr Downer
ran through his ten favourite cities in the world – Sydney is
number one – and then announced the absolutely worst place
he'd ever had to visit. It wasn't Afghanistan; he'd just been
talking about how much he'd enjoyed bravely choppering in to
visit the Australian troops. No, his winner for the world's worst
shithole was, you guessed it, Nauru.

We drive on to Buada Lagoon, one patch of real green on
the island. Most of it, however, looks very dry and grey-green;
they've had a long drought. The locals grow fruit around the

lagoon and I buy a bag of mangos from two young girls; they're tiny and not very good. The mangos, not the girls. There's an old Japanese World War II prison to look at and then it's back to the Oceanside and the harbour, where kids are playing on a floating jetty and a large collection of small outriggers are moored. I haven't seen any out on the water. There are two more phosphate cantilevers here, one of which has collapsed. So they still have one of the four in operating condition.

Finally, I'm dropped off at Capelle to pick up a rent-a-car. Capelle & Partners is the island's big general store and I immediately bump into Sean Oppenheimer, who seems to be the boss here. I was sitting next to him on the plane this morning, although I didn't realise I'd soon be meeting him again.

Sean is very upbeat about Nauru. 'The new government is honest,' he reports, 'and the NRC is doing what they should have done about rehabilitating after the phosphate was extracted years ago.'

'But rehabilitating the place doesn't pay the bills,' I suggest.

'Yes, but there is still another year and a half of primary phosphate they can extract,' Sean continues. 'Then there's years of secondary phosphate extraction possible, and after that they're working on doing something with all that rock pinnacle. They can be cut and polished, they're like marble slabs when that's done.

'Plus the fishing around the island is fabulous,' he enthuses. 'We used to bring in twenty game fishing groups a year.'

Once upon a time.

'Scuba diving is possible too,' Sean insists, 'although when you get beyond the reef edge it drops straight off for a long, long way.'

There's currently no scuba operation on the island, which is a pity as I'd brought my scuba equipment with me from the Solomons.

Sean even has some very comfortable apartment rooms at Capelle's. 'We rent them out to those people trying to visit every country, they all know about it.'

Not Albert, it seems.

The next day, with my Capelle wheels, I set out to explore the island on my own. It's small enough that once you've started out in one direction you might as well keep going that way – 18 kilometres later, you'll be back at your starting place, without wasting energy on a U-turn. On my first circuit I stopped at Aribare Harbour, the island's second artificial harbour, and got out my map to work out how far I'd come. Then I looked up and realised I could see the Menen Hotel, just a few hundred metres down the beach.

Back up on Topside there seems to be quite a maze of roads, far more than the girls took me along yesterday. I end up on a minor road that goes on and on, getting worryingly rough for my streets-of-Yokohama (it's clearly a Japanese secondhand import) Toyota. Eventually I stop, but walk on a little further and find the road drops down to the coast, so I carefully follow it to the end.

I drive back towards the airport and up to the Buada Lagoon again. There are no children selling mangos today and I soon exhaust the possibilities of the island's one little patch of green.

So it's on around the island and up to the other refugee centre, State House. This one is being used as a school, after the school near the Civic Centre burned down, so it's not open for refugee camp tourists like me. I'm beginning to run out of sightseeing possibilities, but just before the hotel there's another road up to Topside and I follow that past some picturesque rocky pinnacles. And then I'm back at the Topside refugee centre.

That night the Nauru President, Marcus Stephens, is hosting a dinner at the hotel, to welcome the new Russian Ambassador to Australia. Nauru falls into his portfolio and he's here for a look; it's probably too late to claw back any of that missing Russian mafia money. As the guests arrive I bump into Rod Henshaw, the government's media man, which means he's the interviewer and DJ on Radio Nauru as well. Sean has told him I'm on the island so I'm on for Nauru drive time tomorrow morning. Tonight I drive out to the island's second-best restaurant – or so I'm told – right by the airport terminal. I'm the only diner.

Back at the government building complex, the next morning, I get my twenty minutes on Radio Nauru followed by a fifteen-minute interview for Nauru TV. I suggest they do it in front of one of the cantilever phosphate loaders, so I can say something about Nauru's possibilities for industrial archaeology. If northern England can sell the tourist possibilities of rust-belt tourism, why not Nauru?

Back at the hotel the pool, which was filled last night for the diplomatic do, is being emptied again. The tide is very low; it's almost dry right out to the reef edge. They say the reef drops straight off to 500 metres deep.

Albert is at the airport. Somehow, after he declined to join my hotel bus tour on that first afternoon, I never saw him again. He borrowed a bike and pedalled around the island. Our Airline's Boeing arrives early. The round-the-island road splits at the airport and runs along both sides of the runway, but traffic on the inner road has to be stopped when flights come in because aircraft taxi across it to get from the runway to the terminal apron.

In the departure lounge I talk to a young Danish guy transiting from Kiribati. After rating Nauru as the worst place he'd ever been, Australia's former foreign minister went on to rank Kiribati as number two. Leaving Afghanistan, Iraq and all those other horror stories to compete for number three and below. The young Dane had been there for a couple of months while his wife was working on an eight-month anthropological research project about water. Places like Kiribati would have to be the cutting edge of freshwater problems – rising sea levels, a low lying atoll, overcrowding and stress on the environment, water in particular. In contrast, Nauru won't disappear – it's not a low-lying atoll likely to submerge if the sea level jumps up a metre or two – but the vegetated coastal fringe is just above the waves; inundate this and all that's left is that inhospitable Topside.

We're ready to go – forty-odd passengers, in an aircraft that seats 132. The plane departs in the opposite direction from what I expect, so I'm sitting on the wrong side, but then it turns to give me a fine view of the whole island as we climb away. An hour and a half later we're off to the east of Honiara, and then a bit later over a very spectacular reef system, the Indispensable Reef. Only another hour and I'm back in Australia. It's unlikely to be quite so simple for those unfortunate refugees, tangled in a new version of Australia's 'scare them away' plan, to take that final step in the trip down under.

PAKISTAN

In Greek mythology the Hydra was a hideous, multi-headed, serpent-like monster. Apart from poisonous breath the beast had the useful skill of regenerating heads as fast as they were cut off. Some versions of the legend insist that two heads popped back for every one that Heracles hacked off with his mighty sword. The ancient Hydra lived in the swamps near the city of Lerna; its modern incarnations live in the Waziristan area bordering Afghanistan, and come in both Afghan and Pakistani Taliban varieties. In place of a sword, the CIA uses drones to sever the modern Hydra's heads, but, unlike Heracles, who quickly realised that this only leads to more of them, the CIA is still launching drone strikes.

Kate Middleton caught without her bikini top seems the only story with a chance of keeping angry Muslims off the front page today. Mitt Romney's latest foot-in-mouth performance in the US election campaign hardly comes close. It doesn't seem to be the best day to arrive in a staunchly Muslim country with a penchant for complaining loudly and often violently about the shortcomings of Western nations. I fell asleep in my hotel in Amritsar, India, just across from the Golden Temple, the most holy spot for the world's Sikhs, and at some pre-dawn hour the gentle 'ping' from my phone wakes me with an incoming email.

It's Maureen, emailing from Paris. 'Is this a good idea?' she queries.

A reasonable question. I was planning to take a taxi out to the India border in the morning and walk across into Pakistan. Then I'd get into Lahore and find a bus to Islamabad, the Pakistan capital. I'd arrive at about the same time Maureen flew out of Paris, and at an uncomfortably early hour the next morning she'd meet me in Islamabad. When I went to bed, just a few hours ago, things didn't look altogether perfect in the Islamic world and now, when I flick on my laptop and cruise around the world's news, they look rather worse.

It's another case of 'upset the Islamic world' idiocy. If it isn't some stupid preacher in the US south threatening to burn Korans it's somebody in California making movies designed to enrage people. The film at the centre of the uproar may have been titled *The Innocence of Muslims* (even that is unclear), but in the Islamic world it has quickly become known as the 'anti-Islam movie'. Either way, it would have disappeared without trace if it wasn't dubbed into Arabic with certain additions that the actors insist were not in the original production. Criticism is one thing, but when you do something purely to provoke, it's ridiculous. My news hunt turns up embassy protests, KFCs burned down – the usual – although the start of this mess, killing the US ambassador to Libya is much more serious. It's later concluded, though, that his murder was not at all connected to the movie protests. But this is all media; I'm pretty confident the on-the-ground reality will – with care – be somewhat better.

'Should be okay. I'll come out to the airport and meet you, even if it is 3 am,' I email back. I turn over and try to get some more sleep.

Pakistan and I go way back. We have history.

My father was working for British Overseas Airways Corporation (later to be called British Airways), and my parents moved to Karachi before my second birthday. My younger sister and brother were both born there. As adults, we may not remember the broad sweep of events, but specific childhood memories can be crystal clear many, many years later. I'm continually surprised by how many sharply etched memories I have of Karachi; it was almost precisely four years later that I left, still a few months short of my sixth birthday. There was that huge whale carcass towed into the harbour at Keamari, the scary jellyfish that would strand on the sands of Clifton Beach, an even scarier lobster that seemed to launch itself off the kitchen bench and block my exit to the door with waving claws. There was a buzzard that used to peer down from atop a flagpole outside the house on Bath Island Road, where we had an apartment, and camel carts throughout the city. There were airport memories: the man who did sleight-of-hand tricks outside my father's office; the baby elephants in the airport hangar, on a stopover from India on their way back to a circus in England; the first Comet jetliner when it came through Karachi. Then there was the old-India-hand, who presumably had spent a little too long in the midday sun and used to turn up outside 4 Bath Island Road every morning to play reveille on the bagpipes. Karachi certainly generated lots of memories for a small child.

It was not until twenty years later that I returned to Pakistan, travelling along the Asia Overland Route, the 'hippie trail' of the 1970s which took me through Afghanistan, over the Khyber Pass and down onto the plains of the subcontinent to India and Nepal. In those idyllic days Afghanistan was all hippies, hashish and handmade rugs, not a place of the Taliban and terrorists.

More years passed before I finally got back to Karachi, clutching a photo of the house where I'd lived so many years earlier. In the family photo album I'd even found a snapshot of a small me standing beside the cook's even smaller daughter. Driving back to Bath Island Road one day, my mother piloting the family Morris Minor, we'd found the girl being pursued down the driveway by a rabid dog. My mother managed to get the car between child and crazed canine and told me to open my door. We dragged her safely on board. Later the dog was lured into a garage behind the house; the police came round, flung open the door and, when the dog raced out, shot it. As any five-year-old would be, I was impressed. From the front, the house looked precisely as I remembered it and when I went round to the back, there was the garage. If the door had opened, forty years later, and the mad dog had rushed out, I wouldn't have been surprised.

My dad used to take me out on a sailing dhow in the harbour, and we'd lower a piece of string to catch crabs that we cooked on deck. On this return trip, I was forty years older – older than my dad was back then – and I walked down to the harbour. Ten minutes later I was out on a sailing dhow and pulling in crabs on a piece of string.

'This,' I thought, 'is amazing.'

Another decade and a half passed and I was back in Pakistan again, this time in the sensitive Kashmir border area inspecting an aid group's work after the disastrous 2005 earthquake. There was one connecting element between all these visits, one shared by many other visitors to Pakistan I've talked to over the years: we've all enjoyed travelling through the country and found the Pakistanis to be friendly, outgoing and helpful. Not quite the image we get in the news, is it?

This time I'm coming back to tick off a trip which has been on my bucket list for far too long. The Himalaya stretches the length of Nepal and on through India before finally fading out in Pakistan, although not before giving the country boasting rights to five of the world's fourteen peaks over 8000 metres, including number two, the deadly K2. The Himalaya blends into the Karakoram Range and then into the Hindu Kush as it gradually falls away westward into Afghanistan. I'm planning to travel the Karakoram Highway, a two-week trip up and over the Karakoram Range ending, if all goes well, at Kashgar in China's far western Xinjiang Province.

On our hippie-trail trip, Maureen and I had crossed the border at Wagah, the crossing point between Lahore and Amritsar. There was no choice: although the border between the two countries stretches for nearly 3000 kilometres, to this day it's virtually the only place you can cross. In 1972, only a year since the war that led to the creation of Bangladesh, relations between India and Pakistan were not very good. They've rarely become much better, but in 1972 the border was only open for three hours a week, on Thursday mornings. All of us, the eastbound hippie-trail troupe, stayed in Lahore on Wednesday night and made the trek, en masse, out to the Wagah crossing point the next morning and, en masse, crossed over into India and spread out in every direction, some north to Kashmir, some south directly to Goa, some just continuing east to Delhi.

Yesterday, I arrived in Amritsar on a train from Delhi and, having dumped my bag at my Golden Temple view hotel, I took a taxi straight to the border although I wasn't planning to cross to Pakistan until the following morning. Compared to forty years ago border crossers between the two countries may be few and far between, but border watchers are big business. Every night the border closing routine has become a major tourist event, on both sides of the border, as the Indian and Pakistani army contingents haul down their flags, slam the border gates shut and close things down until the next morning.

Their boots came down with a resounding thump; then, across the border, there was the briefest handshake before the soldiers spun round and set off on another march, inspired, perhaps, by Monty Python's Ministry of Silly Walks. Monty Python is a natural inspiration when you're wearing a particularly outrageous hat and trying to kick it off your own head. I used to say that when wars were decided by whose army dances the best my money would be on the North Koreans, after seeing a Mass Games in their gigantic stadium in Pyongyang, but after an hour of watching the Indian and Pakistani armies at Wagah, I have a feeling the North Koreans may only be dancing for the bronze medal. Finally the flag was lowered, the Pakistanis slid their gates shut so violently they bounced back, the Indians swung their gates shut with equal temper, and it was all over until tomorrow night.

I found my driver and we cruised back to Amritsar. Having a hotel a stone's throw from the holiest Sikh temple made it easy to follow the important advice to visit the temple at different times of day to appreciate its appearance under varying light. In fact, my afternoon, night and early morning visits could also have been summarised as 'seeing the temple under different rainfall'. I managed to experience everything from a light drizzle to a monsoonal downpour.

I also managed to fit in another prime Amritsar experience – the free vegetarian meal in the shrine's community dining hall. Every day 60,000 to 80,000 meals are dispensed and the production line is amazing. I took a metal bowl and cup, queued up with the Sikhs and squatted on the floor to enjoy the rice, vegetable curry, dhal and chapattis. It was indeed a major operation feeding everybody and the dishwashing line-up was even more impressive. Afterwards, I wandered the brightly lit, crowded streets of the old city around the temple.

This morning, after a broken night's sleep, I head out to the border. I was given conflicting advice as to what time the border opens and I arrive an hour early. I'd have had time to go find some breakfast in Amritsar, but a guy dispensing cups of sweet Indian tea to the Indian immigration officials brings me one as well. One other traveller turns up: Toby is German and is returning to Pakistan. He's come across to Amritsar for just one day, to start another ninety-day spell on his double-entry Pakistan visa. So it can't be that bad.

There's nobody else going in or out so the big, modern buildings seem rather redundant. A bus drives the two of us from the Indian office to the Indian side of the border. We walk the 100 metres where all the military prancing took place last night and then, in the matching Pakistan building, there's a slight delay from a power outage until their immigration computers work. Altogether the crossing takes a bit over an hour, most of it just sitting around, and although an Indian visa guy did take a long, long time looking at my passport, everyone was very friendly.

Toby looks like he could have been a hippie-trail survivor, time-warped in *Back to the Future*-style from that forgotten era. While we wait for the power to come back on, the Pakistani officials ask if he'll show them what he has under his Rasta beanie. He pulls it off to reveal scraggy dreadlocks, the tangle reaching all the way to his ankles. I share a taxi with Toby to the Daewoo Bus Station in Lahore, and then it's almost 400 kilometres on the surprisingly fancy and uncrowded – perhaps because it's a toll road – expressway to Islamabad. There's just one brief stop and then we're at the bus station in Rawalpindi. Toby reckons he's only seen about fifteen foreign travellers in his three months in Pakistan; tourist-wise the country has been deserted.

If there was plenty of security when Maureen and I stayed in Islamabad on our last visit, there's a lot more today. My taxi can't even approach within a block of the hotel; only 'approved' vehicles are allowed to go all the way in. I'm ready to walk the last stretch, but a hotel minibus comes by and picks me up. When we arrive, there's the usual mirrors-under-the-vehicle, inspect-the-engine, check-the-baggage routine, and at this stage you're not even driving into the hotel. You approach it on a parallel road and have to be cleared before you can turn into the hotel, where there are multiple gates allowing just one vehicle at a time, and big flip-up barriers to ensure nobody simply ploughs through. Finally, if you are cleared to drive up to the front entrance, there's a slalom of planter boxes. All of this is overseen by armed soldiers in elevated lookout towers.

In late September 2008 a suicide truck tried to drive into the Marriott Hotel, where Maureen and I had stayed a year and a half earlier. The security guards managed to stop it and the CCTV footage shows them milling around the smoking truck for the next four minutes before it explodes. Although the explosion and subsequent fire killed more than fifty people and gutted the building, the hotel reopened three months later. On our last night at the Marriott, on that earlier visit, we had enjoyed a lengthy meal in the lobby café, which was wiped out by the attack. Australia was playing South Africa in a down-to-the-wire cricket match, and there was no way the waiters or the kitchen staff – cricket fans to a man – could concentrate on their jobs.

Islamabad is a modern planned capital, like Brasilia or, from an earlier era, Washington DC. It's remarkably like Canberra, Australia's planned capital, right down to the surrounding mountains and hills. And, like these other planned capitals, Islamabad sprawls, a city better for drivers than pedestrians.

I do indeed get out to the airport for Maureen's pre-dawn arrival and Najam ul-Haq Khan, who will be our driver for the Karakoram trip, picks us up and we follow the freeway to Murree, the hill station above Islamabad. From GPO Chowk – technically a town square although here it's just a crowded open area below the post office – we walk along The Mall to Pindi Point and back, admiring the Murree curiosity, little 'strollers' used to push children and those too old, or lazy, to walk. Murree, I discover, is not where they brew Murree Beer, the local brand. The brewery started here in 1860, but it long ago moved to Rawalpindi. It must be tough as Pakistan's only (legal) manufacturer of alcoholic beverages; after all, they can't cater to the Muslim population, which accounts for ninety-seven per cent of the country. Even foreigners are forbidden to indulge if they're Muslim, but, despite this seemingly impossible market restriction, the Murree Brewery is one of Pakistan's top listed companies and in recent years sales have been steadily climbing. Clearly, the 'can't drink' restrictions are not too fiercely enforced. Unfortunately for these clever brewers, they're also forbidden to export their ale; the catchy slogan 'Have a Murree with your curry' is waiting to be rolled out should the export restrictions ever be lifted.

Back in Islamabad we drive up to Shakarparian Hills, a local park with great views over the city. The park features the Pakistan Monument, and the Natural History Museum, outside of which stands a huge whale skeleton – could it be from the one I saw in Karachi back in the 1950s? I look at the plaque. No, it was found in Balochistan in 1967. We cross town to the modern Shah Faisal Mosque; Pakistanis joke that the CIA mistook its minarets for missiles, presumably aimed at India. With the media full of stories about the worldwide 'blasphemous American movie' protests, I'm a little cautious about being the only non-believers in town, but two young guys welcome us to Pakistan when they spot us.

There's no bar back at the hotel, but as a 'non-Muslim foreigner' I'm able to order a Murree Beer from room service that evening. Even at an expensive hotel the half-litre bottle only costs $1.50, although there is another fifty-cent charge for issuing my liquor certificate. Once upon a time, a Pakistani liquor certificate implied you were a hopeless alcoholic and needed a beer to keep you alive; not surprisingly they were popular souvenirs for visitors to Pakistan.

The next morning we leave Islamabad on the Kashmir Highway, then onto the Motorway, then the Grand Trunk Road before we finally turn onto the Karakoram Highway, also known as the KKH. A sign announces that it's 804 kilometres to the Khunjerab Pass, the highest point of the road and the border with China. The first stretch of the highway is very picturesquely lined with tall eucalyptus trees, but we admire them through a late-monsoon-season downpour. We puncture a tyre even before we reach Abbottabad, but it's quickly fixed in a roadside repair place, the whole crew crowding around us for a photograph.

Najam is unenthusiastic about my suggestion to turn off the road for a look at the site of Osama bin Laden's rather unremote hideaway. Of course, there's nothing to see now; the house was demolished less than a year after the US raid in order to prevent it from becoming a 'sacred building for jihadis'. Long before they caught him, I'd joked that the car Maureen and I drove from London to Afghanistan, and then sold in Kabul, forty years earlier was probably Osama bin Laden's getaway vehicle. I don't think there was any sign of it outside that Abbottabad compound. The turn-off on Kakul Road to the house, less than 2 kilometres from the main road through Abbottabad, also happens to be the turn-off to the Pakistan Military Academy, which is marked by a tank standing menacingly by the roadside. Named after its British military founder, Major James Abbott, the town still features a number of churches, and we pause so I can photograph St Luke's. We also stop for lunch; there's no shortage of restaurants, although I'm pretty sure that Mr bin Laden never popped out for a quick curry, and he certainly wouldn't have asked for a Murree Beer to go with it.

Remarkably, CNN reporter Barbara Starr's quote, six months before the US raid, that a 'senior NATO official' had told her that 'nobody in al Qaeda is living in a cave' went unnoted. Her report continued that, in fact, bin Laden 'was living in relative comfort, protected by locals and some members of the Pakistani intelligence services'.

Abbottabad today is first and foremost known as the town where Osama bin Laden was tracked down. But even before his appearance, it was an important enough centre to justify a reasonable amount of guidebook coverage. My Lonely Planet Pakistan guide commented on its 'orderly tree-lined streets, European architecture and grand parade ground', the three active churches and the half-dozen recommended restaurants, although it also noted that for cyclists pedalling down the Karakoram Highway from China it was just a pause before the final traffic-laden stretch to Islamabad.

The rain continues to bucket down through the afternoon and there's a stretch where the deluge has prompted some nasty rockfalls. We'll see more of that as we travel north and it doesn't always take a downpour to trigger a landslide. The traffic thins out and we start to encounter security checkpoints.

I've come prepared with multiple copies of an information
sheet with our passport numbers, dates of birth, visa numbers
and other vital military information. Handing these over at
the roadside checkpoints saves the trouble of stopping to fill in
all the information for their records. Driving through French
West Africa a few years before we'd called similar information
sheets a fiche. The final afternoon security point insists that
we take an armed police guard for the last stretch to Besham,
which means it's after dark by the time we arrive. We depart
soon after dawn the next morning so we scarcely see the busy
transit stop.

Shortly before Besham the road joins the Indus River on
its long journey from western Tibet to the Arabian Sea near
Karachi. The Karakoram Highway follows the Indus for the
next couple of hundred kilometres, where we'll divert off the
highway and continue to trace the Indus for another hundred
kilometres up to Skardu.

We're off bright and early; the weather looks much better
and we pick up another Kalashnikov-armed guard almost
immediately. He's not just looking after us – a minibus heading
up the road to a hydro-power project also enjoys his protection,
and we occasionally have to pause and wait for them to
catch up. At the end of the day we pick up a protection van
for the last few kilometres to the border between the North-
West Frontier Province and the Gilgit Agency. The Agency
is a British colonial term which survived for a time post-
independence and is still used unofficially today. Najam says all
this security is quite standard on this stretch, but who are they
protecting travellers from? There's trouble all over Pakistan,

but up here in the north it's all well to the west of our route, whether you're talking about the Waziristan trouble zone, with its local Taliban as well as infiltrators from Afghanistan, or all those American drones patrolling overhead.

Just a month ago three buses were stopped near here, and passengers were pulled off and shot. There had been two similar incidents in the previous six months, but when my German border companion Toby related these events to me he was remarkably nonchalant. 'It's just a Muslim incident, foreigners aren't threatened,' he'd insisted.

That was indeed the situation: the passengers hauled off the buses and executed – even the children – were all members of Pakistan's Shia minority. Or were mistaken for Shia. Pakistan's population may be overwhelmingly Muslim, but this is split between approximately 30 million Shia and 150 million Sunni. Until the 1980s the two communities rubbed along, but in recent years things have gone much less smoothly. In part it's a function of growing Shia activity and demands – Shia are the majority community in Iran, Iraq and Bahrain – in part it's general instability, as a result of the rise of the Pakistani and Afghan Taliban, and in part, as usual, it's the Saudis stirring things up.

The Saudis, with their Wahhabi beliefs, are way off to the puritanical end of the Islamic spectrum – keep women in their place, chop off hands and heads, label non-believers as infidels. So they're more likely to see other varieties of Islam, Shia in particular, as close to apostates. Plus, they're in ongoing conflict with the major Shia power, the Iranians, and have their own fractious Shia minority, which inconveniently happens to be concentrated in the regions of Saudi Arabia where all the oil is found. Worst of all, the Saudis have plenty of money to throw around and lots of it is spent on pushing conservative views. Much of the growing antipathy between Sunni and Shia Muslims in Pakistan can be credited to the Saudis and it's the Shia who pay the price.

'So all the problems are between Shias and Sunnis?' I ask Najam.

'No, that's only further along, in Gilgit and Hunza,' he insists. 'Round here it's mainly political, one party is disputing with another so they block the road. Then you're stuck for two or three days.'

I contemplate our timetable up to Kashgar, where we have flights booked, and hope we don't get stuck.

We stop to wait for the hydro-power group at the Soomro Shaheed Bridge. *Shaheed* means something like martyred or sacrificed – killed unjustly, anyway – and that's certainly what happened to the brave Colonel Soomro. An inscription beside the bridge explains that he was 'drowned along with his beloved daughter while saving her life'. A sentence which doesn't quite seem to work. From there the valley is steep-sided and rocky; it's said that blasting through this stretch of the highway took a year's solid work and cost more lives per kilometre than any other part. Sumar Nala is a small settlement with an Aga Khan–sponsored watermill at a sharp bend in the road, where a smaller river joins the Indus.

At Shatial we have our first reminder that for all the Islamic passion today, the Muslim religion is a comparatively recent arrival on this scene. A collection of Buddhist petroglyphs overlooks the river, showing a Buddha figure, a stupa and other illustrations, plus graffiti, some said to date back to the first century AD. The valley widens out by this point and there's more guard swapping and a protection van before we arrive at our hotel, on the main road and a couple of kilometres below the town of Chilas. Our hotel has a fine stretch of garden with a view over the Indus and a talkative shop owner – with so few visitors these days, it must be a thankless task. With all the highway checks, we're rapidly running through my information sheets so we drive up to the town in search of a photocopier. Najam insists that the town does not have a good reputation and I shouldn't think of going there by myself. Another group of Shia were pulled out of a bus and murdered by a Sunni mob in Chilas a few months ago.

There are more Buddhist petroglyphs soon after we leave town the next morning. It's a dramatic drive following the Indus, with superb views of mighty Nanga Parbat. At 8125 metres, it's the ninth highest mountain in the world and its sheer Rupal Face accounts for its name, 'naked mountain' in Urdu. The mountain's most famous climber only got as far as surveying the peak. German climber Heinrich Harrer had the misfortune to arrive in Karachi after his visit to Nanga Parbat just as World War II broke out. He was interned by the British and, after several escape attempts, finally made his way to Tibet, although the war was over by the time he arrived in Lhasa. Nevertheless, he became a tutor to the Dalai Lama and his bestselling book *Seven Years in Tibet* has been filmed twice, with Brad Pitt playing Harrer in the 1997 film.

Nanga Parbat was eventually climbed for the first time in 1953. The third successful ascent, and the first via the daunting Rupal Face, was made in 1970 by the Italian Messner brothers. Reinhold Messner later became famous for his high-speed, lightweight ascents without supplementary oxygen, but this climb ended in tragedy when his younger brother Günther died during their descent.

Back on the road we reach a point marked as the junction of the Himalaya–Karakoram–Hindu Kush, and just after Jaglot and not far before Gilgit we turn off the Karakoram Highway to follow the Indus River to Skardu, the main town in the Baltistan region and a jumping-off point for trekking and mountaineering expeditions. If you want to climb K2 you'll probably come this way. This will be a three-day side trip, but we've only come a short distance when we encounter a landslide and the road is blocked. I think about our flight out of Kashgar and whether we'll make it. We hang around at a roadside café for a bit, with a bunch of Japanese volunteers who have been working at an aid project in Skardu. They were heading back towards Islamabad but had to abandon their vehicle on the other side of the landslide.

We have lunch, but decide it's not worth waiting to see if the road can be reopened today, so we redirect to Gilgit. Along the way groups of Chinese road-builders work with the Pakistanis. At dinner, at the hotel, there's a contingent of be-ribboned Chinese military, presumably here with the road engineers.

Afterwards we retreat to the lounge to read the newspapers. It's interesting how measured – sensible, even – their op-ed columns are, particularly in contrast with the televised madness on the streets. One columnist regrets that Muslim sensibilities are so easily aroused, while another asks why the Americans insist that they can't simply arrest somebody for making a dumb film when they can put people in Guantánamo Bay indefinitely without charge. Why can't they put offensive filmmakers away? Or offensive Koran burners? I like the idea of Reverend Terry Jones, the Florida holy book burner, being renditioned, popped into an orange jumpsuit and rushed off to Cuba (not far to go) to be locked away.

The next morning we stop at the landslide café for a tea break. We've learned to ask for *halke kali chai*, black tea, but light. Najam counts seventeen separate little slides as we drive across the bulldozed landslide area and past it, up the incredible Indus Valley towards Skardu. No question this is one of the most spectacular roads I've ever travelled along. It's very narrow much of the time – the silty river just racing by, the road often hacked like a rocky slot out of the sheer valley side. Then there are patches of bright, irrigated green against the rocks and dainty little suspension bridges feathering across the Indus to settlements on the other side.

There's more chicken, dhal and chapattis – it's becoming the standard Pakistani meal – at our lunch stop before we pause at a monument to Zulfikar Bhutto, Pakistan's president through the 1970s, who came here to praise the stalwart road builders. Lots of them died on this stretch of road, just as they did on the main Karakoram Highway.

We drive straight through Skardu – we'll return a day later – and arrive in Shigar just as a polo game concludes. The scattered town almost disappears into the forest, which in turn fades into the rocky hills beside the valley. Our accommodation is a beautiful old fort, restored and converted into a museum and boutique hotel. The location is stunning, the rooms interesting, the staff efficient and friendly and it has a great riverside location. Plus it's much cooler here – we're now at well over 2000 metres above sea level, after being around 1000 metres since we left Islamabad. We're not alone – a group of German tourists are also staying here – but this place is so delightful it should be packed out every night.

We spend the next morning walking around Shigar. There are some historic wooden mosques, the ruins of an old fort overlooking the more recent one we're staying in and, with the help of a local guide, we find the 'remains' of an old Buddhist monastery. If there are, in fact, any remains I can't make them out, apart from several Buddhist petroglyphs.

We make the short drive back to Skardu after lunch. En route a flight of suicidal sparrows dives across our path and we console Najam, who seems genuinely upset that he has killed one. The hotel in Skardu is another PTDC – Pakistan Tourist Development Corporation – establishment and it's a rather more utilitarian outpost than some of the fine places we've stayed. The TV in the lobby is tuned to 'angry Muslims'; they seem to be rioting all over the country after the government announced a public holiday for people to express their love of Prophet Mohammed. It's not clear if the government has also distributed directions to the nearest American embassy to express this love, but people seem to have had no trouble working out how to get there regardless. The PTDC Motel may be utilitarian, but the internet connection is good enough that we can keep up with the riots as they unroll.

In Islamabad the protestors have been prevented from approaching the US embassy, so they've moved the love-in site to the hotel we stayed at a few days ago. The guests are trapped inside. In Karachi, in particular, love of the Prophet seems to involve bullets, and by the end of the day twenty-one people around the country have been killed, most of them in Karachi.

Karachi has always been a difficult city. When I lived there as a small child it was an Arabian Sea port suddenly flooded with refugees after partition and pressed into service as the temporary capital. That role only lasted for ten years, but the city remains the country's financial and business centre and the population has ballooned from around half a million at partition to over 20 million today. It's a city often torn by violence, either between political parties, between ethnic groups or between the Shia and Sunni religious communities. Partitions are rarely clean – the division of Czechoslovakia, perhaps, is an exception, but other recent splits, like Sudan and Yugoslavia, have been unpleasant affairs. The partition of India and Pakistan lies very definitely in the unhappy category.

Whoever is involved in the current violence, they usually have no shortage of weapons. During the Russian interval in Afghanistan, the US flooded Pakistan with weaponry to support the mujaheddin in their anti-Soviet campaign. Of course, lots of those nasty WMDs – Weapons of Minor Destruction, usually much more damaging than the elusive Mass variety – never made it to Afghanistan, instead ending up in the hands of a grab bag of Pakistani troublemakers, including Karachi gangsters. The Russians also did their bit to supply the local arms trade. They came back from their unhappy stint in Afghanistan with a lot of heroin addicts and lot fewer Kalashnikovs, left behind in trade for that Afghan smack.

The next day we set out for Gilgit only to be turned back at a checkpoint less than an hour down the road. The road ahead is blocked by protesters and we must go back to Skardu. It appears the local branch of the angry Muslim movement has already blocked the road for a day and they intend to continue for a second. There's no indication why this news has not got back to Skardu, perhaps because the blockade seems rather selective – it doesn't apply to locals, military, police or government officials. Exactly who it does apply to is a fair question, but at this point it seems to include the two of us and our patient driver.

So we head back to Skardu, noting as we drive through the strung-out main street the complete absence of women. In three transits of the town we have not seen a single woman. We settle back into our room, and catch up on the latest news, which is headlined by Pakistan's Railways Minister, Ghulam Ahmad Bilour, who pops up to announce he is offering US$100,000 to whoever will kill the film's maker, whoever he might be. Quite where the Railways Minister will find US$100,000 out of his own pocket doesn't seem to be of interest to the Pakistan media. It would emerge later that two-thirds of the country's members of parliament didn't even bother to file tax returns, let alone think about paying tax.

Blasphemous movies aren't the only reason Americans are unpopular in Pakistan. Topping the list is one I can definitely understand: drones. At some point in the future, I'm willing to bet, there will be a collective realisation that the drone is one of the dumbest weapons ever invented. A gun that every time you pull the trigger shoots you in the foot. Some people have already come to that realisation. Cameron Munter, US Ambassador to Pakistan from 2010 to 2012, is popularly believed to have resigned – or been pushed out – because he was less than 100 per cent enthusiastic about drones. 'Do you want to win a few battles and lose the war?' he asked.

You can argue about whether or not drones make sense – they're 'legal, ethical and wise', according to John O. Brennan, President Obama's top counter-terrorism advisor. You can also argue about the by-kill, how many innocent bystanders get wiped out for every militant target: up to ten civilians for every high-ranking militant, according to a Brookings Institution report. The Bureau of Investigative Journalism, which keeps meticulous track of every attack, took the drone strike count past 300 in late 2012: between 2500 and 3400 people were killed, of whom 500 to 900 were reported to be civilians and nearly 200 were children. If New York University graduate student Josh Begley had his way, you could have kept up to date with all this on your iPhone – he created the app Drones+, which sends an alert every time another drone strike hits home. Apple didn't like it, rejecting it on the third occasion for crude or objectionable content. No surprise – killing real people rather than Angry Birds is obviously objectionable.

Those 3000-odd drone deaths in Pakistan tie in all too neatly with 9/11 deaths – 2996 – and it's a comfortably larger figure than US military deaths in Afghanistan – approaching 2000 at the end of 2012. Personally, I find the use of drones as a means of execution – without any due legal process – reprehensible, and it seems that US opinion is also starting to question the program. But the idea of vigilante justice hasn't just popped out of nowhere. For years we've absorbed it from Hollywood, in its 'licence to kill' promotions. And these films, in turn, feed off real-life military positions – for instance, Israel's targeted assassinations, or even bin Laden's killing. By applying the 'War on Terrorism' label to justify actions like drone killings we're tossing aside the rules of law that have been the basis for our civilisation.

There's a counterpoint to the angry Muslim reports on the TV. The US is running ads with Barack and Hillary, insisting that Americans are nice people, really, and highly respectful of the religious sensitivities of others. Shame about this one 'moronic bigot', as *The Economist* described him. Unfortunately, the US then goes on to undermine the 'one-off lunatic moviemaker' notion, by bringing out the CIA's own lunatics. The mobs are beating at the embassy door, so if you're the CIA, what do you do? Right, you launch another drone strike, which kills four 'suspected militants'. The frustrating thing is that the real issue here is not lunatic filmmakers, but lunatic drone strikes.

Back in Skardu my heart sinks at this latest hare-brained move. At least the suspected militants were in a car out on the road and not within striking range of wedding parties or assembled schoolchildren. Drones have made Americans very unpopular, and I can understand that. If some foreign power were hovering over my backyard night and day, threatening to launch a missile strike if I stepped outside, I'd be pretty unhappy with them too. Worse, from the average Pakistani's point of view, that instead of complaining bitterly about the basic infringement of their rights, their own government took America's money and let them get on with it. Love for the Prophet was a small chance for the government to show they're doing their bit to stand up to America.

So, while the protests continue, we kick our heels in Skardu, watching the latest riots on TV and wondering, anytime we stepped onto the streets, what people were thinking about us.

Our extra day in Skardu does give us more time to look around. We visit Satpara Lake, its picturesque island recently submerged by a hydro-power project. Just off the road is a big rock carved with images of Buddha – a seated figure surrounded by twenty smaller images and flanked by two large standing ones – more evidence of the early appearance of Buddhism in the region. Buddhism came through during the Gandhara period and then, in a second wave, from Tibet around the eighth or ninth century AD. These bas-reliefs probably date from that later period. In the hotel garden there's an Italian K2 museum tent. The French may have climbed the first 8000 metre peak, Annapurna I, in 1950, and the British may have been the first to climb Everest in 1953, but in 1954 it was the Italians who first climbed K2, often listed as the most difficult of the lot.

We opt for chicken and chips for dinner, as a change from chicken, rice and dhal, and Najam interrupts to say that although the road may still be closed tomorrow, we can go through. The District Commissioner will phone the checkpoint to say we're cleared to proceed. Before we depart the next morning there's another confirmation call to the DC, despite which we're again halted at the checkpoint. More talk, more phone calls, until finally the DC has to contact the SP (Superintendent of Police) and it's decided we can continue, with a Kalashnikov-toting military policeman riding shotgun. So to speak.

All of this consumes an hour at the checkpoint, but we're finally off and the trip is, of course, trouble-free – no protests, no roadblocks, no landslides. Shengus, where the roadblock was supposedly set up, is such a small village they'd hardly have enough people to block a road. Four heavily laden foreign bicyclists pass in the other direction; no sign of a guard for them. We drop ours at the bridge just before we rejoin the Karakoram Highway.

Our planned first stop out of Gilgit the next morning doesn't happen. The Kargah Buddha is just outside the town, but in the present circumstances it 'may not be safe'. I bet that if we'd gone there'd have been no trouble at all, and I ask if we can get another armed guard, but that gets me nowhere. Instead we have a brief look around the bazaar, which is not actually open yet; a visit to the very small British Cemetery, which comprises G. W. Hayward, killed by dastardly natives in 1870, a New Zealander backpacker who had a fatal fall and five British mountaineers; and then it's down to the Chinar Bagh to see the Gilgit Uprising Monument, which commemorates the local refusal to follow the Maharaja of Jammu and Kashmir into India at the time of partition in 1947. It was a key event leading to the region being divided between India and Pakistan.

It's no great distance to Karimabad, but it takes quite a time. At first the valley is wide and the road is good, and we stop at a Karakoram Highway monument next to a graveyard for road construction unfortunates. The memorial sign declares that it's 'in memory of those gallant men who Preferred to make the Karakoram their Permanent abode.' Like hell. Then there's a tea stop at a pleasant little roadside café, with soft drink bottles cooling in a water channel. We pass a number of arched concrete covers converting short stretches into tunnels, in order to keep landslides off the road.

To our right, Rakaposhi comes into view even before we stop for lunch at the Rakaposhi View Point Hotel. If gold medals were awarded for truth in advertising this place would deserve one. From our outside table there's an uninterrupted view of the whole face of the Rakaposhi glacier and its sheer, snow-capped peak. You'd like lunch to last longer; the view soars in one unbroken sweep all the way from our table at 2015 metres to the summit at 7885 metres.

Almost immediately past Rakaposhi, we're stopped by another landslide roadblock, this one already being cleared by a digger and dozer, supervised by Chinese workers in hard hats. We're stuck for close to an hour, although at least Najam has muscled straight to the front of the queue of vehicles.

'Have you often been stuck because of road problems?' I ask.

'Oh yes, frequently,' Najam replies.

'What was your longest delay?'

'Twenty-one days.'

'Twenty-one days! What happened?'

'It was in July 1993. Three bridges were washed out, we had three vehicles and a group of tourists coming down to Islamabad. We got them out over temporary bridges, but I had to wait with the vehicles. Food became very expensive.'

'And otherwise?' I ask.

'Oh, usually just two or three days, for landslides, floods or political roadblocks.'

I've already heard about Pakistani political disputes leading to the road being closed, and we'd soon find the road blocked by Chinese politics.

Past the landslide it's not far to Karimabad, an attractive mountain foothill town with considerable tourist appeal, which could easily be the Kathmandu of northern Pakistan. Except there aren't any tourists. We count four Japanese, one elderly Australian hippie lady from Townsville, and us, which makes a total tourist population of seven. Still, there's the trendy little Café de Hunza, a bunch of little craft shops and a handful of places to stay and eat.

After one of the café's cappuccinos, we walk up to the imposing Baltit Fort, which is both very spectacular and very spectacularly situated overlooking the town. From stone foundations, sheer whitewashed walls soar to an eclectic collection of wooden terraces and lookouts. As we walk back through the town, we stop to chat with the shop owners. .

'The people from the Hunza Valley have had close relations with China since the Silk Road days,' one man explains. 'All I need is a pass to go up to Kashgar and I can continue on as far as Urumqi. I don't need a visa or a passport. This only applies to Hunza people, not to other Pakistanis.'

Our hotel in Karimabad feels half-finished and is totally empty; we're the only guests. There's also no power. 'It will come on later,' we're told when we check in. Now, it's getting dark and there's still no power, so no hot water, no wifi. Another hour passes and we're still sitting in the room in the dark. 'Perhaps tomorrow the power will be on,' one of the three guys behind the front desk – in the dark – explains.

'We'll be back in the morning,' we say, leaving for the hotel down the road, where the power is on, construction is complete and there are even a few other guests.

When I get up in the morning and look down over the Karimabad Valley, the view is just beautiful. Lots of lush green, lots of poplar trees and the sun just hitting the Baltit Fort, above the town. The surrounding hills and snow-capped mountains overlook the fort, in turn, and everything is crystal clear. It's a good-to-be-alive morning.

We've arranged for a Jeep to pick us up for a glacier excursion. The road to Hoper, often lined with marijuana plants, has been well travelled today – when we reach the village there's an assembly of Jeeps and the biggest group of tourists we've seen in Pakistan, nineteen of them, all from Latvia. We follow them up to and across the Hoper Glacier, the ice tumbling down from a 7000-metre peak. It's a remarkably short walk from village to glacier, but foolishly, Maureen and I continue up a steep hill to catch a glimpse of the 'white' Barpu Glacier. It isn't white and also isn't as impressive as the Hoper Glacier so apart from some excellent exercise, it wasn't the best use of our rather limited time.

Back down at the highway we make a short visit to the interestingly restored old village of Ganish, a curious mixture of

home and museum. Then we continue up to the Altit Fort, only
a couple of kilometres below Karimabad and its matching fort.
I wish we had longer to stay; Karimabad has been a delight.

The next morning we stop just out of town to look at
more petroglyphs, this time more a scattering of travellers'
graffiti than religious images. These early visitors were clearly
impressed by the sight of ibex. We've travelled 1700 kilometres
with Najam, and today he leaves us to head back to Islamabad.
He couldn't take us if he wanted to – the next stretch of the
Karakoram Highway is by boat.

On 4 January 2010, a gigantic landslide covered not just
the road, but the entire valley from one side to the other.
Including the river. This was a biggie, not something you could
bulldoze away in a few hours or even a few days. Over the
next six months the river backed up behind this instant dam
until a lake stretched back for 22 kilometres, submerging the
Karakoram Highway for that distance along with bridges, three
villages and part of the town of Gulmit. The locals had plenty
of time to pack up and get away, but slowly, inexorably, their
homes disappeared beneath the water. Any talk of clearing the
landslide seems to have been shelved, and nearly three years
later there is still no solution to what looks like a permanent
rupture in the Karakoram Highway. In the meantime, a band
of boat builders, carpenters, engineers, mechanics and boat
pilots arrived in Hunza from the Punjab. There were more than
100 boats on the new lake, shuttling back and forth in just
over an hour. What hasn't appeared is anything big enough to
carry vehicles back and forth, but even that looks imminent.
Later we would see a convoy of collapsible pontoon-style barges

heading south from China. For now, the boats are big, heavy, wooden affairs with a beam across the back supporting twin generator-like diesel engines with a long propeller shaft, like a Thai longtail boat.

The lakeside is a busy scene of loading and unloading and two policemen come over to ask if we have permission to cross the lake. Permission? It turns out we just have to sign a disclaimer – if the boat sinks and we drown we won't blame the Pakistani government. We soon find a charter boat with a couple of Chinese heading back home. The cost rapidly drops as more people offer to join us. It's a forty-five-minute trip up the lake to Gulmit, and we've no sooner arrived at the rather rundown Marco Polo Inn than there's an urgent phone call from Sust, our next stop and the final town in Pakistan before the Khunjerab Pass and Chinese border. Our visit to Gulmit is about to become a very short one indeed.

Our progress up the Karakoram Highway was halted by nature (landslides) and the Pakistanis (American movie protests). Now the Chinese would have a go at stopping us from getting to Kashgar. We're still standing at the hotel's check-in desk when the call comes through from Salah ud Din, who works for the Islamabad travel agency that found us Najam and our car. He's in Sust meeting a group of British tourists coming down from Kashgar.

'You must come to Sust immediately,' he insists. 'The Chinese are going to close the border the day after tomorrow.' The day we intend to cross into China.

'That's not a problem,' I reply. 'We'll hang around here and cross the border the next day. We'll just arrive in Kashgar a day late.' Our schedule has been chopped and changed enough times, one day less in Kashgar isn't going to matter.

'No,' he warns, 'they're not just going to close the border for a day. It's going to be shut for eleven days.'

'Eleven days! What on earth for?'

'Chinese Independence Day,' he says. 'They often close the border for Independence Day, but this year they're going to close it three days before Independence Day and then leave it closed for another week.'

'Didn't you know this was going to happen?' I ask in disbelief. 'Surely they gave you some warning?'

'No, we've only just found out. Tomorrow is the last day you can get across the border.'

Amazingly, the Chinese authorities may have given the Pakistanis only twenty-four hours' notice, but they haven't given their own citizens any warning at all. When I text the news to a Chinese contact in Kashgar, it's the first he's heard about it.

It's fortunate we're so close to the border when this news comes through. We can abandon Gulmit, make the short trip up to Sust this afternoon and cross the border tomorrow, the day before it shuts down for nearly two weeks.

Raja Hussain Khan, the hotel owner whose business has already been decimated by the downturn in Pakistani tourism and then the road flood, is now going to see the first two customers in god knows how long disappear before they even get to their room. He insists we still have time to look around Gulmit and have lunch before we depart. Nearby, there's a tatty little museum of dusty memorabilia, which he runs through item by item. Then it's on to the Korgah carpet-weaving centre, where eight women are busy weaving small rugs. We feel obliged to buy one, a little square with what looks like six computer-game animals. Next, we bump into three sisters who take us back to their house for a look, their rather old and rather eccentric father delighted to have visitors. The house seems to be just one central room with alcoves off it. It's carpeted, but there's no furniture apart from a TV and a music system. I've no idea if the latter works, but the TV certainly does. The oldest sister is back in Gulmit for two months, after six years in school and university in Islamabad. As in Karimabad, the people here are Ismailis, followers of the Aga Khan and much freer, more outgoing and more exuberantly dressed than other village Pakistanis. The mere fact that we're in their house, sitting and talking with two adult women, is a clear sign that this is not Muslim Pakistan as usual.

We're back at the hotel having lunch when two Italians – Caterina and her son Angelo – turn up and quickly decide to also go to Sust today. Raja Khan announces that he'll come with us the short distance up to Sust; he wants to find out what's going on at the border and what the Chinese are up to. From Gilgit north we've seen so many Chinese, supervising road maintenance and construction or actually working on it. It's because the highway trade balance is overwhelmingly in China's favour, he suggests.

'They have no religion,' he complains. 'All they think of is money, money, money. Or perhaps money is their religion?'

Pakistan's interaction with China may be all business and trade, but that's clearly a better situation than they have with the US. Road construction or drone strikes – it's a no-brainer that the Chinese are much more popular than the Americans. The choice may not be love or war, but business or war is a reasonable substitute.

At the landing area at the end of the lake we encounter a couple of New Zealand cyclists who have just arrived, having pedalled down from Kashgar. They've cycled all the way from Singapore.

Sust is a border town – just one street and not a single woman anywhere on it – and we walk the length of it. There's an 'Old Sust' up the hill overlooking the highway. We field plenty of offers to direct us to the Pakistan bus station, but the buses don't intend to go to China tomorrow because they'd be stuck there for eleven days. Instead, we try for a private car or minibus, without success, but it looks like we can get tickets on a Chinese bus. I'd prefer to avoid it, even if booking something privately costs a lot more, as there's no guarantee you're going to stop to see anything on a bus. German friends who travelled the highway a couple of years ago reported that their bus zipped straight over the pass – 'there's the Khunjerab Pass, high point of the Karakoram Highway, border between Pakistan and China', swoosh, gone.

The trouble is nobody from the Pakistan side – whether it's with a bus, car, Jeep or minibus – is keen on getting stuck in China tomorrow. Eventually we find a guy who'll take us; if we make an early departure he'll get back across the border the same day. The promised Land-Cruiser turns out to be a tatty old Hiace minibus with a worryingly dodgy clutch. The Italian pair from Gulmit could have joined us, but they've already grabbed the 'last' tickets on the Chinese bus and it appears once they've drawn up a manifest you have to stick to the vehicle you're listed for.

So our passports are stamped out of Pakistan and off we go, up up up, then a one-hour delay for roadworks. It's not a landslide; I think they're keeping us off the newly sealed bitumen or else they can't be bothered to start up one of the bitumen spreaders that are blocking the road. There's also a stop at the Khunjerab National Park entrance so we can pay the park entry fee, which is much more expensive for foreigners than for Pakistanis, and is free for Chinese, who seem to be something else entirely, neither Pakistani nor foreign. So what do we see for our eight bucks each as we drive through the national park? Nothing.

Finally it's across the pass at 4724 metres, driving through the huge gateway and waving goodbye to the smiling Pakistanis. A few minutes later and just below the pass we're at a distinctly unsmiling Chinese army check-post. It takes a long time to go through security, but when we're ready to go, after an hour, the bus turns up, and we have to wait for them and depart simultaneously. So another hour passes and, damn me, another bus – a Pakistani NATCO one – arrives. So much for Pakistanis not wanting to cross today. Three hours pass and, double-damn me, another bus arrives. We wait for a while, but finally go without them. Our driver is very worried that it's now too late to return today.

Through all this waiting, the Chinese army guys have been almost pointedly unhelpful. They keep telling us to get back into our vehicles, while 10 metres away, beyond the road barrier, hordes of Han Chinese tourists come and go, to see the border. Finally we leave, with a Chinese soldier in our vehicle riding shotgun for the whole group. He slumps asleep almost immediately, wakes to retreat to the back of the minibus to have a cigarette, and then returns to the front to fall asleep again. So we travel in convoy, don't make any stops, arrive at the same time as the other two buses and wonder what we got for our private vehicle expenditure.

Tashkurgan, the first town since the border, is where we really enter China. On the outskirts of town there's a huge immigration and customs building where we're put through more nonsensical paperwork with a ridiculous number of uniformed personnel. They've got every bit of equipment under the immigration and customs sun – computers, X-ray machines, iris scanners, metal detectors, you name it. The process is long and slow.

We head straight to dinner before we even check into the hotel, where we meet an energetically humorous Spaniard and his wife. He's hoping to cross the border southbound to Pakistan tomorrow, but seems not too concerned about getting turned back and having to retrace his steps to Kashgar. Our hotel is typically back-blocks-of-China, simultaneously gaudy and tatty, with a shower squeezed between toilet and sink so it can pour water into both easily. I go out for a quick wander around town and find an ATM that warns me to be careful my PIN number is not 'peeked' at and then regrets that my cash request has failed, 'for some reason'.

Next morning, I have a quick wander around town and bump into Hamid, our driver from yesterday who is much happier since discovering he can cross back to Pakistan later today. We've acquired another driver, car and a young guide, Yusuf, who is a Uighur, the Muslim majority population of the far-western Xinjiang Province. After breakfast, which, like dinner last night, is soup, tough meat and steamed dumplings, we set off around Tashkurgan. The big attraction is the surprisingly interesting mud-walled fort overlooking a grassland, where wooden walkways loop and arc with excursions to a swaying suspension bridge and two big waterwheels, which scoop up the water and slosh it out again, to no purpose.

As we're wandering the paths, we encounter a Chinese group with a small puppy that decides it would prefer to depart with Maureen. Perhaps it spotted the much larger dog loping by, being exercised by two guys on a motorcycle, one of them clutching the leash. Yusuf comments that dogs are the latest sign of Chinese wealth.

The drive to Kashgar starts at 3300 metres and climbs to 4000 metres along a wide, flat, open valley. Tajikistan is only a stone's throw to the west; there's another big, modern immigration and customs building at the turn-off. The valley may be wide and flat, but it's flanked by impressive snow-capped mountains all the way, with Muztagh Ata at 7546 metres the most impressive of the lot. Just past it we stop for lunch at Kara Kul Lake, a tough-bits-of-yak-and-soup-in-a-yurt affair, presumably set up to fleece passing Han tourists. The lake is edged by a long ridge of mountains, each separated by individual glaciers.

We're at yak altitude and Mount Kongur, at 7719 metres, is the next important peak, but after a final narrow and steep-sided stretch, reminiscent of the highway back in Pakistan, we're soon descending out of yak country and down into camel land. Finally it's down to Kashgar at 1300 metres, through farmland, on roads lined with poplar trees. Kashgar has always been the classic Silk Road meeting place – it appeared on all the early maps, was written about by all the early explorers and traders, and featured in the Great Game, the diplomatic chess match between the empires of Britain and Russia,

The hotel in Kashgar continues the tatty-bling collision we encountered in Tashkurgan. Our room is a riot of flamboyant decoration, dazzling colour and complete chaos. Maureen decides that if it was refurnished, cleaned and properly lit, it would look absolutely terrific. In the hotel's popular café I have a large bottle of Sinkiang Beer, my first alcohol since the Murree Beer in Islamabad.

The next day, Yusuf and our phlegmatic driver, who looks like he could moonlight as a surprisingly easygoing nightclub bouncer if necessary, collect us after breakfast and we go to see Kashgar. We start with the Abakh Hoja Tomb, where Yusuf has problems. It appears he's not a registered local guide, because while he speaks Tajik, Uighur and English he doesn't speak Mandarin. To be a registered guide the Han have specified that you have to speak Mandarin; you can probably forget about the local languages and English. So he has to leave the tomb separately and we reconvene on the other side of the car park. The main building is an endearingly dog-eared but glorious mishmash of unmatched and wrongly aligned ceramic tiles

housing forty-odd tombs, including the Imperial Fragrant
Concubine, whose imperial fragrance (no perfume necessary)
becomes a running joke for the rest of the day.

We continue past other minor tombs and mosques, all
closed, to the very blue tomb of Uighur author Yusuf Has
Hajib, much bashed about during the Cultural Revolution
– the tomb not the author. There's also a visit to the main
square, where a big statue of Mao stands, and we wander
around the forlorn remnants of the old town. It's really a
bust; poor Yusuf is hustling to make a tour out of this. Having
knocked down most of the old town, the Chinese are now
trying to charge visitors to walk through the remaining
fragments. They're so ineptly half-hearted about it that we
find ourselves exiting – free – by the pay-five-dollars entrance.
There are some parts of the old mud city wall left, but so
sequestered you can't easily reach them.

The afternoon wander is more interesting, starting with the
very yellow Id Kah Mosque, the largest in town, and followed
by jaunts through a hat street, a music street, and a very
rickety teahouse, where we sit out on the verandah sipping tea
before the night market sets up. Sadly, Kashgar is, as everybody
says, a sorry shadow of its former self, the old town much
diminished, a lot of new Han structure crowding it out. The
dusty, polluted, grey atmosphere of the rest of China has been
imported straight from Beijing.

We bump into our Italian friends in the hotel's café and
compare visa notes. Our Pakistan and China visas were
both nightmares to procure, requiring multiple visits to the
Pakistan High Commission in London and the Chinese visa

office in Melbourne. As soon as the Karakoram Highway was mentioned, the Pakistanis went into panic mode, although in fact the visas they finally issued didn't note that they were specifically valid for the regions the highway passed through. Besides, nobody ever checked it. If we'd simply said we were going no further than Lahore and Islamabad, the whole process would have been much simpler.

For the Chinese, it was our plan to visit Xinjiang Province that gave them a panic attack. The only place in China they're more touchy about is Tibet. Once again, if we just said we were going to China, nowhere special, I doubt we'd have had any problems when we crossed the border from Pakistan. Again, our visa had nothing on it to indicate it covered Xinjiang, although we might have had to show inbound flight 'bookings' to somewhere safe like Beijing or Shanghai.

Clearly not everybody had been as foolishly honest as I had, and, as a result, other visitors didn't have to jump through so many visa hoops. Toby, my long-haired border-crossing companion, had been wandering all over Pakistan for months. The Pakistan embassy in Germany hadn't insisted on tracking his route through northern Pakistan, although he was assigned an armed guard to sit next to him on the bus all the way from the Iran border to Quetta in Balochistan. Same goes for Italy, where you would hardly expect anybody to fill in a visa application with scrupulous honesty. 'We are Italians, of course we don't,' our friends tell us.

We've timed our arrival in Kashgar so we're here for the famed Sunday market. We start by driving out of town to the livestock market, which features donkeys, cows, oxen, yaks and

camels, but mainly a lot of goats and sheep. The animals are
lined up extraordinarily neatly, roped together by the neck,
in alternating directions so they go head-tail-head-tail. From
there we go back into town to the Sunday market, which is in
fact held every day of the week, it's just bigger on Sunday. We're
back at the hotel in time for a late lunch, during which a dust
storm sweeps through the open restaurant, leaving everything
covered in a film of grit.

'In a few weeks we will close for winter,' the waiter says.

For dinner, at another restaurant featuring tat and bling, we
create a different form of chaos. We order the chicken, chillies,
potato and noodles house speciality, but the bowl of food is
huge, the noodles are cold and extraordinarily long, and there
are no utensils apart from miniature chopsticks. The only
additional plates we're given are tiny saucers. It's a recipe for
an incredible mess, and we oblige.

Our hotel, the Seman, was built on the grounds of the
former Russian consulate of the Great Game era, and the
consular building still stands at the back corner of the
compound. The next morning we walk past the neglected
stretch of city wall to the Chini Bagh Hotel, where the British
consulate from that time of imperial rivalries once stood.
Again, the consular building is still standing, although a new
multi-storey five-star Chini Bagh has sprung up in front of it.
Staying at the Chini Bagh was, once upon a time, an important
part of the Kashgar experience. Today the only hint of Kashgar
history – apart from the forgotten consular building out
back – is a series of bas-relief panels illustrating incidents of
Kashgar history (including the Imperial Fragrant Concubine)

along the entrance drive. The text, in gold on black marble, is in Chinese, Uighur and English, but the English tales are the usual incomprehensible garble. There might be money to spend on the gold inlay and marble, but the translation budget is obviously wanting.

Across the road from the Chini Bagh the bulletin board in the Karakoram Café features stills from the movie of the bestselling Afghanistan novel *Kite Runner*. It was filmed in Tashkurgan and Kashgar, and the stills are a vivid reminder of how authentically central Asian these towns look. They can stand in for Kabul with remarkable accuracy. We spend the rest of the day wandering around Kashgar, but our Karakoram Highway travels have ended. The next day we'll take to the air and fly to Urumqi then Guangzhuo and finally on to Europe. Flying China can involve just as many roadblocks, security checks, unpleasant officials and weird delays as travelling the highway. But that's another story.

Despite my childhood connections and long interest in the country, Pakistan is a puzzle difficult to understand and full of 'facts and figures' that can prove seriously misleading. Muslim Pakistan is always juxtaposed with Hindu India, but in fact India could easily rank ahead of Pakistan as the world's second-largest Muslim nation – Indonesia is comfortably number one. Their Muslim populations are nearly identical, and if Pakistan's Sunni Muslims really were to launch an all-out genocide against the Shia population, India would quickly overtake Pakistan. Bangladesh comes in fourth in the Muslim population stakes, but after that it's a long way down in numbers before you reach the other biggies like Egypt, Nigeria, Iran and Turkey.

The population is also overwhelmingly Muslim in neighbouring Afghanistan – and both countries have a Shia–Sunni divide – but Afghanistan is tiny in comparison. There are six Pakistanis for each of the 30 million Afghans, so it's no wonder that Pakistan as a failed state is a much more worrying prospect than a failed Afghanistan. Getting foreign, and particularly American, troops out of the country may be a major demand for Afghanistan, but it's an even bigger pressure in Pakistan. It's the single issue almost everybody in Pakistan agrees on.

India's large Muslim minority may not do as well as the Hindu majority, but Pakistan's tiny Hindu fragments really are a depressed minority. There are lots of places where small minority populations do surprisingly well – the Farsis and Jains of India, Jewish minorities in numerous countries, even the Protestant minority in Catholic Ireland. In recent years it's not only the Shia minority who have suffered in Pakistan. The situation for other minorities, Christians in particular, has been dire.

Pakistan's language is another source of confusion. Officially Urdu is the national language, just as Hindi is the national language of India. Conveniently, the spoken form of Hindi and Urdu are remarkably similar, even though they are written in entirely different scripts. So an Urdu-speaking Pakistani can happily enjoy a Hindi Bollywood movie, but not a Hindi novel. Urdu, in fact, is a recent import; it came in from India at partition and, while it's spoken with some facility by most Pakistanis, it's a first language for only a small minority. Far more Pakistanis – nearly fifty per cent of the population – speak Punjabi as their native tongue. The small but powerful elite who control so much of Pakistan's government and business speak English as their first language, just as the controlling elite do in India.

It would be easy to dismiss Pakistan as an economic basket case as well as a political failed state – there's no dynamic high tech industry in Pakistan; it's India that has the cutting-edge software companies and call centres. Despite this – and despite the huge economic difficulties of operating in Pakistan – the country is not a basket case. In fact, Pakistan's economy is well ahead of the 'cow belt', the huge swathe of deeply Hindu northern India.

Pakistan's people and the country's current events are equally complicated, confused and perplexing. The television images show enraged, tribal mobs, but in Islamabad we meet educated, English-speaking Pakistanis who are considerate, thoughtful and informed. As in any country there is no uniform citizen, and no uniform stance on issues. En route to Pakistan this trip I'd stopped for a few days in Kuwait, where most of the taxi drivers are Pakistani. They're always happy to talk about their lives, their working situations and, of course, cricket. My last driver spoke about how tough it was making ends meet and sending money back to his family in Pakistan. Then he spoke warmly of a couple of young Americans working in Kuwait, presumably in the military, who had befriended him, regularly inviting him out to social occasions.

Then the events flip the other way. A troublesome movie that from a Western perspective is nothing more than the pathetic effort of a misguided man, but to the Pakistan street population is a national and religious insult orchestrated from the top level of US government and business, causes chaos. In the weeks after we leave Pakistan there's yet more madness on the streets. Malala Yousafzai, a fifteen-year-old schoolgirl, is shot in the head by Taliban gunmen for suggesting that education – for girls – is a good thing. A few more weeks pass and Taliban gunmen target health workers trying to clean up one of the world's last reservoirs of polio. They're killed for trying to protect children from a completely preventable disease.

I've been intrigued by Pakistan ever since my early childhood years there and once again I found it a fascinating and thought-provoking country to travel through. As a visitor, it's deeply interesting (for history, politics, art and architecture) and often stunningly beautiful (those soaring snow-capped mountains, those plunging rocky valleys) and yet I've encountered only a handful of fellow travellers enjoying these riches. Most potential visitors have been scared away. At the end of the day, Pakistan is a scary country, a place that combines antediluvian thinking with a stockpile of nuclear weapons, where we are supposed to trust the military to keep this weaponry out of terrorist hands, despite the fact they couldn't track down bin Laden when he was living next door. And all the while the drones keep droning overhead.

PAPUA
NEW GUINEA

There's no end of fairytales about the misery that gold can bring, whether it's losing your child to Rumpelstiltskin or, like King Midas, discovering that you are left with nothing of substance, nothing to eat or drink. The only escape from gold's unhappiness is from good luck – as in Rumpelstiltskin, where the mischievous imp is overheard revealing his name – or by renouncing your foolishness – as King Midas does. On the island of Bougainville, gold was only a by-product – copper was the important mineral – but even in small doses it brought plenty of unhappiness.

I've always had a nagging fascination with the possibilities of 'drifting away', the Pacific Islanders' tendency to set off in a small boat with an outboard motor, from Island A to Island B, only for things to go awry. Perhaps the motor fails or the fuel runs out, perhaps they weren't even planning a voyage, just a late-afternoon fishing trip, but when it comes time to leave the motor doesn't start. Or a little squall blows through and when things clear it's dark and the island is nowhere in sight. They 'lose the land', as one Pacific drifter I encountered put it.

I spent a couple of weeks in the islands of Tuvalu in 2001 and it seemed like every second islander had at some time drifted away. Sometimes they only drifted for a few weeks before turning up on the French island of Wallis. Sometimes it was several months before they were rescued by a fishing trawler or, for one lucky drifter, a Greek cargo ship en route to Japan for a spell in dry dock. Every drifter seemed to pass me onto another until eventually I met Laki (pronounced Lucky) Salapu, who managed to drift away not once, but twice from late-afternoon fishing trips. On one of his unplanned voyages he took six months to drift to American Samoa, where he was initially arrested as a suspected illegal immigrant.

So, a few weeks before my trip, I was not very encouraged to read a *Solomon Star* report about eighteen islanders who had drifted away on the same route I'd be taking. They'd set off from southern Bougainville, intending to get to Ghizo in a day, so they were travelling rather further than my planned Shortland to Bougainville jaunt. They motored past Shortland, crossing the 100 kilometres or so of open ocean heading south, but as they approached Vella Lavella, just north of Ghizo, they ran out of fuel. For the next six days they drifted south and west, into the empty stretch of sea towards mainland Papua New Guinea.

Fortunately a Taiwanese fishing boat spotted them, towed them close to Ghizo and gave them fuel to get ashore. The paper reported that they had been given medical check-ups and were recovering. The Minister for Education and Human Resources, Dick Ha'amori, was worried about them, the paper continued, since his wife and three children were among the voyagers.

'We managed to eat mangos we took from Bougainville and coconuts that floated on the sea,' one of the survivors said.

On top of my mild drifting concerns is Maureen's quite understandable attitude that my trip is strictly a boy thing, or an old-man-pretending-he's-still-a-boy thing. Which is essentially why I haven't told her that I'm planning to travel to Papua New Guinea via the Solomons. Not that she listens anyway. Or perhaps that should be 'wants to listen'.

This sort of adventure is just more 'Tony, always doing stupid things'.

As long as the outboard keeps running my trip will only be 30 kilometres, straight north from Shortland in the Solomon Islands to the southern end of Bougainville, the much troubled island in Papua New Guinea. I'd made one previous visit to Bougainville – way back in 1978 I'd flown in to Arawa and taken a tour of the gigantic copper mine at Panguna. Operated by international mining company Rio Tinto, it was one of the most profitable mines in the world. Not only was it the biggest single component in the country's economy, but Rio Tinto, so the story went, covered its costs with the gold and silver that emerged from the site, before they even got around to the copper, which was what the mine was all about. Then it all went wrong and that huge hole in the ground became the focus of an extraordinarily nasty and long-running civil war between the central government far away in Port Moresby and the disgruntled islanders, yet another of those vicious little conflicts that somehow never made it onto the front pages, never appeared in living colour on the TV news. Even though it was only a stone's throw north of Australia.

Papua New Guinea is a handy little synopsis of all the problems that can afflict one small developing nation. First, there was a confusing colonial history. By the time the European powers got around to this corner of the Pacific most of the easy spoils had been shared out. So the Dutch grabbed the west half of the island of New Guinea and tagged it onto their Dutch East Indies colony, Indonesia today. An arrow-straight border, with just a little kink for the mighty Fly River, divided the Dutch half from the British and German colonies to the east. On that eastern side of the border, the Germans took the north, the British the south, separated by a line drawn on the map. Nobody had ever been into the centre of the island where that line crossed; it was assumed to be uninhabited jungle.

Then World War I came along, and the Australians marched in, kicked the Germans out and took over their colony. 'Might as well have the southern half as well,' the British suggested, although the Australians continued to run the place as two separate colonies right up to independence in 1975. To further complicate matters there were other islands apart from the big one. The scatter of islands to the east, all of them part of the German colony, concluded with Bougainville, named after the colourful French explorer. All this colonial squabbling had its confusing conclusion with the end of the colonial era after World War II.

Logically Papua New Guinea should be one country. It may be a 'parliament of a thousand tribes', as Osmar White coined it, and home to nearly as many languages, but the people are all Melanesians, unrelated to the Indonesians and Malay people to their west. Still, when the Dutch East Indies became independent Indonesia, it was almost inevitable that the half of the island also previously governed by the Dutch would go with it. At the other end of the country, in Bougainville, the people may be Melanesians, but even a quick glance at the map shows that the island is naturally part of the Solomon group. Culturally, linguistically and even physically they're closer to the assorted tribes of the Solomons than to the highlanders and other tribes of the main island. But the Solomons were a British colony while Bougainville was part of the territory won from the Germans by Australia and so, come independence, the international border separated Shortland Island in the Solomons from Bougainville Island in Papua New Guinea. A border I hope to be crossing in a few days' time.

I fly north from Honiara, the capital of the Solomon Islands, to Ghizo, where that drifting boat found safety just a few weeks earlier. From Honiara's airport on Guadalcanal Island we lift up over Iron Bottom Sound, named after the US and Japanese warships that dotted the seabed from the fierce naval battles of World War II. We head north-west along the Slot, the channel that Japanese ships raced down to supply their troops on Honiara, and along which American ships moved north as the conflict inched back towards Japan.

I find a room for a couple of nights at Fatboys, a friendly little resort one island south of Ghizo that caters to divers keen to explore the World War II wreckage which litters so many of the islands' beautiful reefs. From my room's verandah I gaze across to Kennedy Island, where the future US president swam to after his motor torpedo boat PT109 came off second-best in a collision with a Japanese destroyer. I do a couple of dives, paddle across the strait to JFK's small island

in one of the resort's kayaks and, over a cold Solbrew, chat
with the American oceanographers getting ready to launch
two ocean current gliders, curious winged torpedoes which
ride on deep ocean currents and surface periodically to send
their discoveries back to San Diego by satellite phone.

The other Fatboys visitors seem to fit all the Solomon Island
visitor possibilities. Apart from the scientists at work, there is
the solo traveller on his way through the country (that's me),
a couple of Australian expats (Drew and Yvette) and a couple
of tourists on holiday. The tourist couple from Canberra are
unusual in that neither of them are divers – diving is the
big attraction for most Solomon visitors – and also that they
somehow arrived without hearing of the island's fearsome
malaria reputation. Healthy travel advice for the Solomons
always starts with warnings about malaria, often insisting
that it is so prevalent and is found in such interesting varieties
that the country is a favourite for malaria research.

From Ghizo I plan to take the weekly flight half an hour
north to Balalae, the airstrip island close to Shortland, which
is the northernmost island in the Solomons, but first I have
a small problem. Leaving the Solomons. Reportedly there is
no immigration office at Shortland, so if I want my passport
stamped out I have to do it in Ghizo. Except there might not
be an office in Ghizo either. Nobody seems to know. I don't
imagine that not officially leaving the Solomons is likely to
cause me any major problem in years to come; if anything
I am more concerned about running into an official in
Shortland who might try to stop me departing without the
appropriate passport stamp.

The morning of my flight I go in search of an immigration office in Ghizo, with a conspicuous lack of success. Drew, the visiting Australian police advisor, told me the police station could direct me, but I'm sent off on several wild goose chases before I give up and drop into the PT109 Café for lunch. A visiting yachtie insists there's an office in town. He's right; indeed there is. It's beside the hotel, a derelict-looking shed with an 'Immigration' sign leaning against the building in the undergrowth. Unfortunately, the immigration guy is away somewhere and coming back who knows when?

Why didn't the police station know this office existed? I shuttle between the immigration office, the customs office, which I've also found (not at all where the police station thought it was) and the Solomon Island Airlines office, before finally sitting in the immigration office to wait for the possible return of the man with the rubber stamp. At which point the other guy in the office announces that what the hell, he knows where the rubber stamp is kept, he'll stamp me out. And does! So I am stamped out of the Solomons, before I even arrive at Shortland.

The airport boat shuttles me over to the Ghizo airport, on another small island a couple of hundred metres across the harbour. There are just seven of us on the Twin Otter, and we're soon landing on the lush, grassy Balalae airstrip. When everybody starts marching off to the beach I tag along and am quickly collared by Dennis, who appears to have come over to Balalae just to see who's arriving. He offers to run me over to Nila Mission on Shortland Island and I've soon signed him up to be my guide and transport for a trip back to the airstrip tomorrow.

'What about Bougainville?' I continue. 'I want to cross over to Papua New Guinea in a couple of days' time.'

'Well, go on Saturday,' he suggests. 'It's market day in Buin and there'll be several boats from the villages crossing over. You can come on my boat if you want.'

This is proving easier than I expected. Dennis drops me at the mission, where I'm soon installed in the extremely basic St Rose of Lima Guest House.

'Is there food?' I ask the girls who make my bed.

'We'll ask sister,' they reply. Since they never return, the answer, presumably, is no. I find the village store instead and stock up on instant noodles, biscuits and tea. There isn't much else and I wish I'd shopped in Ghizo; the fresh fruit at the waterfront market looks very good in retrospect. I wander around the mission and the village for a bit; Japanese seaplane wreckage lies scattered among the trees and the *Pacific Ace*, a real tramp of a tramp steamer, is moored at the mission dock, where kids dive off the bow. A rather drunk guy staggers back and forth shouting and looking for a fight.

'He wants the CDO to supply a barrel of petrol,' someone tells me.

Who the CDO is and to whom he should be supplying petrol I have no idea.

Is there electricity? I wonder, back at the guesthouse. Yes, from just after 7 pm, which is when I discover I've chosen a room – one of four – with a mosquito net, but no lights. Two other rooms have lights, but no mosquito nets. I swap to the final room, which has both. The Solomons used to be one of the best places in the world for meeting virulent strains of malaria, but it's reportedly much less of a problem these days. Still, I don't plan to research those chances and, besides, malaria might be down but the dengue fever figures are said to be up.

The electricity is on for just two hours, so I go to bed early and sleep surprisingly well. I don't even hear another guest arrive; he takes the lightless mosquito-netted bed I've vacated. In the morning I'm up for tea and more instant noodles for breakfast. Sister walks by and tells me it's her nephew who turned up in the night unexpectedly.

Dennis arrives and, after pausing over a seaplane in shallow water across from the mission wharf, takes me back to his village on an adjacent island. His son (Joe) and nephew (Emilio) then take me back to Balalae to look for wartime wreckage. The boat, with its fifteen horsepower Tohatsu outboard (and zero lifejackets), is the one we'll take to Bougainville tomorrow.

Balalae, like so many Solomon Island airstrips, was built by the Japanese during World War II, but it has a particularly nasty history. After the capture of Singapore, the victorious Japanese shipped 600 British prisoners of war to Rabaul and then 517 of them on to Balalae to build the airstrip. Many of them died from exhaustion, disease and Allied attacks on the island, but any survivors were executed once the work was completed. Bayoneted or decapitated, report the islanders. When the war ended, the Japanese troops on the island insisted the POWs had been shipped off to a prison camp in Japan after the airstrip was completed. If they hadn't arrived in Japan then the ship must have been sunk en route. The truth was only revealed when the Australians who secured the island discovered a mass grave. The pit contained 436 bodies. There's a small memorial plaque beside the airport apron, but the island carries a bad spell; to this day nobody will live here.

There was a lot of wartime wreckage left on Balalae, but much of it has been salvaged by collectors in recent years. An assortment of Japanese wrecks, including most of a Betty bomber, are now housed in an open shed on the west coast. After we check it out we go back to the terminal and start down the runway. Back in Ghizo, Drew reported a largely intact Betty bomber just off the runway on the west side, which I assume is where we're headed. Instead we spend an hour, probably more, aimlessly wandering around the jungle, with some mumbling about wreckage being stolen. I'm getting cut and scratched, and very fed up.

We do see a couple of flying foxes – also known as fruit bats – and Joe and Emilio catch and kill a possum to take home to eat. Apart from the elusive Betty, Drew also had a hair-raising story of encountering a large crocodile in one of the island's ponds, which are mostly likely bomb craters from US attacks. When we come upon ponds, I approach the water with some trepidation.

Emerging back onto the west coast, we walk round to the start of the runway and head back towards the terminal. Then Joe finds wreckage on the east side of the runway: a disorderly assortment with the tail of a Betty – well, I assume that's what it is – with a tree grown right through it, like a modern version of that jungle-throttled Angkor temple. Nearby is more jumbled wreckage, including three Betty tail assemblies. I take another fall over a vine tripwire, and Joe forays off the west side of the runway and there, sure enough, is Drew's Betty. Battered and bent, but remarkably complete.

The boys shuttle me back to the mission where I heat up more instant noodles for lunch, washed down with a Fanta. In the afternoon it rains on and off and the young guy who'd offered to guide me to the big Japanese guns on the ridge above the village turns up too late to make the walk today. I wander over to the church to offer a prayer for good weather tomorrow morning before my fourth instant noodle meal in a row, this time accompanied by a tin of tuna. A battered cat turns up to scrounge the remnants. As thunderstorms pass outside I pack up and write a note in the guesthouse visitors' book; there have been other guests, but often months pass between their visits.

My prayers don't seem to work very well. It rains on and off most of the night, accompanied by gentle lightning and thunder, although outside it's very still – there's no village activity, no jungle soundtrack. I don't sleep well and eventually get up at 4 am, which was when Dennis said he'd pick me up. He insisted that leaving while it was still dark was a good thing; the early arrivals would find it easier to get transport from the beach up to Buin, on Bougainville.

'Isn't there a risk that we'll bump into other boats in the dark?' I ask.

'No, they're all going in the same direction,' Dennis replies. When I get into Buin, he continues, I should be able to get my passport noted and stamped by the police, until I get to a real immigration point. I'm breaking the law – this isn't an official

arrival point into Papua New Guinea. Perhaps wisely, I've
lined up a visa in Australia; I told them I'd be flying into Port
Moresby, and that's exactly what I hope to do eventually, just
not from the conventional, Australian, direction.

There's no Dennis at 4, 4.30 or even 5 am. Are they not
going at all because of the weather? It seems to me he has
some commitment to going – there are other people besides
me heading across and Dennis talked about what he was
taking to trade at the market. And they're used to rain in
these parts. It's warm enough, but I regret leaving my Gore-
Tex jacket behind; once you're damp there's wind chill despite
the warmth. So I read a bit, worry a bit, think a bit, mentally
repack my bag a bit, and listen to the rain, counting the
distance from lightning to thunder as I imagine the sound of
approaching outboards.

Finally, just before 6 am, it starts to clear and when I
walk down towards the jetty and beach there is the sound of
Dennis's outboard. 'It's going to take half an hour to get the
boats ready,' he tells me, adding that somebody will meet us
at the beach on Bougainville. I go back to the guesthouse
to make some tea, tiptoeing around, trying not to wake the
other guest.

At 7 am we finally get away, Dennis and his offsider are
in his boat, the puny Tohatsu outboard replaced with a more
impressive thirty horsepower Yamaha. The second boat has
his son Joe, another offsider, two young women, a small girl
and me – and a forty horsepower Yamaha. After my nagging
drift-away worries, the journey's an anticlimax. The sea
isn't rough, the rain stays away, and while there are heavy

downpours off to the east and black clouds directly ahead, they dissipate before we get to them. A rainbow arcs to the west. An hour and a half after leaving Nila we're pulling the boat up on the beach, in a different country. Our only hiccup, when the engine suddenly stopped with just 10 kilometres to go, was just for a routine refuel. Dennis arrives soon after us and I help unload our cargo onto the beach; it principally consists of about a hundred twenty-four-can slabs of SolBrew whisky & cola, to add to PNG's drinking problems.

A Land Cruiser zooms us the short drive into town and I'm soon at the Buin police station, where Paul Kamuai, the station commander, is initially a little sticky about my unofficial arrival, but switches to being completely helpful when I drop Nick Unsworth's name. Nick is a Brit, working with the police in Buka at the north end of Bougainville; a friend who was with him in Kenya a few years ago has put me in touch with him, and we've arranged to meet up when I reach Buka.

So why didn't I come to Bougainville via Buka in the first place? There are regular flights from Port Moresby, the Papua New Guinea capital; I could have flown in that way without any paperwork or immigration problems. I'd have had no concerns about drifting away either. So why go to all the trouble of arriving here from Shortland in the Solomons? Well, I've always been fascinated by back door routes between countries; arriving by boat on a beach is always going to be more interesting than the airport arrivals lounge. The route from Shortland has always been there, though unofficially; it simply became more illegal and, at the same time, more important, during the civil war, when it was used for supplying the rebels, the Bougainville Revolutionary Army, or BRA. And the activities of the BRA are on my list of things to see.

These days, visitors entering this way are few and far between, so I suspect the police response would have switched to cooperative even without my friend's influence. I'm a rare opportunity to wield the rubber stamps.

Equally important, I discover that turning up unannounced from the Solomons gives you immediate street cred.

'So when did you fly from Port Moresby?' people would ask.

'Oh, I came in by boat from Shortland,' I'd reply, and immediately a smile would appear on my questioner's face. I'd come the 'right' way.

There was another reason I wanted to explore the southern end of Bougainville. I wanted to track down where US enemy number one – until Osama bin Laden came along – had met his end. Admiral Isoroku Yamamoto was the mastermind behind the Japanese attack on Pearl Harbor. If bin Laden was gung ho about his attack on the States, Yamamoto was far from convinced that striking the US so decisively was a good idea. It's unlikely that he actually said the words attributed to him by Hollywood, 'I fear all we have done is to awaken a sleeping giant', but he undoubtedly had misgivings about his meticulously planned mission.

After Pearl Harbor the Japanese advance across the Pacific was turned around at Guadalcanal in the Solomons and the Americans were now advancing north. On 13 April 1943,

Yamamoto set out on a morale-boosting tour of Japanese front-line positions from his base at Rabaul on the Papua New Guinea island of New Britain. In a twin-engined Mitsubishi G4M bomber, known as a 'Betty', and accompanied by another Betty and six Zero fighter escorts, Yamamoto planned to fly from Rabaul to Balalae, then to visit Shortland by boat, return to Balalae and fly to Buin before circling back to Rabaul, arriving nine hours after his dawn departure. Unfortunately for the admiral, the Americans had broken the secret Japanese code and deciphered a navy message detailing his plans.

As Yamamoto flew south, sixteen US P38 Lightnings were heading north from Honiara to intercept him. Right on schedule, Yamamoto's Betty descended towards Balalae – where I had landed just a few days earlier – and the US aircraft arrived with equally meticulous timing. The result was Yamamoto's Betty crashing into the jungle just west of Buin, killing all twelve on board.

Not until 2011, sixty-eight years later, when Osama bin Laden was killed in Pakistan, would there be a similar targeted killing of US enemy number one. Yamamoto's death did great damage to Japanese morale, but until it was announced the following month the Americans were unable to publicise their victory – if they had, they would have revealed they'd broken the navy code and known who they'd shot down.

Getting to Yamamoto's wreck site was top priority for the next day. The manager at my guesthouse, Nashon, who is originally from Goroka in the highlands of the main Papua New Guinea island, latches on and guides me around town.

Not that there's much to see; a sadly worn-out and hidden-away Japanese war memorial is about it. If I weren't being kept here by Yamamoto I'd move on as soon as possible. I bump into Dennis (taking six girls back to Shortland), watch a rugby game at the local school and encounter assorted drunks in town.

'They're drinking JJ – jungle juice, the local homebrew – as well as beer,' Nashon explains.

I mentioned my plan to find the Yamamoto crash site when I was at the police station, and word must have got around town. As I walk through the market somebody approaches me and says if I want to get there I should talk to his friend Albert. I meet Albert and write down his mobile phone number, although he's remarkably uncommunicative. Back at my guesthouse I suddenly find myself organising a Yamamoto outing. Paul, the affable guesthouse owner, has never seen it, despite the site's proximity to Buin. He's eager to go, and organises a car and driver. Nashon wants to come too, and Wilson, a cheerfully rotund guy from the University of Technology in Lae, becomes quite intrigued by the story of the interception of the Betty and is also keen.

Dinner at the guesthouse is enormous. I already had my fill of rice at lunch, but even if I'd started with an empty stomach there was still a double serve of rice, twice as many chips as I could normally manage, mighty hunks of chicken and a stack of overcooked string beans. I manage to eat the chicken, some of the beans and half the chips, and settle in for a noisy night of drunks chorusing their disputes as they march past the guesthouse, often with a musical accompaniment from their boomboxes. I'm so tired after the previous sleep-deprived night, it hardly matters.

The next morning, the 'short cut' route to the wreck site involves multiple river crossings and seems more like the long way round to me. Straight line, it's only 15 kilometres. I read there was a sign by the road indicating where you turn off to the crash site, but when we get there the sign has gone, and just the poles remain. It's an indicator that there's a landowners' dispute, and getting there won't be as easy as everyone thought. Why they have to wait sixty-nine years from the crash and have their argument just before I arrive is beyond me.

I sit inconspicuously in the car while a long discussion goes on. It appears the villagers won't let us go in unless we also get the agreement – unpaid – from the villagers of the other side of the dispute. We drive to the other village contingent and another endless discussion takes place. The result seems to be that each group insists that only they have the right to decide who goes in. I offer to pay both sides of the argument, but if group B gets paid, group A won't let us go and vice versa. They're adamant; they'd rather have their dispute than the money. To come all this way and face a stop sign just four kilometres from the wreck seems very unfair.

As we drive away I try to be philosophical: you have to lose some. But there is one last hope – Albert, the strong silent type. Nobody knows who Albert is, but a couple of kilometres towards Buin we move into mobile phone range and call Albert's number. It turns out he's in the next village along, and what's more he's the local BRA commander.

'No problem,' Albert announces after we've tracked him down. 'Take my sidekick and tell them Albert says you can go.' Or words to that effect.

The trouble is his fey, dreadlocked, Monroe-mouthed (lots of betel chewing) sidekick doesn't look like someone with a lot of authority, not like Albert. Our driver, John, big enough to have some authority himself, insists we must take Albert. So Albert grabs a very big knife and off we go. *Crocodile Dundee*'s 'Call that a knife?' moment would have been instantly sidelined by this machete. *This* is a knife.

By now there are ten of us in the group and when we drive back to the starting point there's no stopping to negotiate with obstructive landowners; Albert just marches straight past. Okay, he does have authority, but he also has a very big bush-knife. The plane is almost 4 kilometres, in a straight line, from the road, an hour's walk through dense jungle interspersed by a couple of plantations. Some wreckage lies by the path a hundred metres or so before the actual impact point, presumably ripped off as the plane plunged down through the trees. At the wreck site the plane is crumpled – where's the front of it? Just compacted? It's also been comprehensively souvenired, with parts taken away, including a wing to Japan. Both engines are still there, with bent props. I've seen a few Bettys by now and I can still clearly recognise it as one. It is an important and interesting site, a turning point in World War II, and I would feel its resonance a few months later when I passed through Abbottabad in Pakistan, Osama bin Laden's final hideaway.

John is driving Wilson on to Arawa so I hitch a ride with them. The trip takes about three hours and overall the road is not too bad. There are a few unbridged rivers to cross, none very deep at the moment, and signs of a fairly recent landslide that blocked the road for some time. This evening the only delay is a bridge with collapsing wood. The metal framework is fine so we spend some time rearranging the bits and pieces of planking before John charges across. Almost all the way we're running through jungle, kid's picture-book jungle, green upon green, climbers upon trees, dense, damp, impenetrable.

The Panguna mine site in the hills above Arawa is my second Bougainville goal, but I've a problem to sort out first. Money. I was told that changing money when you arrive from the Solomons is near impossible so I came with what I thought was a healthy wad of kina bills; the Yamamoto wreck land rights dispute not only jacked the usual visitor price up by a factor of five, but it also meant I had to pay both sides of the argument as well as Albert and his assistant. So I've got to find somewhere to change money before I find transport up to the mine site and get permission to pay a visit.

I trek round to the police station where Nick, my very useful Buka contact, said there are some New Zealand police advisors in residence. Rob Arnold, the chief Kiwi cop, is enormously helpful and drives me around town in search of money changers and a car to rent. The Kiwis have two Land Cruisers, the local police just one but it's stuck in low-ratio four-wheel drive so they can't do more than 25 kilometres per hour, making the pursuit of any local baddies a non-starter. It turns out there's no shortage of bad guys in town. As we drive,

Rob starts telling me the dramatic tale which has unrolled around the police station during the past week, but I'll hear a lot more about it from Chris Imba, a local police officer who takes a day off work and comes up to the mine site with me.

Having got some cash – there's not much interest in credit cards in Bougainville – I go in search of wheels. The first price I'm quoted is an unbelievable US$400 a day, but with some asking around I find a reasonable little four-wheel drive for half that. Still a very hefty price. Then I need permission to go up to the site, where Bougainville's recent sorry story started.

Just before Papua New Guinea's independence in 1975, Bougainville made its own unsuccessful bid for a separate independence and, when that didn't work, made a pitch to join the Solomons rather than the rest of PNG. The island was eventually incorporated into newly independent PNG, but the mine soon became a big problem. Bougainville Copper Limited, a subsidiary of the giant Rio Tinto organisation, had started mining at Panguna in 1969 and almost immediately became the single biggest component of the country's economy. Rio Tinto did very well out of the mine and plenty of money found its way back to the politicians in the capital, Port Moresby. In return, the lucky Bougainvilleans got a tiny share of the mine's wealth and 100 per cent of the inevitable pollution and environmental problems. In 1988 local leader Francis Ona announced that they'd had enough and within a year his Bougainville Revolutionary Army's attacks had closed the mine down. Heavy-handed intervention from the Papua New Guinea army only made matters worse and in 1990 the army withdrew, leaving the BRA in control of the island.

Or sort of in control. In fact the island soon became divided between warring factions and the struggle dragged in the neighbouring Solomons. The island of Buka immediately to the north broke away completely, supported by PNG government troops. PNG clashed with the Solomon Islands after accusations that the Solomons government had been backing the BRA, supplying them via the same Shortland Island route that I'd taken into the country. PNG troops periodically intervened on Bougainville, but never succeeded in subduing the BRA. Worse, the struggle turned very nasty, particularly for isolated villages, a horror story dramatically told in Lloyd Jones's book (and later movie) *Mr Pip*.

Meanwhile prime ministers came and went in Port Moresby, and Australia and New Zealand dithered about supplying peacekeeping forces. In 1996, Julius Chan, prime minister since 1994, ordered his army commander, Jerry Singirok, to lead the PNG army back into Bougainville and sort the mess out. The invasion was a total failure and the following year Chan decided to call in foreign mercenaries from Sandline International. Singirok proved much more adept at rounding up mercenaries, most of them from South Africa, than Bougainvilleans, and when news of the plan leaked to the Australian media, the resulting scandal brought down Chan's government.

The Sandline Affair may have been a failure, but a ceasefire did follow and an international peace-monitoring group brought the worst of the conflict to a close. A new regional government was established in Buka, but the Panguna mine site remained in rebel hands and very few outside visitors were allowed in. In the past couple of years the rebel remnants have started to allow access and an international band of scavengers have descended like vultures and started to ship out anything of value. Technically, Rio Tinto's Bougainville Copper division still owns and operates the place; the business is still listed on the stock exchange and the company still puts out annual reports. 'Not much happening' is the usual account.

The BRA morphed into the Mekamui, and Francis Ona crowned himself king. Although he died in 2005 and a regional government was established in Buka, the mine is still under Mekamui control so I need their permission to go up there.

'Lord William Munta, the local Mekamui head – he's the man to ask,' I'm told.

I track him down in an ordinary-looking little suburban house and he writes me a letter to Colonel Alex Dakamari up at the mine. The BRA and its successor seem very fond of noble and military titles and ranks; Dakamari was only a Commander in an article I read a week or two ago. Greater access or not, it's still going to cost me to get into the Panguna forbidden zone and the sky-high 200 kina (US$100) charge – well, it does cover return visits for twelve months – has just jumped to 300 kina.

I collect Chris Imba from the police station. His father was a Panguna bus driver and used to transport workers up to the mine from Arawa at the start of each shift. Filling up my four-wheel drive indicates just what's happened to the town. I buy petrol in a wire-fenced compound where it's pumped out of a drum into a 5-litre glass container and then drained into the tank. I'd already noticed the fading, but still modern-looking, ex-Shell and Mobil stations around town. The Shell sign still stands over the station entrance, the symbol cracked and punched out, green vines clambering through the broken plastic.

'When I was a kid there was even an escalator in one of the shopping centres,' Chris says. Once upon a golden time.

A few kilometres out of Arawa we reach the Morgan Junction checkpoint for the mine. The guys manning the boom read my letter from Lord Munta and wave us through, no money asked.

'It's all bullshit,' Chris reckons, 'the whole Lord and Colonel business, the roadblocks, the cash demands. They're all just a way of scamming money.'

It's a great drive up, through dense, verdant jungle, the sweeping road still in generally excellent condition although the guardrails look their age and have taken a beating. There's very little traffic. On the way up we pass local mining operations, cut into the hillsides with muscle power and nothing more.

Just before the top we pass the bus depot, where Chris's dad used to park his bus every day. There are still a couple there, rusting away. The mine would make a great post-apocalypse movie set; *Mad Max* comes regularly to mind and I start saying 'amazing' far too frequently. First there's Panguna town, with skeletons of the living quarter blocks, and the empty shells of apartment buildings, some of them with people camping out in the windowless rooms. Then there's an Olympic-size, open-air swimming pool, empty, its tiles shot through with vines, creepers and bushes, but it's the cinema which is the most touching reminder of the past. It's a tangled, burnt-out wreck, but you can still see the rows of seats, only their metal frames remaining, and the three projector apertures. It would be a contemporary-looking cinema right now – if it were still in operation – but in fact it's been a blitzed shell for twenty years.

The mine workshop areas have mainly been stripped out although the Asian scrap-metal dealers – Filipinos, Singaporeans, Koreans, Chinese – are still at work. At some point somebody will decide the building frameworks could be used for bridges and they too will be stripped. Then there's the mine itself, the gigantic hole in the ground, untouched for nearly twenty-five years now, vegetation beginning to cloak it in places. There's the blue stain of copper sulphate streaked down the walls and a bright blue lake, draining away in the centre.

'If it wasn't continually draining out, the crater would gradually fill with water,' Chris explains.

It's the gigantic trucks that really fascinate me, a long line of them parked nose-to-tail up one road out of the pit, a line-up of them down in the pit bottom. All looking as if they were parked after the last shift, waiting to be rolled out again as soon as this little squabble is sorted out. In fact, they're rusting away, their tyres destroyed, glass broken, instruments removed, each of them massive, and impassive. We continue to the valley where the tailings were pushed out, a huge slope gradually swallowing the valley from side to side.

Then it's back down towards Arawa, where the Morgan Junction boys ask for the cash this time. Fortunately they're uncertain as to how much they should be asking and readily agree when Chris suggests it should be 200 kina. We divert to Loloho, where the copper concentrate used to be loaded on ships. Again, it's a post-apocalypse scene; the metal scavengers have been through cutting out beams so the place has collapsed. Nearby, the power plant that used to supply Panguna is another scene of crumbling devastation. Some of the gigantic transmission towers beside the road to Panguna are still standing; occasionally lengths of power cable droop between them, dropping down into the jungle.

Chris is a personable young guy who's just had a part as an extra in the filming of Mr Pip. He played a PNG soldier – so a bad guy – although in the book both sides, PNG soldiers and BRA rascals, are all bad guys. The film was made in a village just south of Arawa, a brave effort to produce it in the real-life setting of the novel.

Chris starts to fill in the details of the amazing – that word again – confrontation at the police station last week.

'I hear the guy was well known locally – in Australia they'd say "an identity",' I say. 'How old was he?'

'James Naveung, he was in his forties,' Chris replies. 'He had a heart attack. That didn't surprise anybody, he was huge and didn't walk anywhere.'

The guys at the petrol depot already confirmed that when I asked them about Mr Naveung. I'd heard the story of his demise and subsequent events even before I left Buin.

'His family accused Tony Oama of killing him with sorcery. So we locked Tony up, for his own protection.'

'And how old was Oama?' I asked.

'About thirty-five. He was nobody special, just an ordinary guy. Naveung's people come round to the police station three times. They demand that we hand Oama over to them. Then the fourth time they break into the station, they haul Oama out and they're about to drive off in a ute when a police officer jumps in the ute too.'

The police couldn't have pursued them in their own car. It's stuck in low gear. The New Zealanders' role is strictly advisory – their brief doesn't extend to chasing armed gangs into the jungle – so their functioning four-wheel drives were off limits.

'So the gang drive away and they start beating Oama with car wheel braces, demanding to know who else was involved in his sorcery. They threaten to kill him and fire a gun right by his head, but our man who has gone with them convinces them that if they kill Oama it's going to make the police look really bad and they'll all lose their jobs.'

'I guess everybody knows everybody in Arawa.'

'That's right, so they release Oama and we take him back to the station lock-up.'

'Not to hospital?' I ask, slightly amazed. 'In fact, why didn't they take him up to Buka? Wouldn't he have been safe there?'

'Well, perhaps that would have been a good idea,' Chris says, 'but they'd just have come looking for somebody else to blame it on. Then, last Wednesday night around 9 pm, Oama's parents' home is broken into and his mother, father and sister are all shot. His mother dies, the other two are taken to the hospital in Buka. The next morning around 10 am the gang turns up at the police station again. This time they're armed with M16s and other guns. They haul Oama out of the lock-up again and drive off with him in the back of a truck. Two hours later, his brother, Joe Sidaung, finds his body on a roadside outside Arawa. He's been cut up and shot. His other three brothers have already headed for the hills.'

'So do you have any idea who did it?' I ask.

'Oh yes, we can identify nine of the eleven people who kidnapped him,' Chris says, 'but what can we do? They have more firepower than us.'

The civil war may be over, but clearly Bougainville is not completely peaceful; there's a lot of weaponry sloshing around and lots of money being made from the Panguna scrap metal. Since nobody – apart from Bougainville Copper perhaps – really owns it, there will inevitably be some trouble over the proceeds.

'It was horrible,' one of the New Zealand cops told me. 'We could see the lock-up from our window, so we saw them drag him out and drive off. There was nothing we could do.'

Chris had the last word on the event. 'There must have been a dozen sorcery cases while I've been in the police and none of them has ended well. We always lock them up for their own protection, otherwise somebody is going to kill them, like this time. Nobody has ever been convicted.'

Of sorcery that is. Although nobody seems to get convicted of killing an accused sorcerer either.

Ron O'Leary had spun his Bougainville tales to me before I set out for the island. He'd worked on the Sabah cocoa plantation. Rex Blow, who owned the plantation, had named it after the district of North Borneo, where he'd been captured by the Japanese during World War II and where, by all rights, he should have died on the Sandakan Death March. Instead, he escaped from the Japanese and made his way to the Philippines, where he operated behind enemy lines for much of the war. Or so the story goes.

After the war, Rex started his plantation and when Ron worked there he employed about 120 people, plus another twenty or thirty to work on the copra.

'I'd line them all up every morning and send them out, ten here, twenty there,' Ron muses. 'Bougainvilleans wouldn't work on the plantation, so we imported Highlanders, Tari wigmen. They were real bush kanakas, didn't even speak pidgin.'

'Bougainvilleans did work at the mine, along with people from other areas of PNG, including Tolais from Rabaul,' Ron continues.

The civil war broke out around the mine, but Ron had headed south, back to Australia, where he settled down near Bendigo in Victoria, the heartland of the Australian goldrush of 1851. Ron turned his hand to this and that, including working over the Victorian era tailings from a disused old gold mine. There was a fair amount of local chatter about how profitable the operation was, but Ron wasn't talking. It was a secret between him and the taxman.

Ron kept some of his Bougainville contacts and news of his mining expertise must have drifted back north because in 1998 a little package arrived in the mail. A pocket-sized sample, a small taster from the BRA.

'It was a film canister of mine tailings from Panguna,' Ron explains. 'I got it analysed and it was one per cent gold. They told me they had 10 tonnes more, just like this. So one per cent of 10,000 kilograms is 100 kilograms of gold.

'They asked me to come up to Bougainville and work over the tailings for them. So I flew up to Honiara – it was tricky getting my equipment in through customs, but they probably knew exactly where I was going. I went up to Shortland and the BRA guys picked me up and took me across to Bougainville. The deal was I'd get two per cent of the gold, but when I got there the tailings were elusive. I don't think they really had 10 tonnes and eventually we only got 20 ounces out of it. If I was doing it again I'd say I get the first x ounces, then you get five, then I get four and so on. In the end they paid me $700 or $800 and they covered the airfares and other expenses.

'Well,' he concludes, 'I had a good holiday. Of course, the whole thing was a mess, the only place they hadn't smashed to bits at the mine site was the laboratory, they'd realised how dangerous some of the chemicals were. There were acids that would eat right through your foot if you spilled them.

'I came back again in 2001 or 2002, but everything was closed, even the plantations had gone by the early nineties – there's no cocoa production anymore, now they're just kanaka plantations, back to coconuts and copra. I came down the coast to Kieta on that last trip, and up in the hills there were little lights everywhere. They'd got electric motors from the mines, fans out of air-con units and rigged up little mini-hydro-power plants to provide electricity in the villages.'

He met an assortment of the BRA names on his visits. 'Francis Ona was a fucking maniac – beady eyes, I didn't like him at all. His son Michael was ten and he'd run around waving a gun at people. The only Westerner who had an interest in the place was Rosemary Gillespie. She was a manic leftie Melbourne lawyer who worked with the Bougainville indigenous women's association. One time she was shot at by someone from a Nomad aircraft,' Ron recalls. 'She'd made lots of enemies.

'I don't think there was a lot of neutrality.' He laughs. 'They may have denied it, but the helicopters Australia supplied were used as gunships; the pilots were kiwis and they'd land them down in the pit, but after they'd been shot at a few times they didn't stick close to ground anymore. Mortars supplied by Australia cost $400 a pop. They used to shoot an awful lot of them out of the pit into the jungle.'

In 2011 it was revealed that Michael Somare, PNG prime minister at independence and periodically ever since, had written a report ten years earlier directly accusing Rio Tinto of causing the war, pushing the PNG government to battle the rebels and supplying helicopter gunships and other equipment. 'Because of Rio Tinto's financial influence in PNG, the company controlled the government,' Somare wrote.

Environmental sensitivity and ethical business practices are concepts that rarely seem to occur to mining companies, although political corruption often seems to be a by-product of mine output. The giant Ok Tedi copper–gold open-cut mine near the Indonesian border, operated by BHP, turned into one of the worst examples of environmental disaster, causing huge damage to the waters and the people along the Fly River. Even BHP was eventually prompted to admit that they were not exactly proud of their management of the mine. The huge natural gas projects currently being developed will pour more resource wealth into the country, undoubtedly prompting more political corruption and ecological disasters. In early 2012 a huge landslide near a new Exxon Mobil project buried a village completely; it may have resulted from cutting corners at a company quarry. In PNG these projects are almost always in remote locations, far from effective government overseeing. If the government is interested in overseeing them in the first place.

Rio Tinto takes its name from its first mining operation in Spain in 1873, where since antiquity a red-tinted river indicated the presence of major iron deposits. Over the subsequent century and a half, Rio Tinto grew to be one of the world's largest mining companies, with dual headquarters in London and Melbourne. Controversy often seems to follow in its wake; the Panguna Mine was only one example. In 2008 the Norwegian government sovereign wealth fund sold its billion-dollar investment in Rio Tinto, due to the company's 'grossly unethical conduct', in particular at the gigantic Grasberg mine on the Indonesian side of the New Guinea island.

After my mine tour I drop Chris back at the police station and drive on to have a look at Kieta, the port for Arawa, before returning the car and walking back to the guesthouse. Dinner is surprisingly good, thanks to the cook, a matronly relative of Chris's, but I've got to be up very early the next morning. My transport to Buka – a Land Cruiser bus service – departs at an ungodly 3 am. Or at least it's supposed to. There's no wake-up from the security guy and no car at 3, 3.30 or even 4 am. We finally get away at 4.30 am, which does mean we do more of the trip in daylight. It's uncrowded (only one other passenger initially, I'm sitting up front), the driving quite sane, and the road is not bad at all. The Japanese have been bridging every river with a standard design concrete bridge, and the construction is almost complete. The last half-dozen or so look like all they need is the ribbon cutting. We're at Kokopau in just over three hours. A couple of minutes later, one of the local PMV boats, dubbed banana boats because of their shape, has shuttled me across the narrow but swiftly flowing Buka Passage.

I contact Nick Unsworth, who drives me around town to see the (limited) sights. We go over to his house on Sohano Island, in the middle of Buka Passage, but only two minutes away on one of the speedy taxi boats. After lunch with Nick and his wife Sally, I wander around the interesting island with its colonial houses, Japanese and Australian war memorials and crumbling cemetery.

After organising flights to Rabaul and Port Moresby, and acquiring some cash, my third Buka goal was getting my passport stamped. That isn't going to happen; there's no immigration office here. Instead I pick up a couple of newspapers – the *PNG Post Courier* seems to find its way from Port Moresby to Buka with remarkable speed – and a cold can of South Pacific and sit on my balcony watching the passing trade on the Buka Passage. This is one of the fastest flowing stretches of tidal water in the world; the little outriggers rush by sideways.

The next day I just kick around, stroll the Buka buai (betel nut) market – the traders are happy to talk business – take a boat across the passage to Kokopau, and wander. I like the music emanating from so many shops and the wonderfully entertaining pidgin advertisements. Then it's back to Buka, where I meet Nick and some other local expats for a very pre-sunset beer at another Buka Passage viewpoint. But my thoughts are already on their way to the next stop.

On one of my first visits to Papua New Guinea, back in the late 1970s, I'd made an interesting excursion to East New Britain, hitchhiking most of the way down New Ireland from Kavieng to Namatanai and hopping across to Rabaul in a light aircraft. Rabaul was regularly cited as one of the most attractive towns in the Pacific, although 'attractive' was clearly juxtaposed with 'dangerous'. The danger didn't threaten you personally; Rabaul was not another PNG township where getting mugged was always a possibility. The threat was to the town itself, in the form of five volcanoes that encircled Rabaul's Simpson Harbour and regularly shuddered, smoked, shook, ejected dust and ash, and generally indicated that Rabaul was living on borrowed time. The harbour was simply the flooded caldera of an earlier cataclysmic eruption and in 1994 Rabaul's time was up.

My flight from Buka to Kokopo, the town that has replaced Rabaul as capital of East New Britain after the 1994 eruption, will take me over the southern end of New Ireland. Papua New Guinea's colonial history was often colourful and the disastrous settlement at Port Breton, right at the southern end of New Ireland, was a perfect example. In 1879 Frenchman the Marquis de Ray announced the establishment of the 'Free Colony of New France' and duped hundreds of people into investing in the colony and setting out for what is now New Ireland; at the time it hadn't even been given its German colonial name, Neu Mecklenburg. When they arrived, there was no thriving settlement, just uninhabited jungle. The Marquis had never set foot on the island. To this day the southern end of New Ireland remains uninhabited, but on my previous visit to Rabaul, the colony's grain-grinding wheel – a symbol of the potential promised to the settlers – stood in a little park on Mango Avenue. Grain was never going to grow at Port Breton. Many of the settlers lost not only their savings, but also their lives, from malaria or starvation. The discredited Marquis died in a lunatic asylum in France.

Buka airport has an absurd security operation: there's no X-ray machine or metal detector, but once everybody has been patted down and checked in, the security guys disappear and you can walk in and out, meet people outside and chat with spectators. The announcements on the flight are made in English and pidgin – it's both a non-smoking and a non-betel-nut-chewing flight. As we're climbing out of Buka I spot a fair-sized cargo ship up on a reef, but once we fly across the southern end of New Ireland, it's mountainous, forested and there's absolutely no sign of human impact or influence at all. In other words, unchanged since the Marquis de Ray's unfortunate settlers turned up.

Kokopo is only 30 kilometres along the coast from Rabaul and it certainly doesn't have any of the drama of the earlier town, but then there's no group of threatening volcanoes huddling over it either. From my hotel I walk into town and, after a couple of false starts, find an immigration and customs guy above the Westpac bank who can stamp my passport – I have officially arrived in PNG!

A little further along the coast I come to the local museum, a disorganised – but very interesting – jumble of World War II wreckage and colonial history. After the sad story of British prisoners of war at Balalae, it was refreshing to discover the story of Jose Holguin, the sole survivor of a B17 shot down during a Rabaul raid in 1943. He was one of the few US aircrew captured in Papua New Guinea to survive the war, and in 1982 he returned to Rabaul and located the wreckage of his aircraft. The crumpled flight deck and the nose art of Naughty but Nice is displayed at the museum, along with the gruelling tale of Holguin's escape.

I followed the tale of Emma Forsayth, aka Queen Emma of the South Seas, on my first visit to Rabaul so I strolled on past the museum to the site of her magnificent home, Gunantambu. All that's left are some of the steps; today they lead up from a golf course, and a new faceless, blocky, dismally bland hotel has been plonked on the top of the rise, with a security fence chopping the stairs and its top landing in half.

Queen Emma was born in Samoa of an American father and Samoan mother. Her first husband died at sea and in 1878 she teamed up with Thomas Farrell, an Australian, to start a trading business. Spotting the potential of the rich volcanic soils of New Britain's Gazelle Peninsula, they established the first real plantation in New Guinea. Farrell died, to be succeeded by a string of lovers, while Emma built up a trading empire of plantations, ships and trade stores. She built her mansion, entertained like royalty and cleverly used her American citizenship to avoid a German takeover when New Guinea became a German colony. 'Queen Emma' may have been a joke at first, but it soon became a name she had earned. She died just before World War I and her home was destroyed during the Japanese occupation in World War II. The stately stairway once led from the waterfront up to her house.

From the sad reminder of Gunantambu and Queen Emma, I walk back to the hotel via the German cemetery. *Ein unbekannter deutscher* – an unknown German – is inscribed on several of the gravestones. Remarkably, Rabaul saw some of the earliest action in World War I. Australian forces quickly overpowered the German colonial command, but the attack also involved the first Australian death in the war. There would be plenty more in Gallipoli and in the European trenches.

I finish the day with a beer on the *Hauswin*, the terrace cantilevered out over the coast in front of my resort hotel. As the sun goes down, there are fine views along the coast to the Rabaul volcanoes.

The next morning I'm picked up by boat from the beach right in front of the hotel and we head down the coast to dive on a Japanese Zero fighter just offshore. It sits on the sandy bottom and the dive is remarkably similar to one I made on an American Hellcat in Ghizo, except it's rather deeper. A little gang of tiny prawns scamper around behind the cockpit and if there was a pilot sitting there today he'd see an anemone with its resident fish directly in front of the cockpit, between him and the propeller.

It's a beautifully calm, clear day, the Rabaul volcanoes on view off to the west, as we head out to the Pigeon Islands. I spend some of my surface interval ashore on Little Pigeon Island – you can walk around it in a quarter hour. Offshore, the reef slopes gently away to an edge and then drops straight off to 50 metres. Round the corner beyond Rabaul at Submarine Base, where Japanese submarines were provisioned during the war, the drop-off is straight to 300 metres. The divemaster has brought along a plastic bottle, crinkling it between his hands to act as a shark caller, but no sharks appear today. Shark calling is a local speciality here in New Britain, and even more so on New Ireland. Towards the end of the dive we see quite a few anemone fish, always my favourites. Sometimes they're hidden away down cracks in the reef and often the boss female fish is big – big for an anemone fish, that is.

After lunch I pick up a rental truck and drive to Rabaul, stopping off at places en route and around the town, even though I'm going to shift from Kokopo to Rabaul tomorrow. The 'prettiest town in the Pacific' was pretty much wiped out in 1994 when two of the five volcanoes around the harbour erupted. It wasn't a lava flow or a disastrous explosion that took out Rabaul, just a steady pile-up of ash until buildings collapsed under the load. Today the east of the town is fairly intact and because the town's deepwater port is vital for East New Britain – there's no port facility to speak of in Kokopo – the town continues, although it's a dusty shadow of its former self. The entire western half of it is just an ash-covered wasteland with a handful of buildings – including the Rabaul Hotel, where I'll be staying – still in operation.

I've got the truck for twenty-four hours so the next morning after breakfast I drive out to the Bita Paka Commonwealth war cemetery. There are more than a thousand graves, more than half of them Indian prisoners of war, mainly from Singapore. The rest are almost all Australians and most of them – Indian or Australian – are so young, and are never coming back to a wife, children, parents. It's so depressingly sad.

I ride back to Rabaul. Why have I come here? I think at first. It's such a dusty, godforsaken site. After lunch I walk down the dusty road – it's hard work trudging through the volcanic ash – to the New Guinea Club with its interesting collection of colonial and wartime memorabilia, all faded and frayed. It's absolutely sauna-hot in the building. Next door to the club building is the site of Admiral Yamamoto's wartime bunker; he would have emerged from here sixty-nine years

ago to clamber aboard that ill-fated Betty and fly off over the
jungles of southern Bougainville.

The sorry tale of the Japanese treatment of prisoners of war
is touched on in the museum exhibits. If you were captured
by the Germans during World War II you had a one per cent
chance of dying while you were a POW. The equivalent figure
for POWs held by the Japanese was thirty-seven per cent! Let
me repeat that: you were thirty-seven times more likely to die
in Japanese hands than in German ones, although if you were
a Russian POW your chances with the Germans were probably
rather worse than the average. This figure for Japanese POW
deaths is an overall one; in some places the death rate was
worse, sometimes much worse. Rabaul was one of them.
Of 126 airmen and coastwatchers captured at Rabaul, only
twenty survived. Of the 10,000 Indian POWs sent to Rabaul,
6000 died. For Chinese prisoners the figures were 756 dead
out of 1504. Of the 620 British POWs sent to Rabaul from
Singapore most would die on Balalae Island in the Solomons.
Not a single British POW would survive the war in Rabaul, but
a handful had been transferred to Watom Island just north
of Rabaul, where conditions must have been slightly better,
because there were eighteen survivors.

Remarkably, despite intensive Allied bombing through
the war, Rabaul was never captured. As the American forces
moved north through the Pacific to Japan, Rabaul was simply
bypassed. The Japanese forces there were powerless, their
aircraft were shot out of the sky, their navy had been sunk;
fighting for survival was all they could do. After the atom
bombs fell on Japan in August 1945, Rabaul surrendered, but

it was not until late February 1946 that the first contingent departed on a battered Japanese aircraft carrier. By the end of June over 90,000 Japanese prisoners of war had been shipped home. Nearly 100 would never get there; they were tried, convicted and executed as war criminals.

Later I walk along the waterfront to the Rabaul Yacht Club; like everything else here it's a shadow of what used to be. Susie at the bar is the owner/manager of the hotel; her Scottish boyfriend works in shipping in Rabaul. Two US yachties turn up and analyse the cargo ship I spotted on the reef as I flew out of Buka. It didn't plough straight onto the reef, they say, just edged on sideways, so it should be easy to get off. The hotel guests include two Austrian women and a Welsh woman. They've spent the day walking around the volcano caldera ridge line. It's a dawn-departure program and Susie tells of a recent visitor who set off without a guide, got lost and spent the night up on the ridge. She was found by the search party the next morning, extremely thirsty.

I'm up very early to drive to the airport. As we fly out it's very forested over New Britain – and over the main island, for that matter – and the guy in the seat next to me becomes suddenly talkative, pointing things out, as we descend over the north coast and the Owen Stanley Range down to Port Moresby.

The PNG capital has a terrible reputation, with endless tales of violent muggings at the hands of 'rascals', as the local ne'er-do-wells are colourfully known. It's a familiar story of a young population, with high unemployment and the loss of traditional village value systems as people abandon their tribal life and head into the big city. All of this set alongside extraordinary wealth as more and more international companies flock in to exploit the country's abundant natural resources. The latest boom, just taking off, is natural gas, which will be compressed and shipped overseas.

Port Moresby is the capital of the country, but Papua New Guinea is often a curiously unstable place. Essentially, voting is all done on a tribal basis and, since there are so many tribes, the government is constantly changing. Coalitions are assembled and disassembled as fast as the political patronage can be passed around. There are, however, a couple of elements that keep the situation from degenerating into complete chaos. Nobody is keen on calling new elections, because the election time churn is very high and politicians don't have great expectations of being re-elected. Getting your hands on political patronage is only possible while you're in power, so once you've been elected and have one hand on the levers of power and one hand in the money bucket, you don't want to risk not being re-elected and having to give up the easy cash.

The tribal instability also means that a military coup is less likely. The military is tribally aligned and facing everybody in the same direction in order to overthrow a government is not that feasible. So, remarkably enough, this tribal instability leads directly to a degree of stability both in government and in the army.

The PNG government comedy routine ran as a multi-act play through 2011–2012. Michael Somare, the country's serial –

though not consecutive – prime minister had been absent for long spells for medical attention in Singapore. The parliament got fed up with its leaderless situation, allegiances were shifted, swaps were made, the seats shuffled and at the end of it PNG had a new Prime Minister, Peter O'Neil. Somare returned from Singapore and convinced the country's supreme court that his replacement had been unlawful and he was still Prime Minister. The parliament decided otherwise, Somare and O'Neil both appointed new police commissioners, and in early 2012 there was even a half-hearted, and soon abandoned, military coup.

The constitutional crisis stumbled on through 2012. Naturally, none of the politicians on either side were enthusiastic about the obvious solution: dissolve parliament and call fresh elections. With all the money currently sloshing around from the forthcoming natural gas bonanza, no politician wants to risk losing out on his share of the loot. And it is 'his' share – when elections were finally held in August 2012, it was a remarkable achievement to get three women into the 109-seat parliament. A bill to reserve twenty-two seats for women was defeated – only one member voted against it, but enough parliamentary members abstained to make it impossible to get to the absolute majority required.

Bushy-bearded Joseph, the first taxi driver in line at the airport, shakes hands, introduces himself and talks about his Highland background as he whisks me into town to an extremely brown-beige-boring and very expensive downtown hotel. It's obviously catering to those international natural resource exploiters. I'm early enough to have breakfast at the hotel, after which I walk around the town centre and down to Ela Beach. That's central Moresby done, and I really cannot remember anything from my previous visits.

In the afternoon I take a taxi with Pewi, another very friendly driver, out to the National Museum. As we approach it he starts to get very concerned, talking about how it can be uncomfortably quiet on a Sunday and how rascals hide in the bush beside the road and could jump out to carjack us if we can't drive straight in through the museum gates. I've just read in the paper about two women off a cruise ship who were mugged outside the adjacent Parliament Building, and their taxi driver's car stolen. We don't have any problems; the museum gates are open and we drive in without pause. Pewi returns for me an hour later.

I was recently at the extravagant I. M. Pei–designed Museum of Islamic Art in Doha, Qatar. The exhibits were superb and beautifully displayed, but it simply didn't feel like there were enough of them to justify the over-the-top building. Here the National Museum is the complete opposite: everything is tattily displayed; the building itself, although fairly new, is shabby and crumbling at the edges; but the collection is superb and you keep wishing it was better cared for and displayed. I'm particularly impressed by the model canoe collection and the full-sized double-canoe from the Trobriands, used in the legendary voyages around the Kula Ring Cycle.

Another effusively friendly taxi driver sails me to the Royal Papua Yacht Club, which since my last visit has moved to a big, new and rather glossy building. Despite all the trouble in the streets, the club is a clear sign that the PNG economy is booming. It's no longer strictly for white expats, either – although the social side is far more important than yachting these days.

The next morning yet another friendly Highlands driver takes me to the war museum, where I don't find any of the Yamamoto reminders I had been led to expect. The collection of miscellaneous junk does include a magnificent old Ford Trimotor, with a corrugated aluminium fuselage and wings, and nine-cylinder radial engines. I've got one final stop in Port Moresby before I fly out to Australia that afternoon. PNG Art houses a warehouse-sized collection of the country's art and it's a solid reminder of what a wonderful place this is for art. It's not just that there's a lot of it, but there's a lot of it from every corner of the country. Just two of my favourites – and I've already got fine examples of each back home – are the intriguing Kombot Storyboards from a village just off the Sepik River and the beautiful wooden bowls from the Trobriand Islands.

Papua New Guinea is a remarkably diverse country with big problems and big possibilities, and I've seen many of them as I passed through. There was colonial confusion in the years leading to independence as the European nations and Australia squabbled, negotiated and fought over its ownership. There were the harrowing years of World War II, when the country remained on the front-line from the start right up to the final day of the Pacific War. There's the double-edged sword of natural resources – certainly they put money in the national pocket, but those riches also bring corruption, ownership disputes and environmental damage. PNG has suffered some dramatic examples of each problem, the cash earned and the costs suffered often travel in very different directions. My travels took me through amazing scenery from jungles in Bougainville to beaches, islands and volcanoes in New Britain, but perhaps Port Moresby, which I'd neatly avoided on my arrival, is the perfect place to depart. Here I collide with one of the country's biggest problems – its young, male-dominated and often lawless city-in-transition position – and at the same time I'm reminded why so many people fall in love with PNG. In Port Moresby I keep encountering an amazingly vibrant artistic culture and straightforward friendliness – where else in the world does every taxi driver introduce himself as you flag him down?

ZIMBABWE

There's no shortage of wicked rulers in fairytales, but the one that always sticks in my mind is from a more contemporary fairytale. Could Robert Mugabe, leader of this Southern African country since 1980, be Lord Farquaad from the movie Shrek? Farquaad, ruler of Duloc and hungry for more power, sets out to rid his kingdom of fairytale creatures, enlisting his men to find, intimidate and ultimately exile them. He is eventually outwitted by an ogre and eaten by a fire-breathing dragon, to the general amusement of the kingdom's citizens. No such fate has befallen Mr Mugabe.

Rigged elections, repression, censorship, corruption: they're all elements of badly governed countries that are likely to prompt unrest and demand for change. But money problems easily top the list, and when it comes to hyper-inflation and a tumbling currency, Zimbabwe has been hard to beat.

Things get pretty tough when your currency is falling through the floor. If you're paid $100 and the next day it's only worth $50, and the day after that, $25, your enthusiasm for work will likely diminish considerably. Conversely, the urge to convert your pay packet as quickly as possible into something useful, like a bag of rice, will elevate considerably. But who wants to sell a bag of rice if the money you're given is soon worthless?

The uprising in Burma in 1988, when Aung San Suu Kyi emerged as the symbol of the population's demands for democracy, was largely prompted by a disastrous currency demonetisation a few months earlier. The military dictatorship, already renowned for its economic ineptitude, suddenly declared that most larger denomination banknotes were no longer valid and could not be converted to the handy new forty-five and ninety kyat notes which were then introduced. Finding that the money stashed under the mattress, which you've worked so hard to save, is suddenly worthless does not make you love your government.

The Burmese government proved comprehensively that messing with your currency is not a good idea. It was hardly surprising, then, that North Korea – another country not blessed with many clever money managers – would try the same trick. In late 2009, the unfortunate citizens of North Korea were told that all their money was worthless, and that less than US$50 of it could be converted into new notes. For once the usually cowed North Koreans rose up in protest, and the government official who dreamed up the plan was set in front of a firing squad.

When the Zimbabwe dollar started to fall through the floor, Mugabe's popularity ratings tumbled with it. Land confiscations, plummeting food production and a failure to pay International Monetary Fund debts kicked off the currency decline, and once the money starts its slide it's very hard to arrest it. In Zimbabwe the slide simply accelerated: new currencies were issued with zeros chopped off the end, but still the Zimbabwe dollar fell. Once upon a time, a single Zimbabwe dollar was a reasonable amount of money; soon you needed thousands, then millions, then billions of dollars to buy anything.

In mid-2008 it took 100 billion dollars to buy a bottle of beer, but an hour later the price had jumped by fifty per cent. By late 2008 the inflation rate was calculated to be almost 100 sextillion (don't ask) per cent a year. Despite the soaring inflation, bank withdrawals were still limited to a figure that worked out to about twenty-five cents US. By early 2009, even billions weren't enough; the $100 trillion note came off the printing presses worth about US$30 and was soon down to less than thirty cents. Of course, by this time nobody was using Zimbabwe dollars – much better to deal in something stable, like the US dollar, the euro or even the South African rand, though using foreign currency was illegal.

Finally, in April 2009, the government admitted defeat and withdrew the Zimbabwe dollar, supposedly for just twelve months, but that time frame was soon forgotten. So if you're going to buy something in Zimbabwe, the US dollar is the currency of choice, and bring plenty with you as this is a much more expensive country than on my earlier visits. The shift from being the breadbasket of Africa to being just another African basket case means that food costs have soared.

It's my third visit to Zimbabwe and a lot has changed since my first, more than twenty years ago. In 1989 everything seemed fine – tourism was booming, as it was on my second visit in 1997 – although in retrospect the whole thing was ready to tip over the edge. Farms were about to be seized, the economy was preparing for freefall and the Zimbabwe dollar was all set to disappear down the hyperinflation slippery slide. So I wanted to revisit some of the places I enjoyed back in 1997, to take a look at what has happened to them in the decade and a half since.

The Chizarira Wilderness Lodge, in the north-west of the country, about halfway between Harare and Victoria Falls, turns out to be the key factor in this plan. It is still in operation, although the owner, Craig van Zyl, confesses that visitors are now few and far between. Nevertheless, if I want to stay there it can be arranged.

'So how do I get there from Harare?' I ask.

'Well, we could fly there in my Cessna,' Craig suggests.

A few more emails zip back and forth and Craig makes an offer too good to refuse. He is having a quiet spell and wouldn't mind a few days in a couple of wildlife parks, as well as visiting Chizarira. If I'd like to pay for the fuel, he'll come along as my pilot and guide.

A couple of days later, I fly into Harare International Airport, grab a visa, zip through immigration with commendable ease, and cruise into town. There's no airport chaos, no taxi drivers fighting to stuff you into their cab; it's amazingly calm, quiet and organised. That impression continues as you drive into town. Where are the potholed, disintegrating roads? Where are the rusting, tied-together-with-wire cars and buses? The traffic lights (mostly) work and cars stop at them. Zimbabwe always looked cleaner, tidier and more organised than most African countries, and in that respect there's no change: from the moment I arrive there's a feeling of 'Crisis? What crisis?'

The feeling continues as I wander around town. Where are the rundown buildings, the threadbare bystanders? I'm amazed at how good everything looks: downtown Harare is modern and orderly, and everything seems to work. The shops are crowded; the shelves are full. It simply doesn't look that bad. And the tourists are coming back – not in big numbers yet, but the statistics seem to indicate that there are far more of them than in recent years. Although, the numbers are still so low that the local hustlers have quite forgotten how to hustle. Nobody is trying to sign you up for safari trips, or sell you bus tickets or jostle you into their business.

Dumping the useless Zimbabwe dollar and substituting the US dollar seemed to turn the economy around in a flash. All of a sudden, the shelves refilled, the pumps dispensed petrol and diesel again, beer flowed, hotels reopened and the economy, after years of decline, began to move forward. It does mean, though, that you have to deal with dollar bills (and, curiously, two-dollar ones) so sweatily damp and worn you feel like disinfecting after every purchase. On the plus side, Harare ATMs dispense crisp new US$100 bills, a note you almost never see in the US. I've been into US shops that are so suspicious of hundreds that they refuse to accept them.

Like Iran and Iraq, Zimbabwe is another developing world country where the press seems to be enjoying a heyday. From early morning the streets are full of newspaper vendors with an array of papers lined up on the pavements. They're all firmly pro- or anti-Mugabe; there's no middle of the road. While I'm in Harare the pro papers (the government-owned *Herald* fronts the push) run with headlines about loyal Zimbabweans lining up to sign a petition against the 'illegal' sanctions against Zimbabwe. These are the sanctions we thought were aimed strictly at Mugabe and his henchmen; the reality, the paper explains, is that they're a Western plot to ruin the Zimbabwean economy, impoverish everyday Zimbabweans and reinstate colonial rule. Meanwhile, the anti-Mugabe papers report that yet another rally for the opposing MDC party (Movement for Democratic Change) has had to be cancelled because the police have belatedly realised that a ZANU (Mugabe's party) under-14 football team was scheduled to play at the same venue.

That night I eat at Amanzi, a surprisingly flash place about 10 kilometres from the centre of town. The artistic garden lighting would impress the Balinese. I've arranged to meet Craig and Dean, a guide at Bumi Hills, there. There's plenty to talk about and by the end of the evening we've mapped out my Zimbabwe stay. Tomorrow I'll pick up a rental car and drive to Bulawayo, 440 kilometres south-west towards the border with Botswana, and stay there for two nights before Craig picks me up in his Cessna 206.

Cecil Rhodes – speculator, mining entrepreneur, colonialist, imperialist and businessman – turned up in southern Africa in 1870 as a sickly teenager, sent here from England to mend his health. Within a year he was in the diamond business with his elder brother and he soon proved adept at grabbing whatever chance came by. Founding the De Beers mining operation – which would give him control over ninety per cent of the world's diamonds – was just one of his coups. He also tagged his name onto a whole country: Rhodesia. Today he's best known for scholarships at Oxford University: Bill Clinton, Kris Kristofferson, Naomi Wolf, Geoffrey Robertson and Bob Hawke were all Rhodes Scholars.

Rhodesia, the southern half of which is now Zimbabwe, never provided the gold-rush riches Rhodes had hoped for, but, with some of the most fertile soil in Africa, it became one of Britain's more successful African colonies. The descendants of those hard-working British farmers would become the focus of the struggle for Zimbabwe today.

Rhodesia eventually became two parts of a three-part colony – North and South Rhodesia, plus Nyasaland – but after World War II the writing was on the wall for all the European colonies in Africa. The British government was pushing theirs towards independence, but if that meant black majority rule then the South Rhodesian whites wanted no part of it. With each step towards independence the whites took another step towards intransigence, finally ending up with Ian Smith, who had been active in Rhodesian politics since 1948, at the controls. In 1964 North Rhodesia became the independent nation of Zambia and Nyasaland became Malawi. The following year, Smith, now the Prime Minister of Rhodesia (the redundant 'South' was dropped), made his Unilateral Declaration of Independence. If British prime minister Harold Wilson wouldn't allow the South Rhodesian whites independence on their own terms, then they'd simply declare independence themselves, and to hell with the British.

Smith quickly banned the two tribally based black opposition parties, Joshua Nkomo's predominantly Ndbele ZAPU (Zimbabwe African People's Union) and Robert Mugabe's Shona-dominated ZANU (Zimbabwe African National Union). Both of them shifted across the border – ZAPU into Zambia, ZANU into Mozambique – and formed military wings. The

Rhodesia Bush War pitching ZAPU and ZANU against Smith's white-dominated government followed, moving into higher gear after a few years, particularly when the Portuguese abandoned neighbouring Mozambique.

As opposition to the South African apartheid policies grew, Rhodesia stood increasingly alone and the attacks on isolated white farms intensified. An Air Rhodesia airliner was brought down in 1978 with a Russian-supplied surface-to-air missile, and the same year the country's main oil storage depot, the most heavily defended site in the whole country, was attacked. Another downed airliner in 1979 emphasised that the end game was in play, but still Ian Smith refused to negotiate.

The opposing parties were finally brought to the table in 1979 and in 1980 Mugabe was elected as the new prime minister (today he's the President). At first he seemed remarkably conciliatory, especially considering Ian Smith had imprisoned him between 1964 and 1974. Mugabe encouraged white Rhodesians to remain in the new Zimbabwe; Ian Smith himself continued to live there for the next quarter century. Only in 2005, two years before he died, did he move to South Africa. Things weren't so cosy between Mugabe and Nkomo, however. The relationship between Mugabe's ZANU and Nkomo's ZAPU parties soon fractured and the relationship with white residents would eventually follow.

Zimbabwe's position, pre-downfall, as African breadbasket was based on inequitable land distribution. It's estimated that at independence whites represented only three per cent of the total population yet they owned sixty per cent of the land. And simple square-kilometre measures of the land didn't tell the whole story either: white-owned land tended to be better, more fertile country. This clearly could not continue and Britain agreed to help finance a 'willing seller, willing buyer' program to redistribute farmland. Unfortunately, this didn't work very well at either end of the scale: poor settlers without the skills and investment to operate profitable farms meant that much farmland shifted back to subsistence agriculture. At the other end of the scale, Mugabe dished land out to his most powerful supporters, who often had no farming skills, and no farming interest. The result was that agricultural exports disappeared, and only food aid kept the population from starving.

Population figures tell the story. Since independence the white population has dropped from 250,000 to 40,000; there was a major exodus after independence and then a lot more after the farm seizures kicked in from 2001. The total population has also dropped, from twelve million to ten million – or worse. While many Zimbabweans fled the country to become a despised second class in neighbouring nations, many of them with vital skills also departed. While Zimbabwe wrestles with worsening health figures in everything from infant mortality to life expectancy, and one of the worst AIDS infection rates in the world, in the UK there are more nurses from Zimbabwe than any other overseas nationality. Park rangers and guides have had to leave the country as safari parks and camps close down, often to neighbouring countries, where wildlife safaris are on the rise.

Mugabe is regarded in somewhat similar fashion to how Chairman Mao was viewed by the Chinese: there is a good/bad split. Mugabe was good: he fought through to independence;

he kicked out the British colonialists. But he was also bad: he wrecked the economy and made his people much worse off. He doesn't seem to worry about flaunting his own wealth; Mugabe motorcades are said to be the longest in Africa – possibly the most dangerous too: in a two-week period in 2012 his motorcades killed three people. Grace Mugabe, his much younger second wife famed for her expensive overseas shopping trips, is definitely not loved.

Before heading south to Bulawayo, I drive to the flash suburb of Gunhill in search of one of Harare's most famous residents, Mengistu Haile Mariam. The Ethiopian dictator ensured a never-ending hatred from Rastafarians by bumping off Haile Selassie after his 1974 coup and, according to Amnesty International, he may have killed as many as half a million people during his 'Red Terror'. Human Rights Watch defined it as 'one of the most systematic uses of mass murder ever witnessed in Africa'. Then the Berlin Wall came down, the Cold War waned, Soviet support began to dry up and, in 1991, the rebels rolled towards the Ethiopian capital in their captured Russian tanks.

One of my absolute favourite Lonely Planet stories is the part we played – however small – in the overthrow of Mengistu. In his book *Zanzibar Chest*, former Reuters correspondent Aidan Hartley recounts how he was with the rebel forces as they closed in on the capital and how the rebel commanders asked him, with some embarrassment, if he had a map of Addis Ababa. None of them had ventured into the city for

many years and many of them had never been there. All he
had was his dog-eared copy of *Africa on a Shoestring* but
that did the trick. It was taken away and photocopied and the
rebels' captured Russian tanks rumbled into the city using our
book as their guide. I've often said that recommending hotels
and restaurants is one thing, a guidebook-given of course, but
helping overthrow a government – that's a whole other level of
guidance!

Mengistu fled the country and has been enjoying Mugabe's
Zimbabwean hospitality ever since. I don't think many
guidebook publishers can claim they helped overthrow a
government so I needed to check out where he had ended
up. I drive past the well-protected villas in the leafy suburb;
every gate warns that guard dogs will attack you, security
companies will intercept you and, if all else fails, the Gunhill
Neighbourhood Watch is on high alert. Garvin Close, where
Mengistu is said to be ensconced, is closed off when I arrive,
with a couple of armed guards keeping dictator watchers at
bay. 'Nobody lives here,' I am told. 'They're all state-owned
properties.' Still, I like to think that Mengistu is a fellow
member of his local neighbourhood watch.

Mengistu inflicted more than just the Red Terror on the
poor Ethiopians. Even more people died as he resolutely
ignored the famine that swept the country in the 1980s and
elevated Bob Geldoff to rock star sainthood. A devastating
drought may have added to the country's difficulties,
but Mengistu, at one time dubbed the 'Black Stalin', had
already confirmed Stalin's and Mao's discovery that farm
collectivisation led directly to starvation, a lesson which

he appears to have passed on to Mr Mugabe. Operation Murambatsvina – translated as 'drive out the trash' – is said to have been masterminded by Mengistu: ZANU thugs razed the homes of 700,000 slum dwellers and pushed them out of Harare.

I'm inclined to exceed speed limits – discreetly, when it's safe, so long as there are no police pointing radar guns, or large wildlife on the road. Here, I know that only donkeys and cattle might wander across the road (lions and elephants stay clear) and I've been instructed to handle any police situation with a simple 'Can we sort this out right now?' Still, I slow down anytime there's a hint of activity ahead and the only radar gun I see pointed at me wouldn't have registered anything problematic. The open road speed limit is 120 kilometres per hour.

The other police presence I note is after I arrive in Bulawayo where a police truck has just rammed through the Bulawayo Club's very solid garden wall, having lost control coming round the corner. Travelling too fast presumably. At the club bar, another drinker has been less fortunate: '155 kilometres per hour at the end of a long straight and then a dip where they were hiding,' he explains. 'Cost me US$20.'

'You should have seen the club before they did it up,' exclaims my new friend, Don Johnson, over dinner. He's Zimbabwe born and has moved through an assortment of local businesses; he now imports something useful from Botswana. Like everybody doing business in Zimbabwe, he's worried about the longer term prospects. 'If they can steal your farm from you five, ten or fifteen years ago, they could steal your business away in another five, ten or fifteen years.'

Presumably, the Chinese are making exactly the same calculations. They're investing in every country in Africa with something to sell, but they burned their fingers badly in Libya in 2011 so they're undoubtedly doing the equations: 'if Mugabe steals farms from white Zimbabweans today what's to stop him stealing businesses from those who aren't even Zimbabwean tomorrow?'

Who is a Zimbabwean anyway? 'My grandfather was born here, my father was born here, I was born here and my children have been born here,' Don explains. 'But now they're threatening to roll out a ruling that all businesses must be fifty-one per cent local-owned, and having a Zimbabwe passport doesn't make you local.

'It's totally racist,' he continues. 'Local means black, you can be third or fourth generation Zimbabwean, but that doesn't make you local. On the other hand, come here from Mozambique or another country in Africa, take out Zimbabwean citizenship and you're immediately a local. As long as you're black, that is. But don't tell a politician that this is racist, they get very upset.'

Zimbabwe citizenship may not get you on the fifty-one per cent side of the local/non-local divide, but it does bring an assortment of problems with it. Zimbabwe does not allow you to keep another citizenship; you have to renounce any other nationality when you take on the Zimbabwean one and acquire your 'green mamba,' the green-cover local passport.

A passport from the developed world brings with it a wide variety of privileges, including not needing visas for many countries. If, on the other hand, your passport is from a developing country – the 'third world' in the old parlance – almost any trip will involve a long round of visa applications, form filling and fee paying.

'So what happens to the farms once they're taken over?' I ask. 'Do the settlers sometimes make them work?' I hardly expect the Mugabe cronies to roll up their sleeves and become hard-working farmers overnight, tied into the international vegetable business or air-freighting consignments off to Europe.

'No, it never happens,' agrees Don. 'But the farms usually go back to work in the end. If it's an A1 farm – one taken over by a government official or someone from the military – they'll generally get an experienced farmer to manage it for them, somebody who will commute to the farm from Harare. It's pretty much the same situation with an A2 farm, where there's been a settler or war vets takeover. A farmer will strike a deal with them to run it. Either way the percentages are the same, the farmer takes seventy-five per cent of the proceeds and has to cover the expenses and make a profit out of that. The local side gets twenty-five per cent for having grabbed the land.'

'So it's straightforward rent-seeking?' I ask. 'No interest in the land or farming, just getting money for having control of the land.'

'Absolutely,' he says. 'And of course there's lots of bitterness amongst the white farming community: your farm is seized and, next thing, your neighbour, whose farm has probably been grabbed as well, is farming it for seventy-five per cent of the output. Unbelievably, farms are still being seized. There are still some white farmers out there who've managed to hang on.'

The empty plinth at the intersection of Eighth Avenue and Main Street, near the Bulawayo Club, was once topped by a statue of Cecil Rhodes. He was quickly removed following independence in 1980, and for thirty years the plinth stood empty.

In 2010 a statue of local hero Joshua Nkomo briefly took up residence. Nkomo led the ZAPU forces in the independence struggle, and Bulawayo is the Ndebele heartland, where support for ZAPU was strongest. A 1980s power struggle between ZANU and ZAPU led to Mugabe sending in his North Korean–trained 5th Brigade; the ensuing Gukurahundi massacres may have taken as many as 100,000 lives, and had a strong whiff of ethnic cleansing about it. As a result, Mugabe is not very popular in the country's second-largest city.

After the Nkomo statue was installed, complaints soon started to circulate. 'Nkomo wouldn't have worn a suit' or 'his head wasn't that small' were typical, but the most serious allegation was that the statue had been sourced from North Korea, and memories of the massacres were still fresh. The Rhodes statue lasted for seventy-six years; Nkomo was only up for a few weeks and, for most of that, under a black shroud.

It's my third day in Zimbabwe and before long I'm in jail, in the grounds of the local prison, at least. To reach the Khami ruins, I'm advised, 'Follow Eleventh Street out of town and keep going for 24 kilometres.' It should be Thirteenth Street, and I compound the error by asking numerous bystanders the way to Khami. It turns out everybody was directing me to Khami Prison, not Khami Ruins, including the hitchhiking nun who rides with me the final couple of kilometres to the prison gate. The soldier at the entrance helpfully suggests that I've come so far in the wrong direction it will be quicker to enter the prison grounds on one side and exit it on the other, rather than retrace my tyre tracks.

The ancient city of Great Zimbabwe, a couple of hundred kilometres to the east, is one of the country's great attractions; it used to feature on Zimbabwe banknotes, when the country had its own currency, and it gave the country its name. It's the Machu Picchu or Angkor Wat of sub-Saharan Africa, and I made my visit on my first trip. Lucky Zimbabwe has a number of secondary ancient sites, though, including Khami, which I finally get to after my prison detour.

The Khami ruins are reminiscent of Great Zimbabwe. They're much less extensive, but with the same curving walls, and – after some solid restoration work financed by the French government – the Western Enclosure wall, and its tiers of carefully arranged stones, looks terrific. There's only one other tourist at the site.

I drive back through town and on to Matobo National Park, stopping for lunch at Amalinda Camp, a classy safari lodge with rooms that blend into the gigantic boulders which litter the landscape. The lunchtime diners include a disarmingly young professional hunter named Adam.

'So what do you hunt?' I ask him.

'Dangerous animals,' he replies instantly.

He's guiding two big guys from Chicago who come to

Zimbabwe to shoot things. It started as a 'once in a lifetime experience' which has now been repeated eight times and on each visit they shoot more and more animals. Their local guide gives me a rundown on what it costs in trophy fees, hunting fees, guides, porters, equipment and travel. You can count on spending US$50,000 to $60,000 if you're planning to bag an elephant, although people pay up to US$250,000 if they want to be absolutely assured of a really big tusker for their billiard room.

From the camp I drive into the park, and on up to Rhodes's grave at World's View; it certainly is a view. Zimbabwe seems to specialise in precariously balanced rocks and from here there's a fabulous outlook over some amazing rock formations. I'd picked up one hitchhiker on my way into the park and dropped her at the ranger station; I've got another on board as I depart.

Back in Bulawayo I've still got time for a visit to the town's wonderful Railway Museum, which features a quite amazing number of old steam locomotives and all sorts of other memorabilia. There's even a heavily armour-plated train designed to sweep for mines placed on the tracks by the rebels. My visit is made even more interesting by a chance encounter with Abdullah Hajit, who used to work here in the railway's heyday. He tells me of the time when the railway workshops worked 24/7 looking after 500 steam locomotives. Today, there are perhaps half a dozen steam locomotives kept in working order, along with forty more modern locomotives.

The drive out to the Joshua Mqabuko Nkomo Airport turns out to be rather further than I'd expected, although I'm only a few minutes late for our 10 am meeting time. Craig's Cessna is parked on the apron, and we depart straight away.

As we fly out, the villages appear as neat little chequerboards of home enclosures and crops. We follow the railway line and the river, and we're soon landing on a long grass-and-dirt airstrip at Hwange National Park. There's a safari vehicle waiting for us, with Brian at the wheel, and almost immediately we encounter some zebras and then, by a waterhole, a big bull elephant in must. 'Must' is a Hindi word and I'm familiar with it from hanging around elephants in Burma and Nepal. It's rather like a male version of being in heat, and happens every year or two. Apart from being edgy, unstable and amorous, elephants in must urinate almost continuously. So much so that they can end up suffering from GPS – green penis syndrome – when algae starts to grow on their penis.

So we watch the bull elephant for a while and yes, with binoculars, I can see its elephant-sized penis is a little green. At this point, a herd of more than thirty elephants appears from the trees and they start marching resolutely towards the waterhole. There's the big matriarch of the herd, a couple of tiny ones, and an assortment of sizes in between. As they move towards the waterhole their speed increases until finally they are positively charging to the water. They look terrific. Slurp, slurp, splash, splash, and straight on from the waterhole to an adjacent, smaller mud bath. Once there, they splash mud and water over themselves with great accuracy. A trunkful down one side, another trunkful down the other, and then they move directly on from mud to dust.

The big bull with GPS sidles over to see if any of the females are interested. They aren't. Within moments they disappear, trailing a great cloud of dust. Everything is done with great speed and urgency, as if there's no time to waste. The whole drink, wash, mud bath, dust bath sequence took less than twenty minutes. Meanwhile, another herd has arrived from the other side of the waterhole and waited discreetly for the first herd to finish before they move in.

I love elephants.

We drive on to Davison's Camp, arriving in time for lunch. It's like other tented camps: rooms that are half-tent, but with attached bathroom, running water, electricity and any mod con you could ask for. And, right in front, a waterhole where you might find elephants wandering past.

I retire to my room/tent to unpack and sort a few things before meeting mid-afternoon. I fall soundly asleep with my laptop on my knee and wake up to find I've typed line after line of *kkkkkk*. We rally ourselves with coffee, and then Craig, Brian and I set off on an afternoon-evening game drive, which turns up all the usual suspects: lots of elephants (the Hwange standard animal), zebras, impala, buffalo and quite a few giraffes.

In other African countries game park visitors must stay safely in their vehicles. In Zimbabwe if you want to get out and go for a wander, well, it's your life. Reassuringly, Craig carries a large gun as we leave the Land Rover and stroll towards the Bulawayo–Victoria Falls railway line, which marks the eastern boundary of the park. As we near the line we can hear a train approaching and speed up to be there as it comes by. There's an elephant standing right on the track. It's one of those perfect, once-in-a-lifetime photo opportunities and I've got my camera with me. Craig has his rifle, but not his Canon. The train toots, the elephant withdraws.

In classic safari fashion, our drive concludes with a sundowner beer and snacks by a waterhole. On our way back to the camp, now after dark, we encounter three vehicles from another camp. Their progress has been halted by ten or eleven lions, which have settled down in the middle of the track and show no intentions of interrupting their rest break just because some Land Rovers have come along. The pride comprises several females, an assortment of cubs and one big male, stretched right across the path and not moving for anybody. They're completely oblivious to us. Take flash photos? No problem. Shine a red spotlight? Big deal. Wake up and move out of the road? No chance. Eventually we drive off-road around them.

Brian identifies the stretched-out male: 'That's Cecil.'

Back at the camp we eat, drink and sit around a fire, watching the nearly full moon while lightning flashes on the horizon. I do like a place where someone with a rifle walks you to your room at the end of the day.

The generator surges back to life just before 6 am, the light flicks on above my head and I'm instantly awake. Thunder and occasional showers woke me periodically through the night, usually with dreams of water and flooding.

Every African game drive brings some new experience.

'When monkeys and other primates see us they climb up into a tree,' Craig explains when we see a bunch of baboons sitting sociably in the shade of a tree. 'Baboons do the opposite,' he continues. 'They abandon a tree and move off. They know we might have guns and they don't want to be stuck out on a branch.'

Sure enough, when we get out of the Land Rover lots of baboons – far more than I expect – climb down or drop straight out of the tree.

Not all wildlife has to be stealthily approached or seen only as a fleeting glimpse. During this Zimbabwe visit I encounter four of the 'big five'. I've already seen lions, elephants and buffalo, and there's a rhino still to come, but the leopard will remain elusive. I'm happy with a consolation prize: a fine big leopard tortoise, which I help out of a muddy roadside hole, probably made by an elephant. It's become mildly stuck.

'Probably about fifty years old,' Craig says as it waddles away in true tortoise fashion.

We also manage plenty of birdlife sightings, including of oxpeckers, the birds that ride around on giraffes and buffalo, cleaning up any annoying insect hitchhikers and working as an extra pair of eyes.

'Hey there,' I imagine them chirping to their four-legged transport. 'Look, there's a human. Move away from the road. Can't you see them in that Land Rover? Come on, move!'

Not good, from our point of view.

Early afternoon we drive out to the airstrip for the flight north to Chizarira. Doug, a friend of Craig's, meets us at the rocky Chizarira airstrip. He's driven all the way from Harare with supplies, but Craig insists that somebody has to come out here a few times a year anyway, to check up on the place.

The airstrip has been burned clear. Craig was afraid it would be totally overgrown and that Doug would have to drive up and down a few times to flatten the grass before we touched down. We drive down the rocky road to the Chizarira Wilderness Lodge. If I was looking for the downside of the Zimbabwe tourism story over the past decade, then here it is.

I stayed here in 1997 with my wife Maureen and our two teenage children. After a spell out in the Okavango Delta, we'd picked up a Land Rover and camping equipment at Maun and spent the next two weeks driving east through Botswana and Zimbabwe to Harare. Nights camping were interspersed with stays at safari parks and surprisingly luxurious game lodges like this one. The Chizarira National Park features a tangle of gorges and valleys and ends with a steep escarpment to the north. The lodge perches right on the edge of this escarpment, with each room teetering above a sheer drop, with a deck that juts out over it. Sleepwalking is not a good idea. One night on that stay, a gale blew up the ravine and through our rooms, shaking everything loose and blowing things wildly around and then out.

There were two lodges and five tented camps in and around the park back in 1997. We stayed for three nights, took walks in the park and enjoyed great food. Some things haven't changed: the food is still very good and the rooms haven't tumbled down the side of the sheer cliff. Stepping out onto a deck suspended over empty space remains a heart-starting moment and that night, cleaning my teeth and going to bed,

I realise that if there's anybody on the other side of the river with night-vision binoculars I'm probably giving them quite a show.

Unfortunately, hotel rooms don't maintain their wonderful status without constant maintenance, and there's nobody staying at the lodge. There was a long empty spell prior to my visit and there'll be another long empty spell after it. When there are no visitors, there's no money and for the park that means there's also fewer means to protect the wildlife. Meanwhile, the number of local poachers only increases. The past decade has not only been unkind to Chizarira's tourist operators, but it's also been very tough on the park's animals.

Craig bought the lodge from the original owner about five years ago and he clearly keeps it open because he wants to, not for any logical (or profitable) reason. He pays half a dozen men from the nearby village a retainer and supplies food. In return, they keep an eye on the place, maintain it a little and show up when the occasional guest, like me, arrives. There's no phone line, no mobile phone coverage, no way to get a message to them, so how on earth do they know we're coming?

'Bush telegraph,' says Craig. 'They will have seen Doug's car coming up the valley. Why else would anybody be coming up here? So they come up to the lodge and, sure enough, it's a visitor.'

They've made the beds and my stay is comfortable, but only a handful of rooms are in use and they're faded, the paint peeling, mosquito nets patched, woodwork scuffed. The other rooms are derelict and the garden is unkempt and overgrown. Structurally, it's all there and okay, and a liberal application of money could bring it back to pristine condition, but that's not going to happen until visitors return.

In 1997 we'd continued on from Chizarira into the Matusadona National Park, where we camped for a couple of nights before driving to the Iwaba Estate near Kwekwe. The Chizarira story may have been a sad one, but what's happened to Iwaba is far worse. Run by Justin and Peter Seymour-Smith, the estate was a 100-square-kilometre private wildlife reserve on the Munyati River. They were pioneers in rhino conservation and, when I visited, they had more than ten black and twenty white rhinos and had provided rhinos to other parks. Their reserve also featured elephants, wildebeest, zebras, giraffes, impala, kudu, sable, crocodiles, leopards and cheetahs. It was a busy place. Breeding and protecting rhinos wasn't an easy operation. Keeping the poachers out was a complex and expensive task, but keeping the rhinos in was also difficult and keeping them happy seemed to be the most difficult job of all. You can't just sling a new rhino in with the established ones; they'll kill it.

Then in December 2006, the army moved in and high-ranking military officers simply took the place over. The Seymour-Smiths, who had been there for nearly fifty years, were given ten days to get out. They have no idea what has happened to the wildlife population they looked after with such care.

At Chizarira we're up bright and early. Doug drives us out to the plane and once we've persuaded three jackals to vacate the airstrip and a herd of waterbuck not to approach it, we're up and away, banking down one of the Chizarira gorges and over Batonga land, where the villages are not as neat and tidy as the Ndebele ones. It's only a half-hour flight to Lake Kariba, and, after dodging a big storm en route, we descend over hippos in the lake, and impala and elephants to its side. Some of the elephants are uncomfortably close to the airstrip; the impala scatter but presumably the elephants are harder to chase off.

A boat shuttles us across the lake to the Rhino Safari Camp. It's on an island joined to the mainland, and to Matusadona National Park, by a small isthmus. Craig and I go out for a drive around the island before lunch; there are elephants on the beach all the way around and as we come back to the camp three of them are cavorting in the water. At times they look like an African Loch Ness monster, swimming along with just the tops of their heads and their back showing above the water. Then they submerge completely and it's snorkelling time. They're clearly enjoying themselves. One of them comes ashore and is a bit shocked to find us sitting on the beach; an angry 'harrumph' and a mini-charge and then he veers into the bush nervously.

There's more excitement that afternoon. Craig spots a black rhino, and we jump across a stream, shuttle across a field, bent over and keeping low so we stay out of sight, before taking up station behind a fallen tree. We're only a stone's throw away from the rhino, but it's completely blind to us and feeding steadily along the riverbanks. The setting is green and lush; it's an absolutely bucolic sight. Eventually the rhino wanders downstream and off into the bush, but I'm euphoric.

The camp's rhino information folder says that if you're charged by a rhino 'the best defence is to find a tree to climb. It is amazing how adrenalin can take you places you would never have thought you could get to!'

We drive back down to the lakeside and take a long sunset trek. We're hoping to find lions. 'If we encounter lions just stand still,' Craig instructs.

'Yes,' I think, 'right behind you.' About three years back a lion killed a staff member in the camp; he was lighting a water heater for one of the rooms and the lion took him from behind.

We only find tracks. Then we drive around some more and, although Craig is convinced the lions are in there somewhere, we don't find any so it's back to camp, dinner and an early night. I don't even read for long because so many insects find their way in under the mosquito net.

The next morning we take a boat back to Bumi Hills and the airstrip. Craig's flying off to Kariba to meet a bunch of friends for a fortieth birthday. Before he can take off, we have to chase a club of impala off the runway; they keep coming back and leaping down the runway, despite much engine-revving and horn-blasting. I'm staying at the lodge before flying back to Harare the next day, but first I fit in two more game drives with Dean, whom I met back in Harare. We spot lots of birds and, once again, lion tracks but no lions, although we do follow a rotting smell to a waterbuck carcass, which would appear to be a lion kill from a few days ago. The next morning is a repeat experience – lots of 'might be', no real sightings. Dean has a bit of a guide-performance style: 'we're so close to this' or 'that might be just around the corner'. In fact, the best sightings are a beautifully electric lime-green chameleon and a sand snake I find by the pool when we return to the lodge.

I've been surprised at how calm and orderly everything is in Zimbabwe; visitor numbers were clearly down, but Harare was neat and peaceful. It certainly didn't look like a disaster zone. The hotels all seemed to be operating efficiently and, although Chizarira was sadly abandoned, the safari camps at Hwange and Matusadona feel as if they were doing fine. The answer, of course, is that the operations that have managed to continue, often by hard work at cultivating a loyal following, are like the tip of a non-existent iceberg. Everything below the waterline has melted away. When the camps departed, the jobs did too.

In fact that's the problem with most of Zimbabwe. You hear about the protests, the political opponents of Mugabe being beaten up and intimidated, but most of the Zimbabwe problem isn't on view. It's been exported. The white farmers, their land seized, have left. As many as two million people have fled to neighbouring countries looking for work or, simply, survival. For the skilled safari camp employees the answer was to move to other African countries where tourism is booming. Lots of Zimbabwe park guides are now employed in Mozambique, a country whose upward arc has pretty much mirrored Zimbabwe's downward fall.

The simple statistics tell the National Park story: all may have been well at Davison's Camp, but in Hwange two thirds of the eighty safari camps have shut down. It's the same story in Matusadona. The Rhino Safari Camp is doing fine, but of sixty-five camps and houseboat operations, sixty have closed. In Chizarira, I stayed at the only place, out of two lodges and five tented operators from my last visit, that is still open, albeit half-heartedly.

It's a repositioning flight to Harare and I'm the only passenger on board. I pay the captain, a young woman, in cash, as we stand on the tarmac beside the plane. Then I stroll across the apron, by myself, and in through arrivals. It's a pleasant contrast to the over-zealous security of first-world airports.

I have time for one final trip, to a part of Zimbabwe I've not visited before: out west to Mutare, near the Mozambique border. So much of the Zimbabwe I've seen has been wilderness, plains and bush without a sign of human life. Where there are cultivation and habitation down below, there are always villages and subsistence farming.

'If there's a tree in a field it's not a commercial farm,' Craig had explained as we flew over the neat villages of Matabeland. The villages alternated between the bare earth of the housing compounds and the green squares of crops. 'Commercial farmers would cut down every tree.'

I depart early and once I'm on the road to Mutare I scoot along, checking the numerous police halts and speed traps along the way. There are so many I start writing them down: 78 kilometres out, then at 118, 164, 181 and bingo at 185 kilometres from Harare I'm nabbed doing 87 in an 80 kilometer-per-hour zone. There are lots of speed limit signs, but no indication when you've left the limited area, at least that's my excuse.

A nicer bunch of speed-trap operators you could not find: everything is neatly processed while they let me look at the speed readout on other cars. The equipment gives more error readings than speeds. My infringement only costs me $10 and I'm given a signed receipt. A young police officer says that if I'd like to marry her she'll leave with me.

It's here, in the west, that the country's commercial farms were located and then, mostly, seized. The Zimbabwean journalist Douglas Rogers detailed his family's resistance to such seizures in his energetic 2009 memoir, *The Last Resort*. It follows his parents' life near Mutare as their backpacker resort, Drifters, collapsed under Mugabe. They struggled to keep hold of the central farm building when other local farmers were pushed off their properties and took up residence in the chalets the Rogers built as holiday getaways.

The Rogers aren't home when I pass by, but Mutare turns out to be a surprisingly attractive place, the wide streets shaded by flame of the forest trees, alive with red-orange blossoms. I continue beyond the town up into the cool heights of the Vumba Mountains and bed down at the swish Leopard Rock Hotel. The Queen Mother and Princess Margaret famously stayed here in 1953, 'keeping Margaret out of trouble back in London,' someone speculated.

The next morning, Newton, the hotel's game-park guide, takes me for an interesting stroll. The park has three giraffes, thirteen zebras (one of them rather tame, having wandered off and lived with cattle when it was young, before returning to the park), wildebeest, eland, impala, bushbuck and blue duicker.

It's only an hour's walk to the Mozambique border, so the hotel was dangerously close to ZANU rebels during the independence struggle and it was attacked with mortars and bazookas on 4 January 1978. Newton was living nearby and remembers running out of his home and hiding when he heard the pre-dawn explosions. The hotel suffered major damage. The coffee farm he worked at was taken over by the hotel in 1994, and turned into the game park in 1998, when Newton switched from farm manager to wildlife guide. A couple of years later, when the farm takeover era began, war vet settlers moved into the game park and couldn't be shifted.

'A couple of lions might have helped,' I suggest, but the solution was rather simpler.

'They didn't have food and nearby people wouldn't supply them,' Newton says. 'So they left the park to get food and while they were away somebody stole all their tents.' He looks puzzled, as though wondering who would do such a thing. 'They left then and didn't come back.'

We encounter more impala on the way back to our starting point, and one of these delicately beautiful little antelopes is only three days old. He's already prancing away, keeping up with the others with no difficulty. 'They're up and running five to ten minutes after birth,' Newton explains. 'When they're ten minutes old you could not catch them.'

Back in Harare there's one final sign of a decade and a half of change. I'd already noted the increasing presence of Chinese businesses all over Africa, including in Zimbabwe, and several people have commented that the Chinese, cosying up to Mugabe and his supporters, could easily find their fingers burnt somewhere further down the line. They're buying up Harare, though, without fear for their fingers.

At the end of my 1997 visit we stayed at the Imba Matombo Lodge. You could call it a Zimbabwean boutique hotel, a big central building that looks like a stately English country home, but with enough thatched roof for a village of English cottages, and, despite this, a distinctly African flavour.

The Imba Matombo is still going strong and still looks magnificent, but I appear to be the only guest. The bar sells only one bottle of Zambezi beer tonight and there's nobody else in the restaurant. Never mind, the receptionist tells me, 'the new owners are going to refurbish all the rooms'.

'So who are the new owners?' I ask.

'They're Chinese,' she replies. 'They've bought three other hotels in Harare.'

ACKNOWLEDGEMENTS

Many people helped with my travel and research on this book, some of whose names I can't mention for assorted reasons.

In Colombia, Germán Escobar was a wonderful and always amusing host and guide in Bogotá and also on the Caribbean coast where we were joined by Patrick Fleming, a terrific companion and organiser for our travels from Santa Marta. For the walk to Ciudad Perdida you could not ask for a better or more expert fellow walker than archaeologist Dr Santiago Giraldo, Global Heritage Fund's director for the site. Vincent Michael, GHF's Executive Director, further enriched the archaeological expertise.

In Congo, Emmanuel Rufubya was my Goma fixer for visiting the gorillas and climbing the Nyiragongo volcano.

I'm coming back for a Congo River trip, Emmanuel. Thanks to Joe Wasilewski and Patrick Kongolo (my Kisangani lawyer!) for bar conversation and advice at Les Chalets in Kisangani and to Thomas Gilchrist of Human Rights Watch for a Goma briefing. Anneke Van Woudenberg's Human Rights Watch reports from DRC are always worth reading.

In Haiti, Jacqualine Labrom was enormously helpful on both my visits and her Haiti experience goes right back to Papa Doc's days. If you want to visit Haiti, her Voyages Lumiere should be your first stop.

I had lots of help in Israel and Palestine, particularly from Michel Awad at the Siraj Center in Palestine, who also organised Nedal Sawalmeh to be my guide on the Nativity Trail walk. Maoz Inon and Suraida Nasser of the Fauzi Azar Inn were wonderful hosts and guides in Nazareth. Dror Tishler and Nitzan Kimchi joined Maoz and me as fellow walkers on the Jesus Trail, at the conclusion of which Israel Shavit was another great host and helper. On the Israel National Trail, Ohad Sharav was not only a fellow walker (as was his son Toam), but also an all-round organiser, explainer, fixer, problem solver and guide.

In Nauru, a big thank you to the passing motorists and motorcyclists who didn't even need to see an outstretched thumb to pick up a roadside hitchhiker, to the friendly staff at the Menen Hotel and to Sean Oppenheimer at Capelle's for rental car assistance and advice.

In Pakistan Najam ul-Haq Khan was an amazingly calm, collected, organised and experienced driver and guide. Kudos also to Jamil Mir of Travel Waljis in Islamabad, who sorted out all the travel problems that popped up. Whether it was landslides, protests or unexpected Chinese border closures, he always managed to organise or reorganise. In Gulmit, poor Raja Hussain Khan of the Marco Polo Inn not only saw his first customers in who knows how long disappear due to that border closure, but he also came with us up to Sust. After we'd left Pakistan, Abdul Wahab of Old Road Tours in Kashgar sorted that end of the trip and provided Yusuf, our expert young guide. And before I even got to Pakistan, when persuading Indian Railways to issue a Delhi–Amritsar railway ticket proved to be mission impossible, my Delhi friend Ashok Khanna came through!

In Papua New Guinea, Nick Unsworth's assistance spread far from his base in Buka. The police station in Arawa provided all sorts of help, particularly from Rob Arnold and the other visiting Kiwi cops, and from Chris Imba, the local officer who showed me round the Panguna mine site. Thank you to Dennis for speeding me across from the Solomon Islands to Bougainville in his boat, and to Paul Kamuai at the Buin police station for diplomatically handling my unofficial arrival in his country. I can't forget Albert, the BRA man with the big machete whose help ensured I didn't miss out on Admiral Yamamoto's World War II crash site. In Australia Ron O'Leary was a wonderful source of information and entertaining tales on Bougainville.

Zimbabwe was made extraordinarily interesting by Craig van Zyl, who was not only a terrific guide (I appreciated the big gun he toted when we were walking in lion land), but also a fine pilot.

Acknowledgements

Getting this book over the finish line required a great deal of expert editing help from Emma Schwarcz.

Finally, and as always, to Maureen. This time she came with me to Haiti and Pakistan and on earlier trips we've visited Israel, Palestine, Papua New Guinea and Zimbabwe together. And when she doesn't join me, she lets me go. What more could I ask for?

OTHER APPEARANCES:

Extracts from the Democratic Republic of the Congo, Haiti and Israel & Palestine chapters appeared as 'A Troubled World' in the Small World edition of *Griffith Review*. The Haiti extract also appeared in the Qantas inflight magazine *Australian Way*. Material from the Israel National Trail account in the Israel & Palestine chapter appeared in *The Independent* in London.

For books I used in researching *Dark Lands* look for the 'Dark Lands Reading List' at http://tonywheeler.com.au/